D0843208

WITHDRAWN

Social Stratification in India

Social Stratification in India

Issues and Themes

K. L. SHARMA

Sage Publications
New Delhi/Thousand Oaks/London

First published in 1997 by
Sage Publications India Pvt Ltd
M–32 Greater Kailash Market–1
New Delhi 110 048

Sage Publications Inc **Sage Publications Ltd**
2455 Teller Road 6 Bonhill Street
Thousand Oaks, California 91320 London EC2A 4PU

Published by Tejeshwar Singh for Sage Publications India Pvt Ltd., typeset by Line Arts Phototypesetters, Pondicherry, and printed at Chaman Enterprises, New Delhi.

Library of Congress Cataloging-in-Publication Data

Sharma, Kanhaiyalal
    Social stratification in India: issues and themes/K. L. Sharma.
       p. cm.
    Includes bibliographical references and index.
    1. Social classes—India. 2. Caste—India. I. Title.
HN690.Z9S6438 305.5′0954—DC21   1997   97–3382

ISBN: 0–8039–9362–5 (US-Hb)   81–7036–607–0 (India-Hb)
         0–8039–9363–3 (US-Pb)   81–7036–608–9 (India-Pb)

Sage Production Editor: Urmi Goswami

To my teacher
Professor Yogendra Singh
from whom I have learnt
the craft of sociology

Contents

Preface

This volume is the outcome of the third survey of literature concerning the sociology of social stratification in India conducted on behalf of the Indian Council of Social Science Research (ICSSR). Though I was assigned the task of preparing a 'trend report' for the period from 1979 to 1989, I appropriated this opportunity to broaden the temporal scope of the study by including some relevant literature on the theme concerning before and after the stipulated period. The nature of this study is both multi-disciplinary and interdisciplinary because social stratification is a focal theme in all social sciences. Hence, social stratification cannot be restricted to disciplinary boundaries of sociology.

An effort has been made in this volume not only to report 'trends' in the study of social stratification, emphasis is also laid on under-standing and explanation of the ideology, structure and process of social inequality both temporally and contextually. The two earlier 'trend reports' by Yogendra Singh have been briefly referred to as 'base lines' for locating 'shifts' in theoretical, methodological, structural and processual aspects in studies of social stratification.

It may be admitted here that vast literature generated on social stratification and mobility in the recent past speaks of the magnitude of the persisting social inequality and the demands for social change and mobility in Indian society. Describing even synoptically such vast literature becomes a herculean task. One can only be apologetic for being eclectic in such a situation.

An attempt is made in this study to analyze theoretical and methodological issues by hammering on the dissolution of antinomies like caste and class, caste and power, power and class, structure and culture, and structure and process, as they could all be seen together as interacting components at the conceptual as well as empirical levels, and as such these are not reducible to each other. Ideal constructions and empirical complexities despite their obvious differences are not divorced from each other.

Keeping this perspective in mind the study analyzes culture and stratification, nature of social stratification in rural–agrarian and urban–industrial settings. An analysis of social stratification among weaker sections, such as the OBCs, SCs and STs, and of gender and social stratification enriches the comparative perspective of the study.

An appraisal of the explanations of social mobility shows that the culturological perspective suffers from serious inadequacies. But the structural perspective alone is unable to explain the entire gamut of structure and change in relation to social inequality. Moreover, culture has materiality in the background, and the latter (class) has culture hidden under it. Uncovering of the underlying layers of formations from the apparent structures brings home the hypothesis that caste inheres class and class inheres caste, and hence caste and class are not antinomies. It is suggested that caste–class–power nexus approach, rather than the causal and dimensional approaches is significantly relevant for analyzing social stratification and mobility.

While reporting theoretical, methodological and substantive 'shifts' in the studies on social stratification and mobility, historicity and change are focused in relation to specific contexts such as rural–agrarian and urban–industrial, and segments of society like the weaker sections and women. The role of the state and its policies is given due significance in the study.

'Description' becomes inevitable in the analysis which is based on reporting of trends over a specific period of time. The available literature, despite this limitation, has been arranged in various categories and focal sub-themes as given in the volume.

Whether the category of women and gender can become a matter of social stratification may be a very relevant question. However, gender is being argued as a significant dimensional input in the theory of social stratification. The chapter on 'Gender and Social Stratification' is included in this book for the pragmatic reason that women in India are placed, though differentially, lower to men, in general, both within the family and in the wider society.

A 'desirable' or 'desired type' of society could be visualized by having deep insights into the ideology structure and process of social stratification vis-à-vis different sections of society, particularly the most disadvantaged ones. This volume modestly claims to offer an understanding of the complexities of social stratification and mobility.

First of all, I would like to thank Professor M. S. Gore for inviting me to undertake the third survey of social stratification on behalf of the ICSSR. I express special gratitude to Professor Yogendra Singh who coincidentally commented twice on this manuscript, firstly for the ICSSR and then for Sage Publications. Substantial revision of the manuscript is based on constructive comments and suggestions made by Professor Singh. I am also grateful to Professor Y. B. Damle for making highly appreciative comments on the manuscript. My students Dr P. C. Singh, Dr S. K. Mishra and Dr Sohan Lal Sharma deserve sincere thanks for helping me in preparing the manuscript. I thank Mr A. N. Kunjunny for typing the first draft of the manuscript, and Ms Shobha Sharma for meticulously typing two revised drafts of the manuscript.

Writing a book like this is a very difficult task. Omissions are bound to occur in encompassing the conceptual issues and substantive concerns, and in establishing the relevant linkages between the two. But it has been a tremendous experience for me. If this book is found useful by students, teachers and researchers, I shall feel greatly rewarded.

One

Introduction

Theoretical and Methodological Issues

There are no neat theoretical formulations and precise methodological devices in social sciences in general and in sociology in particular. The multi-dimensional and fluid nature of social reality is a prohibitive factor in arriving at an objective analysis and understanding of the social phenomena. Social stratification is a generalized aspect of society and approaches to its study inevitably become a part of larger theoretical constructs. The main approaches to the study of social stratification are the Marxian, Weberian, functional, social-psychological and structuralist. Each of these approaches refers to a specific viewpoint by which structures and processes of social stratification are viewed and patterns of hierarchic social relations are ascertained and valued.

Conceptual Schemes and their Operationalization

Yogendra Singh (1977: xi) observes in his book *Social Stratification in India* that:

The theoretical and methodological issues which one observes in the studies of social stratification in India relate mainly to formulation of conceptual schemes and operationalization of these schemes through indicators of status, levels of equality and inequality, occupational differentiation or degree of homogeneity and heterogeneity of groups in status hierarchy and of interactional variables such as pollution–purity (through exchange of food articles, co-dining, etc.), dominance, fusion, fission, etc.

Singh finds systematic theories such as functionalism and Marxism more powerful than the conceptual schema. Using a two-dimensional property space in the context of caste, all approaches are classified by Singh as universalistic–particularistic and cultural–structural (ibid.: xii). Singh analyzes caste as a universal reality and not as a typical Indian social reality on the one hand, and as a cultural/ideological system versus a system of social relationships on the other. The conceptual schemes like the closed and open and segmentary and organic systems of the caste stratification (Bailey 1963; Béteille 1966) also fall under this broad rubric of the functionalist analysis.

Studies of class stratification in particular have used the Marxist models employing interactional categories and concepts. Ramkrishna Mukherjee (1957), Daniel Thorner (1976) and several others have studied agrarian relations in interactional terms focusing upon the nature of the mode of production in Indian agriculture.

Besides being a fundamental reality and a fact of life, social stratification is a sensitive subject as it refers to social ranking of people in high and low positions in society. At times it seems that social ranking is deterministic or one-dimensional, but in reality it is multi-faceted and multi-causal. Caste, class, race, ethnicity, etc., are certainly different forms of social inequality, but what is apparent in them is not found in substance. Caste is not just a system of social stratification based on ritual purity and impurity of people, things and occupations. Economic and power dimensions have also been the central foci of the caste system. Class and ethnicity are also found embedded in each other, sometimes distinction between these two even gets blurred.

Thus the multi-faceted and multi-causal nature of social stratification calls for a multi-disciplinary treatment. A good number of economists, historians and political scientists besides sociologists and anthropologists are engaged today in analyzing the nexus between caste, class and power, both historically and contextually. Multidimensionality certainly implies multicausality of social inequality, and yet one can see a dominant causality by ascertaining the relative power of various factors and forces over a period of time and also at a given point of time. One can visualize a simultaneous coexistence of social, economic, political and cultural factors in status-determination, and also any one of these can be found more effective than the remaining ones. What is important, therefore, is not the counting of factors as such, but the *dominance* of one or two factors over others and the nature of nexus between different factors and changes therein.

Sociology of social stratification seeks to analyze the structure, process and ideology (Singh 1977) of social inequality. No society is stagnant, hence ideology plays an important role in social change and mobility. Sociology of knowledge perspective, norms and values guide the structure and process of social stratification and the State, in shaping and reshaping the society, also becomes an imperative tool for a deeper understanding of the structuring of social inequalities.

The question of relevance comes up with the formulation of categorizations, theoretical constructs and approaches concerning the studies of social stratification. Why is a particular set of concepts, categories and approaches preferred instead of an alternative set(s) as a theoretical and methodological device? The question of relevance also attracts the serious scholars because of the hiatus between the apparent and the hidden social reality. Today, debates on feudalism, mode of production in agriculture, and notions of caste, class and power are sufficiently indicative of the distortions. Since these are being debated, drifts from the implicated meanings of these concepts and categories have slowly been emerging. However, despite the drifts, structural–functional, structuralist, structural–historical and Marxist orientations and constructs continue to overshadow studies of social stratification.

A critical review of these studies on social stratification indicates that caste is treated as a system of rituals and ideas. Class is perceived as a system of relations between the rich and the poor and as groupings of people simply based on their common economic and occupational interests. Power is understood mainly either as the resourcefulness of an individual(s) or a phenomenon emanating from the state and its apparatuses. These formulations provide clues for analyzing the connexion between the prevalent concepts, frameworks and paradigms vis-à-vis Indian society.

Concepts such as vertical mobility (Srinivas 1952), and horizontal mobility (Majumdar 1958), reference group (Damle 1968; Lynch 1969), and caste, class and power (Aggarwal 1971; Béteille 1965; Bhatt 1975) have been uninhibitedly applied to the study of social stratification. The implicated meanings of these concepts do not help much in the understanding of social inequality in India. Vertical mobility, for example, presupposes availability of avenues for structural changes in the system of social stratification with the individual as a unit of ranking. But such a concept is hardly relevant because of the lack of requisite openness and the absence of the individual as the unit of social ranking in Indian society. This, however, should not be taken to mean that Indian society is monolithic, unchanging and stagnant. Social mobility is both a historical and a contextual social reality in Indian society.

Caste as a System of Social Stratification

The varied notions of caste—either referring to it as a rigid, unchanging, archaic and oriental system though functionally inevitable (Furnivall 1939; Ghurye 1961; Hutton 1946), or as antithetical to class (Davis 1957: 364–91), or as a unique system of ideas encompassing all other aspects of society (Dumont 1970)—are not only contradictory in terms, but also imply denigration of Indian society (Sharma 1986: 16–39). How can a rigid, unchanging and archaic system be functional for the entire society, for individual members of a caste and for caste as a whole? How would it prove to be an effective mechanism to face the challenges and forces of change from within and outside Indian society from time to time?

Caste has never been static as it has been said to be, and it has also not been functional as reported by several scholars. Thapar (1974: 95–123) observes that caste and class divide in ancient India was never rigid because society was not rigidly structured. Society was dynamic, and change in one aspect affected the other. It is evident from Thapar's observation regarding the prevalence of mixed castes and the hiatus between actual status and ritual status that social mobility in ancient India was possible. Uma Chakravarti

(1985: 356–60), based on her study of Buddhist sources, mentions about status incongruities. Kosambi's emphasis on production rather than kinship (1956: 86–87) for the study of social formation in ancient India also substantiates the multi-dimensional and multi-causal character of social reality. Hence, the application of the caste model (Béteille 1969: 17) for studying Indian society has sent wrong messages about its historicity and specificity.

Interdependence and interpenetration of caste, class and power in India's social formation at any given point of time and over a period of time not only highlights the limitations of monocausal explanations, but also throws light on the composite character of social reality. The use of application of nativistic concepts and categories, and the varied Marxist categories could be viewed as a reaction and alternative to the one-dimensional approach. Indian tradition is being considered as the sole basis in the first case; however, the general Marxist concepts find a preferential treatment in the second. These approaches too are not free from ideological moorings and narrow implications.

The Meaning of Social Inequality

Social inequality is a perennial problem as it causes high and low positions and the principles on the basis of which it exists determine the distribution of societal resources among individuals, families and groups. Despite its ubiquity, it has ramifications in terms of its causes, consequences (both functional and dysfunctional) and dynamics. Dahrendorf (1969: 17) poses four relevant questions about the problem of inequality. These are:

1. Why is there inequality among men?
2. Where do its causes lie?
3. Can it be reduced, or even abolished altogether?
4. Do we have to accept it as a necessary element in society?

Despite these being ubiquitous questions, there are differential patterns and expressions of social inequality all over the world. Legitimacy to social inequality, its functionality and inevitability are the focal points in all the formulations including the one proposed by Dahrendorf. Dahrendorf refers to natural distinctions (of kind and rank) based on what functionalists like Parsons (1954: 69–88, 386–439) call biological or non-social criteria. Social differentiation (positions of reputation and wealth) is referred to as social stratification based on the normative orientation of society. The universality of inequality does not make it inevitably functional. Dysfunctional consequences (Tumin 1953; 1955; 1957; 1969) of social stratification have been highlighted time and again. Further, functionality is a relative phenomenon. What is considered as non-social in the industrial Western world could be genuinely social for particular pre-industrial societies (Smith 1964: 141–76). Sex, age and kinship are the only bases of high and low positions and power in tribal communities. On the contrary, property, land, education and other such factors might not necessarily be significant determinants of social status in these communities.

It has been analyzed elsewhere that 'no debate on inequality can ignore the element of equality as an important component of all human societies and social movements therein' (Sharma 1994: 4). Derecognition of power and privileges based on birth and caste rank has created a sense of equal citizenship and equality of opportunity. Encouragement to the sections aspiring for equality to demand their share in national resources has brought about a new social language of interaction between the traditionally privileged and the emergent new strata. Derecognition of and challenge to the institutional set-up and the privileged groups and families are found historically and contextually in Indian society despite persistence of social inequality therein in varied forms and practices.

Thus social inequality is multi-dimensional and dynamic. It is not monolithic. There is constant structuring and restructuring of social inequality. Inequality is not opposite of equality theoretically as well as empirically. It is a 'relational' phenomenon, and not an absolute one. It is to be seen in relation to one another at the levels of individuals, families and groups. Family, for example, consists of both inequality and equality among its members. And inequality among its members is based mainly on age, sex, kinship and deference rather than on income, education, occupation and office held by individual members. However, the latter criteria too have always remained crucially significant in intra-family ties.

Criteria of social inequality such as income, competition and education alone do not explain the entire gamut of social stratification in Indian society. The underlying assumption of these criteria is of an industrially advanced society in which supposedly contest rather than sponsorship is of the prime value. Individual, like the Western society, is not the central unit of actual social ranking in the Indian society. However, individual remains the main reference point in India's Constitution. It is also not that ranking based on group alone is the basis of status and power. A critical appraisal of Louis Dumont's view on India's caste system throws the following questions:

1. Is the notion of Homo Hierarchicus synonymous of India's caste system?
2. Are there no elements of Homo Equalis in the Indian system of social stratification?

If the answer to the first question is in the affirmative then caste becomes an absolutist, unchanging and holistic system remaining totally unconcerned with its own contradictions and also with the external forces of change. There is a long epochal history of discontinuities, breakdowns, contradictions and changes in India's caste system. In response to the second question one may refer to several movements as crusades against the hegemonic supremacy of the upper castes, feudal lords, usurers and exploiters. Thus, the answer to the second question is in the affirmative, whereas it is negative in regard to the first question.

Notions of both inequality and equality are built into the ideology and practice of the caste system, and these two are not only closely interrelated but have changed over a given period of time. Change occurred both in the nature of and in the nexus between inequality and equality. Both the ideational and the structural forces have enabled the persistence of some aspects of the caste system despite murderous onslaughts on it. There were strong in-built balancing mechanisms in India's caste system which have no doubt now become quite weak. For example, Brahmins performed priestly functions and rituals while remaining at the top of the caste hierarchy, and the lower and untouchable castes functionaries also used to perform certain rituals on occasions like birth, marriage and death. Both Brahmins and lower castes enjoyed ritual or priestly status, and both were paid in cash and kind in lieu of their services. They were considered as essential components of the caste system. These points of similarity, however, did not imply equality of the two.

A Brahmin remained ritually superior to a lower caste functionary irrespective of the fact that both performed rituals and that too on the same occasions. In the same way both *jajman* (patron) and *kamin* (servant) were parts of the *jajmani* system, and the two were required to work in unison but the two had been granted different specific unequal rights and duties. At the same time the dissatisfied *kamins* could refuse to render their services to the *jajmans* and prevent the fellow-*kamins* to work as substitutes for them. Caste-councils (*biradaries*) defended the rights of their members and more so in the case of the functionary castes.

These points of similarity thus do not explain absolute supremacy of the patrons under the *jajmani* system. However, the upper-caste patrons, because of their superior economic standing, could compel the lower castes to work for them on the unilateral terms and conditions. In fact, two situations can be: (*a*) the lower castes expressed their dissatisfaction and annoyance; and (*b*) the upper castes resorted to force and violence, boycott, denial and withdrawal of land and employment.

Approaches to the Study of Social Inequality

Approaches to the study of social inequality are not only thought constructs, they are also rooted into the real world, the world of structural aspects of society. As a mere ideational phenomenon, an approach is a world of thoughts and dominates the world of things. Dumont (1970) perceives hierarchy as the domination of thought rather than of things as it is the ideology of pollution–purity that determines high and low in society in regard to people, clothes, occupations and positions. On the contrary, following the Marxian view it can be stated that the existential conditions determine hierarchy and inequality. To quote Marx and Engels (1968: 36): 'As individuals express their life, so they are. What they are, therefore, coincides with their production, both with *what* they produce and with *how* they produce.' Marx speaks of both *structure* of existential conditions, and also of the *process* of change in these conditions.

Through his analysis of evolution of society, state and forces of production Marx provides a vivid account of socio-economic differentiation. Antagonism and contradictions are the causes of differentiation and change, and these have been inevitable phenomena of change in the system of social stratification in India. Caste, for example, has acquired a new form, and it has also become a different sort of system of relations. What was considered as immutable and rigid has become quite flexible, and what was considered as an inevitable part of the system has become optional or it has disappeared. New dimensions have been accredited to it mainly because of some unintended and unanticipated consequences of both structural and ideological changes. Similarly, the class character of Indian society has also considerably changed since independence particularly due to the emergence of the middle class disproportionate to the upper and the lower classes.

The emergence of the new middle class disproportionate to the forces of production, and also to the size(s) of the upper and lower classes has forged a new nexus between caste and class. The embourgeoisement of the principal agricultural castes has established a new direction between caste, class and politics. The divide between the traditionally dominant and the emerging sections has acquired a new character.

Thus, structuring of social inequality is a continuous process. It is a life-process of the placement of individuals, families and groups. What people do as members of their families and collectivities (castes and communities) is not independent of their existential conditions. What they do in structural terms is their social life. What is its mode of production? What units (classes, groups, collectivities) are produced as a result of certain social (material) conditions? What is the nature of social interaction between the groups produced through this social and historical process? These basic Marxian questions despite the globalization of world economy and the considerable weakening of Marxism in the erstwhile socialist countries remain relevant for exploring the nature of social stratification in contemporary India. A possible key to find answers to these questions may be found in the proposition: Each generation continues the traditional activity in completely changed circumstances, and modifies the old circumstances with a completely changed activity. The Marxian perspective can explain the following:

1. Continuity of tradition and emergence of modernity side by side in the field of social stratification;

2. Determination of social relations by the direction of social change; and
3. Coexistence of the structure and process of social stratification.

Though Max Weber represents a considerably different perspective while compared with Marxian thinking, yet Gerth and Mills (1970: 46) observe: 'Much of Weber's own work is of course informed by a skilful application of Marx's historical method.' Weber criticizes Marx for an untenable monocausal theory, a segmental perspective and reducing the multiplicity of causal factors to a single-factor theorem. However, Weber's work is commented by Gerth and Mills (ibid.: 46–50) as an attempt to 'round out' Marx's economic materialism by political and military materialism.

Weber (1970: 180–95) in the well-known essay—'Class, Status, Party' considers 'classes', 'status groups' and 'parties' as phenomena of the distribution of power within a community. Power is understood by Weber (ibid.: 180) as 'the chance of a man or of a number of men to realise their own will in a communal action even against the resistance of others who are participating in the action'. The individual becomes a significant unit in Weber's definition of power. The principle of rationalization also finds its due place in Weber's thinking. Weber observes: 'Economically conditioned power is not, of course, identical with power as such' (ibid.: 180). Further, Weber makes it clear that the emergence of economic power may be the consequence of power existing on other grounds. Man does not strive just for economic power. Power may be valued for its own sake. Quite often the striving for power is also conditioned by the social honour it entails. And not all power entails social honour. There are other bases too of social honour. The three orders, economic, social and political/legal, are not identical, and yet they are closely intertwined. The subjective element (satisfaction/frustration) becomes an important dimension along with provision of goods and external conditions of life (ibid.: 424) in Weber's perspective on class status.

Now the question is: How far have the multi-dimensional studies of social stratification emphasizing caste, class and power/politics accounted for Weber's principles of rationalization, individual and his action (subjectivity) and interpretative understanding? Several points concerning the notion of rationality, historical specificity, cultural moorings, methodology and levels of application and analysis are necessary ingredients in the application of Weber's approach to the study of social stratification.

Pierre Bourdieu (1991) argues that symbolic productions are to be treated as instruments of domination. The Marxist tradition ignores this and lays great emphasis on relating the symbolic productions to the interests of the dominant class. 'The dominant class is the site of a struggle over the hierarchy of the principles of hierarchization' (ibid.: 168). The dominant class imposes the legitimacy of its domination to appropriate the social world for its own benefit. The capital (economic, social, cultural or symbolic) which provides the basis for position to the agents is placed at the top in the principles of hierarchization. Capital is power, and power relations are not reducible to the intentions of individual agents or even to direct interactions between agents (ibid.). The distribution of power is multi-faceted and a relative phenomenon. The kinds of capital are powers which define the chances of profit in a given field. This view marks a break with both Marxian and Weberian traditions. However, Foucault's concept of power is somewhat closer to the one given by Weber. Empirically, Foucault conceives power as the interaction of warring parties, as the decentred network of bodily, face-to-face confrontations, and ultimately as the productive penetration and subjectivizing subjugation of a bodily opponent. Foucault considers power as a paradoxical operation, and it includes synthetic performances. Power constitutive of discourse is *will to truth*, having transcendental generativity, and also self-assertion at the same time at the empirical level. Habermas observes that what 'difference' is for Derrida, 'power' is for Foucault (1987: 266–93).

Social stratification viewed from a structural perspective implies ordering and reordering, and distribution and redistribution of people and resources, respectively. Change emanates in a given society partly from the endogenous forces, namely, the incompatibility of the parts of the system, and partly from the wider forces. Thus, there are manifold problems in the conceptualization of social stratification and social inequality and in the formulation of the relevant approaches with specific reference to the study of caste, class and power in India.

The Main Points of the Studies on Caste Stratification

Generally, caste is considered to be a closed system denying social mobility in Hindu society. Connubiality and commensality are

considered as the cardinal principles of inter-caste relations based
on the ascription of caste rank by birth. A number of studies (Bailey
1957, 1963; Bougle 1958: 30; Dumont 1970; Ghurye 1961; Hocart
1950; Hutton 1946; Madan 1972; Marriott 1965, 1959: 92–107;
Mathur 1964; Mayer 1960; Shah 1982; Srinivas 1955, 1984; Weber
1970: 180–95) highlighting the ascriptive basis of caste ranking could
be mentioned in this context. Caste continues to be a pivotal force
in guiding social relations in Indian society as perceived and reflected
in these studies. Pollution–purity, caste endogamy and lately caste-
based ethnocentrism and mobilization are articulated as the main
points in support of the super-organic character of the caste system.
Caste, in these studies, is equated with social stratification encompassing economic and political aspects of social status.

The foregoing studies focus on caste as the sole institution of social
ranking considering caste as an extreme form of class (Kroeber
1930: 254–57; Myrdal 1944; Weber 1970). Socio-religious and ritualistic considerations have again found a prime place in the studies
of social stratification in the 1940s and the 1950s (Ghurye 1961;
Hocart 1950; Hutton 1946). Srinivas (1952), Dube (1955: 54–62),
Marriott (1955), and Dumont (1957, 1958, 1966, 1970) in particular
have considered caste as an institution of social stratification. Caste
is seen as the basis of inter-group relations based on the principle
of pollution–purity. Ritual impurity, normal ritual status and ritual
purity (Srinivas 1952) constitute the social hierarchy. Thus, the main
criteria for the ranking of castes are ritual and not economic (Dube
1955: 54–62). Both ritual and political power are rooted in the
religio-ritualistic order of the caste system (Dumont 1970).

F. G. Bailey (1957; 1963: 107–24) considers caste as a system of
closed organic stratification, whereas Oscar Lewis (1958) finds
caste as an integrating and cohesive factor in the village community
as it encompasses kinship ties and political and economic relationships. Mayer (1960) observes that caste and kinship ties involute
other relationships. Caste ranking is a part of the social structure
(Mayer 1965: 3). To date caste is the sole institution of social
ranking in India (Dumont 1970).

The Myth of Caste as an Encompassing System

A number of studies do not substantiate the hypothesis relating to
caste as an encompassing system as they have reported regional

variations in regard to the rigidity and pollution–purity dimension of the caste system. McKim Marriott (1965) uses the term elaboration as a parameter or comprehensive measure to work out a continuum of rigidity-flexibility in five regions, namely, Kerala, Coromandel, upper Ganges, middle Indus and Bengal delta, signifying maximum rigidity in Kerala and minimum in the Bengal delta. These regional variations are also linked up with ethnic differentiation within and between the regions. Prevalence of lesser elaboration of caste indicates the role played by economic and political factors in status-determination.

Horizontal mobility in the caste system implies a consideration of some factors other than caste. Caste has undergone a sea-change over the last two centuries. The relative deprivation faced by the backward castes (including untouchables) has generated sentiments against the upper castes. Education, reservation of jobs, legal and constitutional provisions and safeguards, developmental programmes and also withdrawal of the status enjoyed by the upper castes are some of the key factors which have weakened upper-caste dominance and the socio-economic conditions of the middle and lower castes.

It has been observed that rank–orders in the village community depended upon the quality of agricultural land and infrastructure for cultivating it (Ruben 1974: 20) rather than on the caste-rank alone. The economy evolved from pastoralism to trade and commerce in ancient India. Romila Thapar (1974: 95–123) refers to changes in elite groups due to invasions and migrations. Due to such changes rules of marriage and status–relationships could not remain rigid and static. Thapar observes that it was not a rigidly structured and frozen society. There were both ritual status and actual status, and the latter was characterized by secular bases of social stratification. Due to the identity based on common economic and occupational interests, mixed castes also emerged further signifying changes in the caste system due to economic considerations. The ritual and the actual statuses were rarely in harmony.

The social formation of the Indus society can be characterized in material terms by applying the Marxian concept of the Asiatic System as the principal mode of production (Chakraborty 1983: 1832–38). Along with this mode, other modes of exploitation existed. There were temple slaves and semi-independent urban producers. A class of *priests also existed*. And above all these groups was a central authority, a ruling class and the state.

Uma Chakravarti's analysis of ancient Indian society based on Buddhist sources (1985: 356–60) not only corroborates Thapar's analysis of status mobility, but also depicts two possible social arrangements: (*a*) the Brahminical division of society was a sum total of Brahmins, Kshatriyas, Vaishyas and Shudras incorporating both varna and *jati*; and (*b*) the Buddhist texts mention about the non-Brahminical primacy in which the Kshatriyas received ascendance over the Brahmins followed by the Gahapatis. This was the *kula* system, and it had gained upper hand over the Brahminical order. The non-Brahminical order represents a division of society into the domains of power, ritual and economy. Particularly due to the ascendancy of the Kshatriyas over the Brahmins there was tension between the· two.

Thus, it is not that caste alone held society together. Economy along with caste contributed to the making· of society (Kosambi 1958: 86–87). Land tenure systems, ruling class, landed aristocracy, big peasants, etc., have affected caste rigidity enormously from the twelfth century AD (Hasan 1979: 17–32). It was a highly structured, complex and yet dynamic society. K. L. Sharma's study of social stratification in rural Rajasthan (1974) shows how a socially patterned taxation system, systems of land control and land-grants existed under the *jagirdari* system.

A caste-rank was never absolute. Besides birth, the rank of a caste depended also upon its *referents* (other castes) with which it interacted. A Brahmin *jajman* or an upper-caste landlord was served by a *kamin*, but the *kamin* was not a *kamin* of an intermediate caste *jajman* or of a Chamar though he performed more or less the same functions for them which he performed for his upper-caste patrons and landlords. A contra-priest is not equivalent at all to a Brahmin priest, and yet he is granted priestly status in those specific situations in which he performs certain rituals particularly in upper-caste families. A contra-priest signifies the coexistence of both inequality and equality, and absolutelessness of power of the upper castes over the lower castes.

Louis Dumont in Defence of Caste

Dumont observes that caste stands for inequality in both theory and practice; but this inequality is not simply the binary opposite of equality. The inequality of the caste system is a special type of inequality. While admitting the pre-eminence of the idealist or intellectualist orientation in his understanding of sociology, Dumont emphasizes the study of 'ideas and values' as the main focus in his study. Thus, Dumont adopts the structuralist method and orientation in his analysis of the caste system.

Like Bougle (1958: 29), for Dumont the notion of fundamental opposition between the pure and the impure is the hallmark of the caste system. The principle of the opposition between the pure and the impure is a 'single true principle', signifying hierarchy in terms of the superiority of the pure over the impure. It also separates the two, hence the division of labour. A necessary hierarchical coexistence of the opposites (Dumont 1970: 43) is basic in Dumont's framework. It is this principle of pure and impure that determines hierarchy; in fact, hierarchy itself becomes a value and a fact both. The caste system is a system of ideas and values, and it is a formal, comprehensible rational system, a system in the intellectual sense of the term. Different castes are related through a system of oppositions.

Dumont also differentiates between *status* and *power*, emphasizing the subordination of the king (power) to the priest (status). Hierarchy involves gradation, but it is distinct from both power and authority. Hierarchy is an all-embracing, comprehensive ideology and concept leading to structured social inequality. Thus the principle of hierarchy not only applies to castes, but also to the notions of values, occupations, food, clothes, bride-givers and bride-takers, etc. Dumont looks for cultural meaning of affinity and consanguinity (Sharma 1983). Yogendra Singh (1985: 37–79) discerns four notions from Dumont's *Homo Hierarchicus*: (a) ideology, (b) binary tension or dialectics, (c) transformational relationship, and (d) comparison. Since everything is seen through the ideology of the pure and the impure, change is *in* the society and not *of* the society. The caste system does not change but changes take place within the system. Srinivas (1984: 153), while agreeing with Dumont, also characterizes 'caste society' as holistic and hierarchical, inimical to individualism except in the form of the sannyasi or renouncer.

Though Srinivas considers *jati* as the sole unit for understanding Hindu society, he is quite critical of Dumont's treatment of caste. Srinivas (1989: 2) writes: 'Dumont has failed to argue convincingly that Hindu caste represents an instance of pure hierarchy in the sense that he uses the term viz., the subordination of power to status (religious rank).' According to Srinivas, Dumont maintains that status and power were separated, and that the latter was subordinated to the former. Power is subordinated to status in both the varna and the *jati* systems. *Jatis* are ranked on the basis of relative purity, a higher caste being purer than a lower. Further, Srinivas articulates that Dumont postulates a homology between varna and *jati*, and considers that *jati* is dependent upon varna by virtue of its being secondary and segmented, and contradictions in the concept of *jati* can be resolved by appealing to the concept of varna. Thus, there was dependence of *jati* on varna in relation to matters of power. Srinivas writes: 'This is the argument of naked expediency and it seems to be the central weakness in his argument. He is really jettisoning his entire case.'

A scaler analysis of purity–impurity as the basis of power as perceived by Dumont was not entirely irrelevant in the past when 'ritual hierarchy' reigned supreme. Today, numerical strength of a given caste, its alliances with other castes, benefits received as a 'backward caste' and caste-based mobilizations account for power actualized in political and other spheres of social life. Both Dumont and Srinivas did not comprehend the situation that exists today in terms of 'resilience' of the caste system. Srinivas finds the process of sanskritization quite 'cohesive' for social mobility both cultural and structural. In essence, however, cultural mobility remains at the centre-stage in his understanding of caste system. In a postscript to sanskritization (ibid.: 22–25) Srinivas, though lately, realizes that female sexuality is also controlled by it. He writes: 'The desire to control female sexuality, promote female reproduction of sons while discouraging the production of daughters, are all built into sanskritization' (ibid.: 23).

Srinivas attributes several notions, institutions and practices to the ideology of sanskritization and ideas of purity and impurity. 'Inherent in the logic of a hierarchical society is the greater need to control the sexuality of women at the higher levels of the hierarchy' (ibid.: 24–25). But what about the very structural processes of change which have not originated directly from the caste system? Adult franchise, land reforms, green revolution, migration, industrialization, etc., have occurred partly as a consequence of global changes and considerably as a result of the nationalist endeavours particularly after independence. Srinivas does not go beyond the notion of the sanskritic tradition to explain cultural changes (ibid.: 56–72), and this is why his framework continues to be Brahmino-centric, ignoring the emergence of the intermediate and lower castes in positions of power and authority.

A paradigmatic change is observable when Béteille (1994: 435) argues 'that certain fundamental changes are taking place in the social mechanism of the reproduction of inequality in which the family and not caste now plays the active part'. The internal mechanisms of the reproduction of inequalities are undergoing significant change. Béteille cites the case of the reproduction of the service class from one generation to another, and the unequal distribution of life chances or access to it. Caste automatically does not influence the distribution of life chances. The family plays a crucial role in the reproduction of social structure (including inequality), and a far more active role than caste. Family is repository of social and cultural capital through the process of socialization of its members (Bourdieu 1991: 114). However, the most significant feature of the caste system is its cognitive continuity and change though in transformed forms. Caste could not check differentiation of property, technological change and occupational mobility, and yet it has survived and even penetrated into nontraditional and new spheres of life (Gould 1988: 1–20). Another point contradicting the views articulated by Dumont and Srinivas is presented by David N. Gellner and Declan Quigley (1988: 1–37). In their study of the Newar society in Nepal they refer to the 'double-headed' caste hierarchy. Claims to high status in complex caste hierarchies are based on multiple criteria which are contested and evaluated differentially. 'In Newar society there is ample scope for opposing views and contested rankings between castes of similar status' (ibid.: 13). Within castes too, the ranking of lower-order groups is also contested. A situation resembling that in the princely states of Rajasthan also prevailed in Nepal where the person of the king had to be seen as superior, or at least not inferior to Brahmins, in some important contexts. In different localities, the same caste may be ranked and treated differently. Some castes are found in some parts of the country only. Gellner and Quigley, hence, talk of several sub-regional hierarchies. The notion of caste 'elaboration' by McKim Marriott (1965) and the studies of caste in India, Sri Lanka and Pakistan (Leach 1960) have also hinted at the rigidity and flexibility of caste in different parts of India and the neighbouring countries.

The idea of 'blocs' or levels in the caste hierarchy with reference to Newars of Nepal speaks of order within the caste. Declan Quigley while summing up the debate on the nature of caste argues by contesting Dumont's view that Newars have only status groups and not caste at all (1995: 298–327). The city in Nepal is the centre of caste and provides the ground for maximum caste activity. Bhaktapur (a town in Nepal) exhibits a full-blown caste society. Another town Lalitpur displays the same caste-based, palace-centred pattern (ibid.: 319). The defining criterion for the Newar social organization is structural, and not cultural (ibid.: 319–20). Quigley prefers to abandon linear, ladder-like hierarchies to represent the order of castes.

Though the Nepalis have themselves arranged castes along a linear hierarchy, but they also represent the caste order in a quite different manner manifesting ambiguous relations between patrons and priestly castes and those between different castes of priests themselves. The apparent linearity is quite spurious at the actual level. The 'contextualizing' of caste in terms of community formation, politics, religion, untouchables, tribes, etc. (Searle, Chatterjee and Sharma 1994) can bring out ramifications of caste hierarchy. What is needed is the emphasis on the nexus between caste and class in the context of continuity and change (Sharma 1996: 130–46) rather than treating the two systems as dichotomous.

Since caste has increasingly acquired a segmental character, it has lost its ritual basis of ranking to a considerable extent. What was pure in yesteryears and remained confined to the *dwij* castes has reached to the lowest of the low castes, and what was impure and was concerned with the untouchable castes has become secular as it is being accepted by the upper castes. Therefore, change is both *in* and *of* the caste system.

Cultural versus Structural Criteria in Caste Stratification

Despite recent efforts for renewal of culturology and indigenous categories in sociology and social anthropology, emphasis has considerably shifted from cultural criteria to structural analysis in the study of social stratification. Inequalities in rural India (Chakravarti 1983: 129–81) are based on structural criteria such as status, economic differences and power, and a lower status in one of these spheres is not necessarily congruent with the other two spheres. Thus, caste as a cultural institution plays a limited and fixed role today in determining social status and inequality. Structural incongruities have been observed in several other studies too (Bailey 1957; Epstein 1962; Gupta 1984; Omvedt 1982; Sharma 1974; Singh 1968). Caste has renewed its nexus with economy, polity, religion, migration, etc. New frontiers in these areas have changed the traditional character of agrarian relations, economic transactions and service-relations resulting in the restructuring of the caste system (Mencher 1974: 469). Role-reversal has stepped up.

However, social inequality is not uniformly structured. Social stratification is observed in diverse forms in different structural and historical contexts. Morton Klass (1980) relates caste with physical force and economic power. Social inequality is measured in terms of the distribution of material resources and power. It is a lived-in experience, an existential reality. But it is always a relative phenomenon (Berreman 1979), and it could be studied in terms of four dimensions, namely, behavioural, interactional, material and existential. These four dimensions would not perhaps be different in essence from interactional and attributional approaches as suggested much earlier by McKim Marriott (1959: 92–107). Behavioural and interactional could be clubbed as interactional and material and existential put together could be termed as attributional approaches.

Dumont, Srinivas and several other scholars see individualism in renouncing the world but not in migration, feuds, competition, bargaining and such other acts in the traditional Indian society. Occupation, education, power and style of life (Sharma 1980: 99–114), ownership, control and use of land in relation to caste (Béteille 1972: 135), and the land grab movement by the poor and landless peasants and the structural and emergent factors resulting in the termination and failure of the movement (Singh 1974: 46) are some of the examples of the changing criteria of status–determination and caste–class nexus.

Rajendra Singh's study (ibid.: 46) of the Basti district in Uttar Pradesh probes the following questions:

1. How have various agrarian reforms affected caste, class and land relations?
2. Who have been the gainers and who the losers are of land as a result of these reforms?
3. What is their caste and class position today?
4. What is the impact of these reforms upon the emerging pattern of power-structure in the district?

Singh's findings show that class solidarity as well as pauperization are the characteristic features of the zamindars in Basti district. A strong lower middle caste rich peasantry also emerged at the same time. Proletarianization and downward social mobility among the landed families and bourgeoisiefication and upward social mobility among the middle and lower middle caste families of tenants, labourers and artisans (Sharma 1974) have been reported in Rajasthan. Singh (1974: 64) writes: 'After examining the Basti situation I find the inadequacy of class as well as caste. The agrarian society in Basti conforms neither to a class nor to a caste model.' Gough (1980: 337–64), Gupta (1984: 2049), Meillasseux (1973), Namboodiripad (1979: 329–36), Omvedt (1980: 145; 1982) and Ranadive (1979: 337–48) have arrived at the following view: (a) caste is not precisely equivalent to class, (b) castes are discrete, and (c) class relations can be analyzed by exploring their connections with caste, kinship, marriage and family. Thus, the shift in regard to caste as a system of stratification is reflected in the dynamics of the nexus that caste has/had in Indian society with class, power and social mobility. Structural criteria have always been central to caste as a system of social stratification.

A Résumé of the Earlier Trend Reports on Social Stratification

Two earlier trend reports on the sociology of social stratification were written by Yogendra Singh (1974, 1985). In the first report (1974), Singh mentions that the sociology of social stratification is concerned mainly with the nature of social order, social equality and inequality, social justice, power and the nature of man. In a broader sense these issues are related to the questions of theory, structure and process of social stratification (Singh 1977: 1). Singh observes that the theory of social stratification refers to *why* of social stratification. The dimensionalistic approach, namely, status, wealth and power, provides specific explanations of social stratification.

Yogendra Singh (1974: 314) poses a host of questions regarding studies on social stratification in India. These are about theoretical assumptions, functional or dialectical postulates, structural foci, units or components, direction, relevance, strategic processes, their causes, consequences and impact on the social system. The first report discusses studies on caste, Scheduled Castes, class structures, agrarian class stratification and change, and elites and social stratification. Studies of social stratification on these aspects involve ideological debate regarding equality/inequality.

We notice a shift in emphasis in Singh's second report on social stratification (1985: 37–79). Singh examines various studies of the decade under review in terms of changing theoretical orientations such as structural, structuralist, structural–historical and Marxist. The spectrum of analysis is quite vast in the second report as social stratification is viewed in relation to the studies in other social sciences. National ideology, self-awareness among social scientists in the 1970s, sociology and social change, social stratification in non-Hindu communities, tribes and Scheduled Castes have been particularly discussed. Singh distinctly observes the following new trends in the studies of social stratification:

1. Increased debates on the ideological moorings of concepts and theories.
2. Efforts to re-emphasize conceptual systems and their presuppositions in the light of shifting programmes.
3. The new substantive concerns in the stratification studies.
4. Fruitful convergence of multi-disciplinary interests, both substantive and theoretical, in the studies of social stratification.

Singh notes that these trends are mainly due to the decline of academic colonialism and positivism of the West. Indigenization of concepts and paradigms gained currency by raising the question of relevance, in particular of the variants of functionalism and Marxism which originated from the experience of the Western society, culture, polity and economy.

Caste, Class and Power as Dimensions of Social Stratification

There is no chronological order in the studies of social stratification based on theoretical orientations such as structural–functionalism, structuralism, structural–historical and Marxism. Studies of the nexus between caste and class (Béteille 1966; Sharma 1974; Singh 1968: 165–86, 186) not only bring out the multi-faceted nature of caste and social stratification in India, but they also explain the influence of the structural–historical perspective on the studies of social stratification. Some of the studies of caste which have a class point of view (Desai 1975; Gough 1960: 11–60; Mencher 1974: 469–93; Omvedt 1980: 1347–50; 1980; 1982) highlight the relevance of the structural–historical perspective for the study of social stratification. However, studies influenced by the structural–functional perspective have not moved away from the hierarchical model of caste, consensus, resilience, summation of roles and statuses at the micro-structural or communitarian scale of reality. The structural–historical perspective not only explains the dynamics and dialectics of caste, class and power, but it also facilitates studies of downward social mobility and the structural processes of change such as bourgeoisiefication and proletarianization.

Studies of caste, class and power (Aggrawal 1971; Béteille 1966; Bhatt 1975) also go beyond the analysis of the principle and practice of Pure and Impure. Caste-free areas have emerged due to the differented structures in modern India. Cleavages between caste, class and power indicate the incompatibility of the principle and practice of the pollution–purity syndrome with macro-structural changes. While analyzing the problems of conceptualizing caste and class in India (Sharma 1986: 26–61), it is suggested that dialectics, history, culture and structure should become essential features of the structural–historical approach for the study of social stratification. It is these that constitute the totality of social formation (caste, class and power), and as such also facilitate the analysis of theory, structure and process—the three essential ingredients of social stratification (Singh 1974: 311).

Today, the debate regarding social stratification in India centres around: (*a*) whether changes in caste and class are transformational or structural; (*b*) whether caste is closed and class is open; (*c*) whether caste is organic and class is segmentary; and (*d*) whether caste is being replaced by class and political power or not. These questions have come up time and again because caste and class have been perceived mistakenly as polar opposites.

S. C. Malik in the preface to *Determinants of Social Status in India* (1986: x) discerns four main approaches: (*a*) emphasis on status stratification; (*b*) the use of Marxian models or their modified versions; (*c*) the use of the varna–*jati* model; and (*d*) the purely empirical approach. However, this categorization suffers from cognitive–logical inadequacy. For example, status stratification is not an approach, but a substantive theme of study. So is the case of varna–*jati*. Varna and caste could be studied from a functional/dialectical/psychological point of view. All these approaches could be empirical/historical, and therefore, there is nothing like 'the purely empirical approach'. Yogendra Singh's treatment of approaches to the study of social stratification (1974: 311–82; 1985: 37–79) provides a comprehensive view of the theoretical/ideological debate and of the substantive issues in the studies of social stratification. However, Malik (1986: 1–24) outlines the following issues as central to the study of social stratification:

1. Ritual values as a determinant of status.
2. Social mobility and status determination.
3. Social status and stratification.
4. The problem of caste and class.
5. Historical situations.

Some questions in general regarding concepts and approaches, and specific and substantive issues regarding India (ibid.: 17–20), have also been raised.

It is difficult to map out the entire gamut of the multi-dimensional studies of social stratification, yet in a broad sense we could incorporate the following points:

1. The traditional pattern of stratification in India.
2. Conceptual problems in the context of caste and class in India.
3. Continuous hierarchies and discrete classes: social mobilization among peasants.
4. Caste and politics.

5. Caste, class and party.
6. Caste, land and power.
7. Social stratification and power.
8. Agrarian classes and political mobilization.
9. Social stratification and rural development.
10. Social stratification and sources of mobility among Scheduled Castes in urban India.
11. Professions and social stratification.
12. Industrialization and social stratification.
13. Class and ethnicity among tribes.

There could be many more areas relevant for the study of social stratification. These may include education, wealth and property, migration, etc. More than the substantive aspects of the study of social stratification are the issues which have crystallized since independence. Yogendra Singh (1986: 325) sums up the main issues regarding the studies of social stratification in the post-independence period as follows:

Among the important features of these studies were: focus upon ritual bases of caste stratification, structural–functional perspective in analysis, collection of data through fieldwork observation and a limited space–time boundary in delineation of the system of caste stratification.

Singh also hints at the neglect of the use of historical sources of data, analysis of the origin or evolution of social stratification and no attempt to view the caste system in the macro-structural perspective of social transformation. Most of the studies were descriptive and reported a microcosmic view of social reality. The issues of concept, ideology or method were not raised. Class analysis as a frame of analysis remained almost ignored.

The Shifts in the Studies of Social Stratification

However, in the past forty years we have witnessed several conceptual and substantive changes in studies on social stratification. Structural–functionalism of the fifties encountered conceptual and methodological challenges in the form of Dumont's structuralist theory and ideology, Marxist theory and method, and Weber's dimensionalistic approach of class, status and party. Singh observes that in the sixties the debates in the studies of social stratification focused mainly on the choices among conceptual typologies versus continuum, historical specificity versus comparison, structure–function versus conflict, and dialectic versus ideology. Studies of social stratification became problem-oriented both conceptually and substantively. The new studies dealt with the problems of caste and class exploitation, domination, poverty, alienation and distributive justice. A rethinking of the concepts of caste and class (Sharma 1986: 29–61) became a focal point of debate in the studies of social stratification. The theoretical focus shifted to structuralism, structural–historicism and Marxism from the traditional British and the American structural–functionalism.

Yogendra Singh (1986: 327–28) further observes that in the 1970s and 1980s the new orientations in the studies of social stratification were concerned with (a) the debate on the role of ideology in the paradigms of social stratification, (b) a revival of historical and evolutionary perspectives, (c) the emergence of the dialectical paradigm as a new theoretical orientation in the studies of social stratification, and (d) increasing realization about the issues of relevance both from social and conceptual points of view. Thus, Singh considers ideology, evolutionary perspective, dialectical orientation and the issues of relevance as the main concerns in the studies of social stratification.

Surendra Sharma (1985: 82–114) provides a comprehensive review of the studies of social stratification in India mainly focusing upon theory, ideology and method from the viewpoint of the sociology of knowledge. The main problem as envisaged by Sharma is that a proper connection between theory, method and data is lacking in the studies of social stratification. The ideological and historical dimensions of social inequality along with the quest for equality remain in most studies unspelt out and unanalyzed. A rethinking of the concepts of caste, class, power, and social mobility is seriously underway.

References

Aggarwal, P.C., 1971, *Caste, Religion and Power*, New Delhi: Shriram Centre for Industrial Relations.

Bailey, F.G., 1957, *Caste and the Economic Frontier*, Manchester: Manchester University Press.

————, 1963, 'Closed Social Stratification in India', *European Journal of Sociology*, Vol. IV, No. 1.

Berreman, G.D., 1979, *Caste and Other Inequalities*, Meerut: Folklore Institute.

Béteille, André, 1966, *Caste, Class and Power*, Bombay: Oxford University Press.

————, 1966, 'Closed and Open Social Stratification in India', *European Journal of Sociology*, Vol. 7, pp. 224–46.

————, 1969, 'Ideas and Interests: Some Conceptual Problems in the Study of Social Stratification in India', *International Social Science Journal*, Vol. 21, No. 2.

————, 1972, 'Agrarian Relations in Tanjore District', *Sociological Bulletin*, Vol. 21, No. 2.

————, 1994, 'The Family and the Reproduction of Inequality', *in* Uberoi, Patricia (ed.), *Family, Kinship and Marriage in India*, Delhi: Oxford University Press, pp. 435–51.

Bhatt, Anil, 1975, *Caste, Class and Politics*, Delhi: Manohar Publications.

Bougle, C., 1958, 'The Essence of Reality of Caste System', *Contributions to Indian Sociology*, No. 2.

Bourdieu, Pierre, 1991, *Language and Symbolic Power*, Cambridge: Polity Press.

Chakraborty, Aparajita, 1982, 'The Social Formation of the Indus Society', *Economic and Political Weekly*, Vol. XVII, No. 50.

Chakravarti, Anand, 1983, 'Some Aspects of Inequality in Rural India, A Sociological Perspective', *in* Béteille, André (ed.), *Equality and Inequality: Theory and Practice*, Delhi: Oxford University Press.

Chakravarti, Uma, 1985, 'Towards a Historical Sociology of Stratification in Ancient India: Evidence of Buddhist Sources', *Economic and Political Weekly*, Vol. XX, No. 9.

Dahrendorf, Ralph, 1969, 'The Origin of Inequality Among Men', *in* Béteille, André (ed.), *Social Inequality*, Penguin Books.

Damle, Y.B., 1968, 'Reference group and mobility in the caste system', *in* Silverberg, James (ed.), *Social Mobility in the Caste System in India*, The Hague: Mouton Publishers.

Davis, Kingsley, 1957, *Population of India and Pakistan*, Princeton: Princeton University Press.

Desai, A.R., 1975, *State and Society in India*, Bombay: Popular Prakashan.

Dube, S.C., 1955, *Indian Village*, London: Routledge and Kegan Paul.

Dumont, Louis, 1958, 'A. M. Hocart on Caste: Religion and Power', *Contributions to Indian Sociology*, No. 2.

————, 1966, 'A Fundamental Problem in Sociology of Caste', *Contributions to Indian Sociology*, No. 9.

————, 1970, *Homo Hierarchicus*, London: Paladin, Granda Pub. Ltd.

Dumont, Louis and **D. F. Pocock**, 1957, 'Village Studies', *Contributions to Indian Sociology*, No. 1.

Epstein, T.S., 1962, *Economic Development and Social Change in South India*, Manchester: Manchester University Press.

Furnivall, J.S., 1939, *Netherlands—India: A Study in Plural Economy*, Cambridge: Cambridge University Press.

Gellner, David N. and Declan Quigley (eds), 1995, *Contested Hierarchies*, Oxford: Clarendon Press.

Gerth, H.H. and C. W. Mills (eds), 1970, *From Max Weber, Essays in Sociology*, London: Routledge and Kegan Paul.

Ghurye, G.S., 1961, *Caste, Class and Occupation*, Bombay: Popular Book Depot.

Gough, E. Kathleen, 1960, 'Caste in a Tanjore village', *in* Leach, E.R. (ed.), *Aspects of Caste in South India, Ceylon and North-West Pakistan*, Cambridge: Cambridge University Press.

———, 1980, 'Modes of Production in Southern India', *Economic and Political Weekly*, Vol. XV, (AN) Nos. 5, 6 and 7.

Gould, Harold A., 1988, *Caste Adaptation in Modernizing Indian Society*, Delhi: Chanakya Publications.

Gupta, Dipankar, 1984, 'Continuous hierarchies and discrete castes', *Economic and Political Weekly*, Vol. XIX, No. 46.

Habermas, Jürgen, 1987, 'Some Questions Concerning the Theory of Power: Foucault Again', *The Philosophical Discourse of Modernity*, Cambridge: Polity Press, pp. 266–93.

Hasan, S. Narul, 1979, 'Zamindars under the Mughals', *in* Frykenberg, R.E. (ed.), *Land Control and Social Structure in Indian History*, New Delhi: Manohar Publications.

Hocart, A.M., 1950, *Caste: A Comparative Study*, London: Mathew and Co.

Hutton, J.H., 1946, *The Caste in India*, Oxford: Oxford University Press.

Klass, Morton, 1980, *Caste: The Emergence of the System in South Asia*, Philadelphia: Institute for the Study of Human Issues.

Kosambi, D.D., 1958, *An Introduction to the Study of the Indian History*, Bombay: Popular Book Depot.

Kroeber, A.L., 1930, 'Caste', *Encyclopaedia of the Social Sciences*, Vol. III.

Leach, E.R. (ed.), 1960, *Aspects of Caste in South India, Ceylon and North-West Pakistan*, Cambridge: Cambridge University Press.

Lewis, Oscar, 1958, *Village Life in Northern India*, Urbana: Illinois University.

Lynch, Owen, 1969, *Politics of Untouchability*, New York: Columbia University Press.

Madan, T.N., 1972, 'On the nature of caste in India: A review symposium on Louis Dumont's *Homo Hierarchicus*', *Contributions to Indian Sociology* (NS), Vol. VI.

Majumdar, D.N., 1958, *Caste and Communication in an Indian Village*, Delhi: Asia Publishing House.

Malik, S.C. (ed.), 1986, *Determinants of Social Status in India*, Simla: Indian Institute of Advanced Study.

Marriott, McKim (ed.), 1955, *Village India: Studies in the Little Community*, Chicago: Chicago University Press.

———, 1959, 'Interactional and attributional theories of case ranking', *Man in India*, Vol. 34, No. 2.

———, 1965, *Caste Ranking and Community Structure in Five Regions of India and Pakistan*, Poona: Deccan College.

Marx, Karl and Frederick Engles, 1968, *The German Ideology*, Moscow: Progress Publishers.

Mathur, K.S., 1964, *Caste and Ritual in a Malva Village*, Bombay: Asia Publishing House.

Mayer, A.C., 1960, *Caste and Kinship in Central India*, London: Routledge and Kegan Paul.

————, 1965, 'The significance of quasi-groups in the study of complex societies', *in* Banton, M. (ed.), *The Social Anthropology of Complex Societies*, London: Tavistock.

Meillassoux, C., 1973, 'Are There Castes in India?', *Economy and Society*, Vol. 2, No. 1.

Mencher, Joan P., 1974, 'The Caste System Upside Down, or The Not So Mysterious East', *Current Anthropology*, Vol. 15, No. 4.

Mukherjee, Ramkrishna, 1957, *The Dynamics of Rural Society*, Berlin: Academie Verlag.

Myrlag, Gunnar, 1944, *An American Dilemma*, New York: Harper and Row.

Namboodiripad, E.M.S., 1979, 'Caste Conflicts versus Growing Unity of Popular Democratic Forces', *Economic and Political Weekly*, Vol. XIV, Nos. 7 and 8.

Omvedt, Gail, 1980, 'Who Should Dalits Ally With?', *Economic and Political Weekly*, Vol. XV, No. 32.

————, 1980, *We will smash this prison*, New Delhi: Orient Longman.

———— (ed.), 1982, *Land, Caste and Politics in India*, Delhi: Authors Guild Publications.

Parsons, Talcott, 1954, 'An Analytical Approach to the Theory of Social Stratification',and 'A Revised Analytical Approach to the Theory of Social Stratification' *in* Parsons, Talcott, *Essays in Sociological Theory*, Glencoe: The Free Press.

Quigley, Declan, 1995, 'Conclusion: Caste Organization and the Ancient City', *in* Gellner, David N. and Declan Quigley (eds), Oxford: Claredon Press.

Ranadive, B.T., 1979, 'Caste, Class and Property Relations', *Economic and Political Weekly*, Vol. XIV (AN), Nos. 7 and 8.

Ruben, Walter, 1974, 'Decline of the Structure of Ancient Indian Society', *in* Sharma, R.S. and Vivekanand Jha (eds), *Indian Society: Historical Probings*, New Delhi: People's Publishing House.

Shah, A.M., 1982, 'Division and hierarchy: An overview of caste in Gujarat', *Contributions to Indian Sociology* (NS), Vol. 16, No. 1.

Searle, Chatterjee and **Ursula Sharma** (eds), 1994, *Contextualising Caste*, Oxford: Blackwell Publishers.

Sharma, K.L., 1974, *The Changing Rural Stratification System*, New Delhi: Orient Longman.

————, 1980, *Essays on Social Stratification*, Jaipur: Rawat Publications.

————, 1983, 'Agrarian stratification: Old issues, new explanations and new issues, old explanations', *Economic and Political Weekly*, Vol. XVIII, Nos. 42 and 43.

————, 1986, *Caste, Class and Social Movements*, Jaipur: Rawat Publications.

———— (ed.), 1994, *Caste and Class in India*, Jaipur: Rawat Publications.

————, 1996, 'Conceputalization of Caste–Class Nexus as an Alternative to Caste–Class Dichotomy', *in* Momin, A.R. (ed.), *The Legacy of G. S. Ghurye*, Bombay: Popular Prakashan.

Sharma, Surendra, 1985, *Sociology in India: A Perspective from Sociology of Knowledge*, Jaipur: Rawat Publications.

Singh, Rajendra, 1974, 'Agrarian Social Structure and Peasant Unrest: A Study of Land- Grab Movement in District Basti', *Sociological Bulletin*, Vol. 23, No. 1.

Singh, Yogendra, 1968, 'Caste and Class: Some Aspects of Continutity and Change', *Sociological Bulletin*, Vol. XVII, No. 2.

————, 1974, 'Sociology of Social Stratification: A Trend Report', *in A Survey of Research in Sociology and Social Anthropology, ICSSR*, Vol. I, Bombay: Popular Prakashan.

————, 1977, *Social stratification and change in India*, Delhi: Manohar Publications.

————, 1985, 'Sociology of Social Stratification', *in a Survey of Research in Sociology and Social Anthropology*, Vol. II, ICSSR, New Delhi: Satvahan Publications.

————, 1986, 'Some emerging issues in the Indian sociology of social stratification', *in* Sharma, K.L. (ed.), *Social Stratification in India*, Delhi: Manohar Publications.

Smith, M.G., 1964, 'Pre-industrial stratification systems', in Lipset, S.M. and N. J. Smelser (eds), *Social Structure and Mobility in Economic Development*, London: Routledge and Kegan Paul.

Srinivas, M.N., 1952, *Religion and Society among the Coors of South India*, Bombay: Oxford University Press.

———— (ed.), 1955, *India's Villages*, Calcutta: Government of West Bengal.

————, 1984, 'Some reflections on the nature of caste hierarchy', *Contributions to Indian Sociology*, Vol. 18, No. 2.

————, 1989, *The Cohesive Role of Sanskritization and Other Essays*, Delhi: Oxford University Press.

Thapar, Romila, 1974, 'Social mobility in ancient Indian society', *in* Sharma, R.S. (ed.), *Indian Society: Historical Probings*, New Delhi: Peoples Publishing House.

Thorner, Daniel, 1976, *The Agrarian Prospect in India*. Delhi: Allied Publishers.

Tumin, Melvin M., 1953, 'Some Principles of Stratification: A Critical Analysis', *American Sociological Review*, Vol. 18 (August), No. 4, pp. 387–94.

————, 1955, 'Rewards and Task-orientations', *American Sociological Review*, Vol. 20 (August), No. 4, pp. 419–23.

————, 1957, 'Some Unplanned Consequences of Social Mobility in a Mass Society', *Social Forces*, Vol. 36 (October), No. 1, pp. 32–37.

————, 1969, *Social Stratification*, New Delhi: Prentice-Hall of India.

Weber, Max, 1970, 'Class, Status and Party', *in* Gerth, H.H and Mills C. Wright (eds), *From Max Weber: Essays in Sociology*, London: Routledge and Kegan Paul.

Two

Culture and Social Stratification

The world in which one lives is not merely created of material objects and events. The meaning-strata are significant as they transform material things into cultural objects and acts of communications (Schutz 1972: 5), hence the stratifications of the life-world. The typications of the social structure provide evaluations of social positions. The degrees of freedom are reflective of the nature of social structure, and therefore, they are distributed socially. The questions of culture and ideology have been central to major streams of thought such as Marxism, neo-Marxism, critical theory, structuralism and post-structuralism, and post-modernism. Culture is perceived as an encompassing phenomenon, independent of any other phenomena, having the capacity to influence power- and social-ranking.

Culture and Power

We look at culture as a symbolic system comprising art, religion, ideology, language, etc. These are used as instruments of domination and power and division of labour (social classes). Bourdieu (1991: 170) observes: 'What creates the pair of words and slogans, a power capable of maintaining or subverting the social order, is the belief in the legitimacy of the words and of those who utter them.' Bourdieu's concept of cultural and symbolic capital(s) could be defined as 'knowledge, skills and other cultural acquisitions, as exemplified by educational qualifications' and 'accumulated prestige or honour' respectively (ibid.: 14–15). These concepts go beyond the Marxian, Weberian and the structuralist explanations of status and power. For Bourdieu, a symbolic power can become a power of constitution, a power of keeping or transforming the objective principles of union of separation, marriage and divorce, association and dissociation which are at work in the social world. It is a power of conserving or transforming the present classifications when it comes to gender, nation, region, age and social status, a power mediated by the words that are used to designate or to describe individuals, groups or institutions (ibid.: 137). He further observes: 'To change the world, one has to change the ways of making the world, that is, the vision of the world and the practical operations by which groups are produced and reproduced' (ibid.: 137).

The indological and the orientalist discourses sponsored by the British (Inden 1990) shaped and reshaped the caste system, Hinduism, the village community and the institutions like kingship, feudalism and rituals. The British rulers imagined India and then initiated symbolic and cognitive discourses to create the 'imagined' country at the ground level. Thus, the symbolic power is based on the possession of symbolic capital; it is the power of imposing on other minds a vision of *social divisions*. Hypergamy, for example, authorizes the wife-takers to claim their superiority over the wife-givers, and also imposes the same by way of making some demands as a right. 'Symbolic power is a power of creating things with words' (ibid.: 138). There is struggle for creating classifications of classes, social divisions and institutions. Those who succeed become honourable possessors of symbolic power and they form a new group of power-wielders as they carry *recognition* to impose their *words* on others.

Caste as a Flexible System of Social Ranking

Edmund Leach (1960: 1–10) argued, long before many advocates of Indian ethnosociology/culturology, that caste is a system of interrelationships and that every caste in a caste system has its special privileges. Structural and behavioural properties of caste do not stand apart from each other. Rank and endogamy alone are inadequate criteria for comprehending the entire gamut of the caste system. The caste system is much more flexible than it is understood to be. The similarity between different caste systems is a matter of structure rather than culture. There is no syndrome of common cultural traits applicable to all societies. However, caste as a structural phenomenon has no worldwide application, and here Dumont (1967) is right when he observes that caste is a pan-Indian civilization. However, Leach's observation that 'Whenever caste groups are seen to be acting as corporations in competition against like groups of different castes, then they are acting in defiance of caste principles', cannot be factually substantiated because intra-caste, inter-caste competitions and rivalries and alliances for realizing some definite goals, have become an undeniable reality. Dumont, however, is wrong when he juxtaposes the purity–pollution frame to the achievement of power. The notions of pollution–purity and power have instead existed side by side, creating room for dispute over questions of value and of role in schemes of hierarchy (Washbrook 1991: 179–203). Washbrook, relying upon several studies of culture and society, argues that 'no position in society possessed an indisputable status, and all groups seem to have existed in competition for precedence over those surrounding them' (ibid.: 185); competition and contention, and rivalries always perpetuated Indian society. Despite these changes, a caste does not cease to be a caste.

Indigenous Cultural Forms and Social Ranking

A number of scholars (Inden 1976; Inden and Nicholas 1977; Marriott 1990; Östor 1980, 1982) have found that kin is not a fixed category, but is transformable through certain transactions of substantive properties in the cultural field. Kinship is now taken as a relational and dynamic system.

A mention of Östor's study (1984) of Bengali society may be made here. Östor in his case study of the town Vishnupur discusses the phenomena of legend, ritual, bazaar and rebellion. He begins with *itihasa* (legend and history), and living realities of *puja*

(rituals), bazaar (market and economy), and takes into consideration the local ideas, practices, categories and action for constructing
domains in society as they are lived, practised, categorized, differentiated and interrelated.

Östor regards *itihasa* as a convenient introduction to the indigenous, cultural and comparative construction of society both as a
reality and as a way of procedure and method. From this nodal
point he reaches to *jati* as well as caste, *puja, jatra* (theatre) and
purana. Thus, relevant symbolic systems are discovered to interpret
the context of everyday life. The realms of *puja, jatra* and *purana*
as indigenous domains are constructed through the practices relating to the Snake Goddess. Östor writes about the domain of bazaar
'as in puja so in the bazaar'. Thus Östor analyzes the problems of
change, transformation and revolution through cultural categories.
He defines the word *andolan* as an indigenous explanation of
change. Relations between these domains are historical, dialectical
and structural (ibid.: 198). What is communicated by the words
such as economics, caste, politics, class and religion does not
commensurate with the meanings and practices relating to the
words like bazaar, *sarkar, puja, andolan, itihasa* and *jati*. Östor
concludes that 'capitalism has neither eroded hierarchical society
nor deformed it beyond recognition' (ibid.: 199). The new society
is neither hierarchical nor capitalist nor even modern/Western
(ibid.: 199). Indigenous cultural forms are still meaningful and do
not fit the Western domains of politics, economics and religion.

Kinship is seen as an aggregation of certain cultural categories
and systematic principles (Khare 1983: v). Khare views kinship as
a platform for studying profound question of the Hindu order.
Cultural analysis of Hindu social organization is made possible by
understanding indigenous ideas and categories pragmatically cho-
sen and interpreted. The purpose to understand the empirical and
the symbolic schemes of classification is to bring out the local
properties that such formulations express or entail. Thus the social
reality is interpreted, and a dichotomization of distinctions between
the real and the unreal does not take place. Hence, pure and impure,
or equality and inequality, are not polar opposites. Khare examines
the symbolic properties of the Indian varna and *jati* scheme to see
how this social classification (groups and their members) entails
an arrangement of symbolic representations and how it is an
exercise in interrelating a whole to its parts—the 'one to the many'

and the general to the particular (ibid.: 84). Concordances and correspondences between the *classifier*, the *classifying* and the *classified* explain the relationships of subordination, coordination and superordination between social groups and their members besides highlighting the varying cultural perspectives and values relating to the classification. Thus, the cultural archetype is central in the understanding of the empirical classification. The archetype may be seen in the ideology of pure and impure, hierarchy, hypergamy, etc.

Elsewhere Khare (1975: 97–114) clearly formulates his perspective on social inequality: 'Cultural principles ultimately structure inequalities of the caste system' (ibid.: 98). Emphasizing a place for the individual within the collectivity in the Hindu framework, Khare argues painstakingly that equality and inequality are relative categories, and inequality entails equality as a complementary component. Hence, he considers the dichotomies entailing pure and impure, and the individual and the collective as an exercise in cultural manipulation which ignores ground reality and its cultural frame. Khare writes: 'Castes express equality within their own group boundaries, and also in a limited manner with those placed above or below' (ibid.: 102). Harold Gould (1967: 197) explains that such a cultural framework is implicit in the *jajmani* system in terms of the concept of the 'contra-priest' and the empirical reality of the ritual function performed by the lower castes for the upper castes. Several instances of the bargaining by the functionary castes for more wages and gifts have been reported. Such bargaining takes the form of refusal to render services such as supplying earthen pots and haircutting (Sharma 1974).

Towards an Indian Ethnosociology

In an interesting collection of essays—*India through Hindu Categories* (Marriott 1990, the essays were published earlier as articles in *Contributions to Indian Sociology*), it is further affirmed that units such as *kin* and *castes* are not to be treated as fixed, but as transformable through certain transactions of substantive properties among them. The volume contributors claim that their analyses go 'beyond purity and pollution' as posited by Dumont (1970). One-dimensional normative analysis and reified versions of structuralism

realizing variance of units like caste, house and person are rele-
gated to the background. The emphasis is on the analysis of the
multi-layered, multi-dimensional contexts of Hindu life. Recognized systems of categories from Hindu categories differently relevant and applicable for different castes and groups of people are
taken as major tools of understanding and analysis. These have
been produced and reproduced temporally and spatially, through
combinations and permutations of known components (ibid.:
xi–xvi). Marriott attempts to construct an Indian ethnosociology to
eliminate both an alien ontology as well as an alien epistemology.

Though *India through Hindu Categories* apparently communi-
cates a message of subordination and symbolic constructions of
Muslims, Sikhs, Jains, Parsees, etc. by the Hindu symbolic world,
yet its relevance is amply highlighted in the rebuttal of the Western
social science paradigms and conceptual constructions. Marriott
discusses the three diametric concepts of purity, dominance and
hierarchy in terms of the two pairs of Hindu concepts, namely,
pure–impure and great–small. The word 'hierarchy' is not only
alien, it suffers from its one-dimensional participation in the three-
dimensional Hindu semantic space (ibid.: 30). In the present volume
it is used in three different ways, namely, referring to (*a*) purity,
(*b*) the dominance or power diameter, and (*c*) the vertical dimension of the three concepts. Likewise, the concept of encompassing
implying both inclusion and exclusion results in irresolution. Marriott writes: 'Encompassment is thus an oxymoron, it asserts that
Hindu society is both split and not split, both ranked and not
ranked' (ibid.: 31). Such self-contradictory usages of encompassment and/or hierarchy create a logical scandal; and Marriott claims
that his model avoids such scandal (ibid.: 31). 'Diversity of ranking
is an intrinsic potentiality of such a model' (ibid.: 31). There are
diverse and shifting three-dimensional views and diverse rankings
in actuality, hence no single-dimensional space (model) can be
accepted.

Another important critique of Dumont's approach is provided
by Inden (1976) in his analysis of marriage and rank among
Brahmins and Kayasthas in middle-period Bengal, and by Inden
and Nicholas (1977) in their study of kinship in Bengali culture.
Marriott and Inden (1974, 1977) and Davis (1983) argue that the
attributional, interactional and purity–plus–power perspectives emphasize the physical nature of caste, behavioural dominance and

encompassment (the attributional element of purity is qualified by the interactional element of power), respectively. It is evident from the writings of Inden (1976), Marriott and Inden (1974, 1977), Östor (1984) and now again from Marriott (1990) that the physical nature and behavioural codes are not distinct and separate phenomena. Hindus regard physical nature and behavioural codes as cognitively non-dualistic features. Each is immanent in the other; each is inseparable from the other; each is a reflection and realization of the other (Davis 1983:2).

Marvin Davis, based on his study of a village in West Bengal, suggests that 'neither physical nature nor behavioural codes are the sole or even the primary criterion of caste rank in Hindu society. Instead, the rank of any caste depends mutually on its nature and code. Ethnography of social stratification by using the indigenous concepts such as *des, jati, lok, gramer raj, sarkari raj*, in the context of space and time is presented in the form of an alternate perspective. The Bengali cosmos and culture do not recognize caste as a unique system of inequality. 'Bengalis view the several worlds of the universe, the various life forms that inhabit those worlds, and all birth groups into which humans in society are divided, as recognized into a series of ranked orders and ordered ranks' (ibid.: 3). Individuals are also thus ranked. 'Rank is an ordering principle of the Bengali cosmos and society as a whole' (ibid.: 3). *Gun* and *dharma* constitute a simple criterion of rank. 'One is but the reflection and realization of the other' (ibid.:3). Thus the attributional, interactional, and purity–plus–power theories of rank are unified, non-distinct, inseparable and non-dualistic, as in the Bengali cosmos and culture the nature and code are recognized as unified.

Like Marriott (1990) the rank is not seen as fixed and unchanging over time by Davis (ibid.: 3–4). Rank can be transformed through the life activities of its members. Thus a unified theory of rank is transformational and it reveals internal dynamics of Bengali society. In the behavioural patterns relating to marriage, diet, food exchanges, and work, flexibility in ranked inequalities and the ideas behind the rank–order is evidenced in the space–time context. Three pertinent questions (ibid.: 4) discussed by Davis are: (*a*) Are individuals properly considered units of rank among Hindus? (*b*) Are they defined and ranked by the same features of nature and code as are the more inclusive birth groups to which they belong?

(c) Can the defining features, and thus the rank of individuals be transformed in much the same way and through similar acts as, say those of castes? Through these questions Davis analyzes a group-oriented Indian society. In fact, the entire analysis is targeted against Dumont's theory of pollution–purity and his notion of the individual's place in the Indian caste system.

Davis discusses that individual Bengalis retain a personal identity, pursue self-interests and self-development and they can be ranked differently from the birth groups to which they belong. Davis (ibid.: 5) writes: 'Individuals, in sum, have a status different from their status as a caste member or any other status deriving from membership in a family or larger kinship grouping'. Thus an individual is the normative subject of thought and action, a microcosm of the universe at large. All the criteria applicable to the ranking of the birth groups are applicable to the individuals as well.

In the case of Bengali society, the cosmos and society are constructed from the combinations and products of given cultural units such as *des, jati* and *lok*. Such an analysis also offers the possibility of cross-cultural generalizations. The argument that the cosmos is in *jati* and the individual, and that both, *jati* and the individual are in the cosmos while retaining their respective identities makes the perspective under discussion holistic and the space–time–context-specific. However, Dumont as well as Inden, Davis, Östor, and Marriott emphasize the unique nature of Hindu and/or Bengali society, thereby undermining the external influences on Indian society. The structural perspective explains how material/physical phenomena can shape and reshape cultural norms and practices. Moreover, indigenous concepts and categories relating to material possessions and political power and people too, have been used in the studies of land relations, elite formation and social mobility (Mukerji 1954; Sharma 1974; Thorner and Thorner 1974).

In a well documented study of culture as an instrument of power (Joshi and Josh 1994:31), it is argued that 'cultural hegemony implies that the overarching societal order is permeated by a particular cultural system or the shared symbols of a cultural enclosure'. Culture is used to construct a new identity in place of the old one. Struggles for cultural assertion with a view to challenging the established hierarchy are taken to be as efforts at establishing *power* by the upwardly aspiring groups of people. A new language, text, set of symbols and metaphors must be seen in the context of the actual conditions of power relationships in society (ibid.: 68). Castes, classes or communities are thus to be seen in terms of the actual cultural and social relations of power rather than in terms of the debates relating to the post-structuralist versus materialist formulation and the cultural-holism versus cultural/regional autonomy/specificity. According to Joshi and Josh 'the struggle for cultural hegemony can be traced historically backwards into time, into the formation of caste society' (ibid.: 69). Caste has been shaped and reshaped by political struggles, and relations of power are culturally constructed. Hence, a paradigm of hegemony or dominance. Culture is power, and the cultural struggle is a power struggle. Such an emphasis on the power paradigm is not visible in Khare, Marriott, Östor and Davis. Cultural/regional specificity heavily burdens their formulations as they mainly draw upon indigenous concepts and categories.

The focal theme of the XXIst All India Sociological Conference at Jawaharlal Nehru University was *Cultural Dimensions of Social Change*. The cultural perspective was quite broadly perceived in this conference as some of the theme papers analyzed communitarian and cultural identities, globalization and social change; secularization and minoritization; culture, ideology and social process in Indian politics, technology, communication and culture change, etc. Yogendra Singh (1994) in his presidential address highlighted the significance of culture in understanding social change in contemporary India. Culture manifests itself in the technological, mental, moral, social, aesthetic and spiritual aspects of human life. Culture accords meaning to man's life and to his relationships with his fellow-beings. However, Singh observes that interaction between the wider models of culture constructs and particular cultural structures, the mixing of the global with the particular, can help resolve the problems arising out of structured social inequalities. Paradigm mixes rather than exclusive structural and cultural perspectives could be worked out for establishing linkages between culture, structure and change.

André Béteille (1992:29) while commenting on Marriott's argument about the transactional and transformational culture of India (1976) argues that it entails an accentuation of the contrast between Indian and Western thought and culture. This accentuation of the contrast impinges directly on the comparative study of caste and race. Béteille accepts the inseparability of substance and code, and of the actor and the action as argued by Marriott, but this is also true of modern capitalist societies like America, particularly in the context of race (ibid.: 30). A return to the indological approach in a somewhat transformed manner would ignore study of hard facts relating to India's economy and polity. Béteille considers this as an emphasis on the book-view as against the field-view of Indian society (ibid.: 33).

Caste–Class–Power Nexus

The caste–class situation in India is varied. Some of the questions raised earlier relating to caste, class and power as separate yet interlinked domains have become obsolete and sterile. Profiles of the caste–class situation in nine states (Sharma 1994), namely, West Bengal, Orissa, Bihar, Uttar Pradesh, Rajasthan, Gujarat, Maharashtra, Andhra Pradesh and Kerala, show that caste and class are not polar opposites and are found in both rural and urban areas. The caste–class nexus, its continuity and change is a historical fact of Indian society and it characterizes the continuity and flexibility of Indian social formation. Caste has been changing rapidly finding a place for itself in non-conventional and secular domains of social, economic and political life. While caste is consciousness, a frame of reference, it is also a reality, a domain of actual social relations. The uninhibiting appearance of caste in one form or other is due to the continuously changing caste–class–power nexus and levels of mobility, that is, mobility at the levels of the individual, family and *jati*. Confederations or alliances of castes for political gain or for seeking reservations in educational institutions and jobs are a recent development particularly in north India. Forwards, backwards, Harijans, *adivasis*, Muslims, etc., are the new socio-political entities consciously created and articulated for achieving well-thought-out political and social goals.

Today the question is not of adherence to the notions of pure and impure, hierarchy and hereditary callings and of protecting the rigid, archaic and oriental character of the caste system, but it is of the absorption of the non-caste issues into the orbit of caste; and the exploitation of caste for the realization of political and economic goals (Sharma 1995:1). Access to political power through caste-based mobilization is common practice, but empowerment generally strengthens and sometimes quite vigorously the caste-based socio-cultural activities. The main difficulty about the neo-culturological view is that it relies more on the apparent or *form* (of the caste system) than on the actual practice of social inequality. It may so happen that the form is not seen in the practice and the latter is hardly reflected in the former. Contradictions, discontinuities and breakdowns relating to the relationship between the form and the practice of caste have become sharper in the recent years, highlighting a new nexus between the apparent and the real. In the realm of social inequality, continuity of the old and the emergence of new values and practices are clearly evident in different permutations and combinations in terms of the space-time context. The nature and direction of social change largely determine social relations today. And there is a coexistence of value frame, structure and process of social inequality. A new rationalization for denigrating the traditional value premises and social relations, and the ideologization for a new society not necessarily antithetical to the traditional one, are finding their ground in different measures in different parts of India.

It is not the ritualistically perceived and influenced world of things, nor is it an economically-conditioned power or merely subjective realization of stratificatory ramifications that matters today; empowerment through access to positions of power, lucrative and secure jobs, honorific statuses, a respectable life-style, command on language as a social asset, are being perceived as the relevant instruments by individuals, families and groups aspiring for upward social mobility. Destabilization of the entrenched dominants through crystallization of electoral strength mainly in numerical terms is more than evident from the recent elections held in some states in India. A new middle class not necessarily having expertise in professions is emerging as a result of its empowerment. The traditional ideology and structural bases of social inequality have not only been severely threatened, but new foci, alternate ideologies and paradigms are being articulated by the empowered sections of society. New substantive concerns such as empowerment of the poor, weaker sections and women, have added additional dimensions to the understanding of social inequality.

References

Béteille, André, 1992, *Society and Politics in India: Essays in a Contemporary Perspective*, Delhi: Oxford University Press.

Bourdieu, Pierre, 1991, *Language and Symbolic Power*, Cambridge: Polity Press.

Centre for the Study of Social Systems, 1994, Theme Papers and Abstracts, *XXI All India Sociological Conference*, 19–21 December, Jawaharlal Nehru University, New Delhi.

Davis, Marvin, G., 1983, *Rank and Rivalry: The Politics of Inequality in Rural West Bengal*, Cambridge: Cambridge University Press.

Dumont, Louis, 1967, 'Caste: A Phenomenon of Social Structure or an Aspect of Indian Culture', *in* de Reuck, Anthony and Julie Knight (eds), *Caste and Race: Comparative Approaches*, Boston: Little Brown & Co.

———, 1970, *Homo Hierarchicus*, London: Paladin, Granda Publishing Company.

Gould, Harold, 1967, 'Priest and Contra-Priest: A Structural Analysis of Jajman Relations in the Hindu Plains and the Nilgiri Hills', *Contributions to Indian Sociology* (NS), 1.

Inden, Ronald B., 1976, *Marriage and Rank in Bengali Literature: A History of Caste and Clan in Middle Period Bengal*, Berkeley: University of California Press.

———, 1990, *Imagining India*, Oxford: Basil Blackwell Ltd.

Inden, Ronald B. and Ralph W. Nicholas, 1977, *Kinship in Bengali Culture*, Chicago: University of Chicago Press.

Joshi, Shashi and Bhagwan Josh, 1994, *Struggle for Hegemony in India, 1920–47, Volume III*, New Delhi: Sage Publications.

Khare, R.S., 1975, 'Hindu Social Inequality and Some Ideological Entailments', *in* Nair, Balakrishna N. (ed.), *Culture and Society*, Delhi: Thomson Press.

Leach, E.R., 1960, 'Introduction: What should we Mean by Caste?' *in* Leach, E.R. (ed.), *Aspects of Caste in South India, Ceylon and North-West Pakistan*, Cambridge: Cambridge University Press.

Marriott, McKim (ed.), 1989, *India through Hindu Categories*, New Delhi: Sage Publications.

Marriott, McKim and Ronald B. Inden, 1977, 'Toward an Ethno-Sociology of South Asian Caste Systems', *in* David, Kenneth A. (ed.), *The New Wind: Changing Identities in South Asia*, The Hague: Mouton.

———, 1974, 'Caste Systems', *in Encyclopaedia Britannica, Macropaediz*, Chicago: Helen Hemenway, pp. 982–91.

Mukerji, D.P., 1958, *Diversities*, New Delhi: People's Publishing House.

Östor, Akös, 1980, *The Play of the Gods: Locality, Ideology, Structure and Time in the Festivals of a Bengali Town*, Chicago: Chicago University Press.

———, 1984, *Culture and Power, Legend, Ritual, Bazaar and Religion in a Bengali Society*, New Delhi: Sage Publications.

Östor, Akös, Lina Fruzzetti and Stene Barnett (eds), 1982, *Concepts of Persons: Kinship, Caste, and Marriage in India*, Cambridge: Harvard University Press.

Schutz, Alfred, 1972, *The Phenomenology of the Social World*, London: Heinemann.

Sharma, K.L., 1974, *The Changing Rural Stratification System*, New Delhi: Orient Longman.

———— (ed.), 1994, *Caste and Class in India*, Jaipur: Rawat Publications.

———— (ed.), 1995, *Social Inequality in India*, Jaipur: Rawat Publications.

Singh, Yogendra, 1994, 'The Significance of Culture in the Understanding of Social Change in Contemporary India', Presidential Address, *XXI All India Sociological Conference*, 19–21 December, 1994, Jawaharlal Nehru University, New Delhi.

Thorner, Daniel and **Alice Thorner**, 1974, *Land and Labour in India*, Bombay: Asia Publishing House.

Washbrook, David, 1991, 'To Each a Language of His Own: Language, Culture, and Society in Colonial India', *in* Corfied, Penelope J. (ed.), *Language, History and Class*, Oxford: Basil Blackwell.

Three

Social Stratification in Rural–Agrarian Setting

There are misconceptions about caste and class in relation to the understanding of social stratification. These misconceptions are as follows: (*a*) Caste and class have emerged as polar opposites. (*b*) While caste is a rural phenomenon, class is an urban one. (*c*) Caste is concerned with ritual ranking, while class is a grouping based on common economic and occupational interests. (*d*) Caste is a collective entity whereas class is characterized by the individual as a unit of ranking. (*e*) Caste is a rigid, immobile and ascriptive institution and class is characterized by flexibility, mobility and achievement orientation.

It is conclusively substantiated through historical evidence that caste and class are not polar opposites, and class is not replacing caste, instead caste is transforming itself in the wake of macro-structural changes which include legal and constitutional provisions. Class is a global phenomenon. Both caste and class are dimensions of the same social formation, hence caste inheres class and vice versa. Neither a caste nor a class view can accurately portray or even attempt to explain reality. Caste and class together could provide an understanding of social stratification in both rural and urban settings. Both caste and class have a structural as well as a cultural dimension.

Approaches to the Study of Rural–Agrarian Stratification

Ramkrishna Mukherjee (1957; 1981: 109–16) analyzes realities of agrarian relations in India through three conceptual frames: (*a*) the property and production relations in agriculture; (*b*) the status categories in rural society; and (*c*) the interactions between the elites and the masses of many denominations. These frames in a broader sense refer to the Marxist and/or the Weberian theoretical orientations. Both are relevant to the understanding of social reality. However, Pradip Kumar Bose (1989: 183–98) analyzes somewhat differently the theoretical problems in the study of agrarian structure, change, and rural–urban interface. He writes: 'The problems encompass both ideological and structural space' (ibid.: 195). According to Bose, three dominant sociological approaches for analyzing the agrarian social structure in India are: (*a*) that which regards tradition as the central element in the study of structure; (*b*) that which uses natural, native or indigenous categories; and (*c*) that which draws its conceptual tools from the established sociological formulations like that of Marxian, Weberian and Durkheimian, etc. (ibid.: 183). Emphasis on the study of tradition and use of indigenous categories are not so central to the classification put forward by Ramkrishna Mukherjee. Tradition occupies a place of significance in D. P. Mukerji's formulation (1958). Daniel Thorner (1976) in his study of land relations uses the indigenous categories. These are not neatly worked out approaches. Tradition has a wide range of meanings incorporating orthodoxy on the one hand and liberal interpretative sources for understanding of socio-economic and political formation on the other. Similarly the nativistic categories are close to the tradition in one sense, and are absolutely secular in nature on the other hand as used by Daniel Thorner.

To generalize the reality of village life, it is necessary to understand the complexity of the relationships amongst the multitude of social, economic and political factors (Dasgupta 1975: 1395–1414; Srinivas 1975: 1387–94). A fairly rigorous study by Dasgupta based on an analysis of 126 villages from fourteen states taking into consideration 234 variables and further classified into thirteen key variables, discusses three major associates of modernization. These are: (a) the proletarianization of the poor peasantry with the increasing concentration of village resources in few hands; (b) the shift in the mode of production in agriculture from family-based subsistence farming to market-oriented hired-worker based agriculture; and (c) the increasing diversification of economic and social life in the village. These new parameters of status and social mobility in the countryside are replacing the traditional criteria related to sanskritization, westernization and the dominant caste. Though economism is dominantly reflected in Dasgupta's analysis, the emergence of new criteria in the countryside cannot be overlooked as reported in this comprehensive analysis.

While analyzing the rise of a middle class and of a bourgeoisie in India, Krishna Bharadwaj (1980) examines the production–exchange relations in the rural and urban India. Bharadwaj provides a classification dividing rural society into: (a) semi-proletariat, (b) small holders, (c) farmers, and (d) rentiers. The urban society is divided into: (a) the industrial bourgeoisie, (b) the middle class or petty bourgeoisie, further divided into upper, middle and lower middle classes, (c) the industrial proletariat, (d) semi-proletariat, and (e) lumpen proletariat. This classification apparently seems to be a neat and convincing exercise, but at least two points require clarification: (a) the nature of synthesis between interactional and attributional criteria in class analysis; and (b) the nature of divide between the rural and urban population in India. How the relations between different classes occur and what is the nature of the interaction between them remains unexplained. And the changing nature of the country–town nexus too, remains unexplicated. A clear rural–urban divide as a conceptual frame and as a reality has become an untenable formulation. Country–town nexus is an appropriate conceptual tool to analyze social relations in rural and urban settings.

During the past decade a shift from the studies on caste and kinship to those on agrarian relations, social transformation, peasantry, rural poverty, agricultural labour, country–town nexus, caste and class nexus, caste and class tensions and conflicts and mode of production in Indian agriculture is clearly evident. In most of the studies the concepts of class and mode of production are used to explain agrarian stratification and its transformation. Rural inequalities are explained in terms of the mode of production in agriculture and policies of the Indian state. Regional variation and disparities are also explained with such a frame of reference (Byres et al. 1976; Adnan 1985: PE-53–PE-64).

A large number of the studies do not focus on the social structure and patterns of class formations and class alignments in rural Indian society (Alavi 1981: 475–86). The classical Marxist analysis of the development of capitalism in Europe cannot explain the development of capitalism between peripheral capitalism and metropolitan capitalism, the former signifying countries like India, the latter a feature of the developed world.

Raising another important question John Harriss (1982b: 9) writes:

> I argue that the expanded reproduction of capital in agricultural production is subordinated to that of merchant and finance capital, in a form of economy like those described by Marx as *intermediate* forms of capitalism. The process of *differentiation* of the peasantry is thus *blocked* both because of the character of the economy and by the ideological structures of caste and kinship which reinforce the existing relations of production and the power structure.

Harriss also discusses the question whether or not the caste system is breaking down or whether it is successfully adapting to the new conditions. The relationship between the processes of material production and the ideological structures is intrinsic to Harriss' study of a village in the North Arcot district of Tamil Nadu.

There is a small class of landowners with extensive interests in trading and transport activities, money-lending and urban property. A majority of the households own limited or none of the means of production—barring the labour power of their members. They, therefore, have to sell their labour—directly or indirectly—through the mechanism of advances from the class of landowner/merchant capitalists.

Bose has studied this pattern of differentiation in the historical perspective in the context of Bengal (Bose 1986). Studies on patterns of differentiation in other parts of the country also reiterate the historical nature of this differentiation. The capitalist farmers are also money-lenders/merchants who indulge in usury, and they find this more profitable than investing in agriculture on a continuing basis (ibid.: 284–85). Thus, ideology, relations of production and social change are interrelated phenomena. The process of polarization of the peasantry into a class of rural capitalists and another of agricultural labourers is constrained by the conjuncture of the particular kind of marriage alliance made by different groups and the operation of merchants' and usurers' capital in the economy. Bose (ibid.: 235) writes: 'The whole is reinforced by the structure of political power, and it cannot be fully comprehended except in relation to the ideology of caste.'

Thus, caste gives coherence and meaning and it structures actual social relationships. Caste is not a mere epiphenomenon of class relations (as it is unquestionably accepted even by orthodox Marxists). Caste is both an actual structure of social relationships and an ideology. As such, caste structure does not rest only upon unequal access to the means of production and the appropriation of surplus by a dominant caste. Harriss writes: 'The dominant caste must be a part, at least of the dominant class, though the dominant class and the dominant caste are not necessarily entirely congruent' (ibid.: 295). There are complementary *unequal exchanges* between members of different castes, hence the hierarchy and the exploitation of labour, poor and lower caste men.

Inequality in Rural India and the Country–Town Nexus

A reference may be made here about inequalities in rural and urban contexts. Michael Lipton (1977) points out that economic growth in the less developed countries has hardly any impact on the mass poverty. Disparity between urban and rural welfare is much greater in poor countries than in the rich countries particularly in the early phase of development. Lipton (ibid.: 67) observes:

> Despite some vulgar Marxisants, the basic conflict in the
> Third World is not between capital and labour, but between
> capital and countryside, farmer and townsman, villager
> (including temporarily urban *fringe villager*) and urban

industrial employer-cum-proletarian elite, gainers from dear food and gainers from cheap food (ibid.: 67).

The industrial workforce is against the equalizing measures as the large masses of the deprived rural poor would also share what 5 to 10 per cent of the urban-industrial workers enjoy in terms of salaried regular employment as a privilege. Thus, Lipton emphasizes the inevitability of urban–rural conflict. C. H. Hanumantha Rao (1978: 1699–1702) finds Lipton's analysis quite unsound and unrealistic. Rao observes that Lipton's diagnosis comes very close to what the politically dominant sections in India have asserted that the rural sector has been neglected and there should be more public investment in agriculture and rural development programmes. Earlier the late Charan Singh and recently Devi Lal have articulated the country–town relations as a social divide between the poor and the rich.

C. T. Kurien (1980: 365–90) argues that the rural scene in Tamil Nadu is far from static, and the rural areas have experienced a dynamism unknown in the past. There have also been induced changes, and while some of the changes have been in the desired direction, others have gone against the targets set for social transformation. Some of the negative social consequences include pauperization of small farmers, the decline in the real wages of the agricultural labourers, and the continuance and increase of mass poverty. But this may not be true about Punjab, Haryana, western Uttar Pradesh, Gujarat and parts of Karnataka and Maharashtra. Unintended and hidden positive social consequences have also occurred there due to various programmes of rural development.

Dipankar Gupta (1988: 2688–96) in his study of the Bharatiya Kisan Union (BKU) finds country–town nexus quite useful as a frame of reference as well as an empirical reality. The BKU has maintained its distance from political parties. It has a strong base in the fairly well-off peasantry and advocates for its betterment by seeking some concessions. But it draws upon national leadership in towns like Muzaffarnagar, Saharanpur, Meerut and Delhi for execution of its policies and programmes. Though unapproving, Mencher's observation (1978: A-98–A-104) is quite significant to understand the country–town nexus. She writes:

The present agricultural policy, with its stress on hybrid grain varieties, commercial fertilisers and pesticides, tractors and food processing mills etc. is intended to make peace between these groups by providing food at a low price for the urban workers without disturbing productive relations in the rural area. As such it has produced a convergence of interests between the rural elite and the industrial lobby.

In another paper, Mencher (1980: 1781–1802) further examines the Kerala model of development by analyzing the life conditions of the agricultural labourers. They are no longer agrestic slaves, and are free to choose their careers. There is still extreme hostility between landowner and agricultural labour. Without intensive industrialization and leadership from the ranks of agricultural labourers, not much change is going to occur. A study of peasant struggles and land reforms in Malabar (Radhakrishnan 1980: 2095–2102; 1981: A-129–A-137; 1982: A-107–A-119) while corroborating Mencher's findings, shows that though Kerala has a relatively better record in regard to implementation of land reform measures than other states, its vast masses of agricultural labourers remain landless and poor.

Historicity of Rural–Agrarian Stratification

Caste by itself was never the determinant of social status in India. It was also not always the dominant factor in everyday life. Power and not caste (Chakravarti 1985: 356–60) was the basis of social hierarchy in ancient India. Chakravarti in her study based on the Buddhist sources mentions social hierarchy consisting of Kshatriya, Brahmin and Gahapati (or *kulas*) in descending order rather than the commonly accepted order of precedence comprising Brahmin, Kshatriya, Vaishya and Shudra. Besides power, the agrarian society had great complexity in the Chola country (Karashima 1984). Burton Stein (1980) emphasizes the role of eco-type regimes in the shaping of agrarian regimes and socio-cultural variations. Based on several historical studies and analyses about social stratification in ancient India, Vivekanand Jha (1990: 1–31) writes:

The overwhelming impression is that of a highly complex socio-economic structure with the city holding a central and commanding position vis-à-vis the countryside which it dominated and exploited, and a definite stratification along class lines within the city itself with the privileged ruling elite enjoying unequal wealth, power and prestige in relation to the mass of common people.

The various ruling social strata found in ancient India were: princes, priests, merchants, officials and scribes. Jha adheres to Piggott's view that there was a state ruled by priest-kings, wielding autocratic and absolute power, controlling production and distribution and levying tolls and customs. Basham (1954) also refers to a single centralized theocratic state. In course of time urban craftsmen became a part of the ruling class. Caste-like groups, untouchability, caste–class nexus, service relationship emerged subsequently.

A somewhat different perspective is provided by Indra Deva and Shrirama (1986: 1–28, 59–129) regarding 'crystallization of the traditional pattern of stratification in India' in the Rigvedic period. Varna or class was the basis of segregation, and the priestly class had emerged though not quite distinctly. During this period distinction between the Aryans and the Dasas also emerged. After the Brahmins and the Kshatriyas, the class of traders or Vaishyas surfaced. Though different varnas had emerged with the order of precedence, people enjoyed the freedom to choose their profession(s) based on their abilities and achievements. Later literature refers to the four-fold varna order in terms of their origin, rank–order and specific duties and roles. Ritualism, a later development, was a contributing factor to the shift in the nature of varna—from class to caste.

Agrarian hierarchy in the Mughal empire (Hasan 1969: 18) is classified into three broad categories: (*a*) the autonomous chieftains, (*b*) the intermediary zamindars, and (*c*) the primary zamindars. Similar observations have been made by Stein (1969: 175–76) and Cohn (1969: 57–58). Cohn observes that the *mahajans* (bankers and traders) were landholders and the latter were also involved in money-lending.

Satish Chandra (1986: 21–28), based on his study of four villages in the former state of Jaipur in Rajasthan, divides 249 households in three categories, namely (*a*) privileged sections, (*b*) cultivating classes and (*c*) service classes. The three categories are 13 per cent, 76 per cent and 11 per cent of the total households, respectively.

'There seems to be a broad correspondence between caste and status.... The privileged and the service classes are roughly equal and constitute about a quarter of the population of villages' (ibid.: 25). Rajputs and Mahajans quite often enjoyed superior status than Brahmins, based mainly on their better economic position. Instead of classifying society on the model of the four varnas, during the Mughal period warriors were given first place, the second place was given to artificers and merchants, the third to the learned, and the fourth to the husbandmen and labourers (ibid.: 51). Thus, there was no perfect correspondence between caste and class. The local landed elements were the most important and powerful group in the village community.

The peasantry in medieval India was not an undifferentiated mass. It was divided on the basis of occupation, caste and economic position. The zamindars, the village officials and the *khud-kasht*, the *pahi-kasht* and the landless labourers formed the agrarian stratification (ibid.: 54). S. P. Gupta (1986: 92–115) uses the concept of agrarian trade considering the mercantile classes as an important element of the agrarian economy of eastern Rajasthan. Gupta also draws a distinction between (*a*) *khud-kasht*, (*b*) *raiyati-kasht*, and (*c*) *pahi-kasht*. This classification represented a hierarchy among the peasants that of superior right-holders, peasant–proprietors, and non-resident cultivators, respectively (ibid.: 116–33). 'The stratification of village society was also reflected in the system of taxation' (ibid.: 123). Similar findings have been reported by K. L. Sharma (1986: 103–27) and Hira Singh (1981). The favoured revenue payers were from among the Brahmins, Mahajans, Patels and Bhomias. According to Gupta, the ordinary peasant, whether *raiyati* or *palti* was under considerable financial pressure. On the other hand the *mahajans*, *bhomias*, *chaudhuris* and *quanungos* (*pargana* officials) and *patels* (village officials) and a class of Rajputs (mainly the Shekhawats) belonged to the privileged class within the village.

The land tenure systems of colonial India, namely, the *zamindari* and *ryotwari* settlements, further accentuated intra-class and inter-class status distinctions. Agrarian relations have undergone a definite change after the abolition of these systems in the independent India. However, due to the capitalist mode of production in some areas distinctions among the peasants in terms of high, middle and low statuses have become quite sharp. Some parts of the country continue to have a sort of feudal/semi-feudal mode of production because the land reforms have remained largely ineffective and the traditional inequalities are persisting in effect with a changed form.

The tendency of the colonial official agrarian policy was clearly designed to perpetuate and even increase the stratification within the village, by making the rich richer and the poor poorer through a system of discriminatory taxation. In Punjab as was the case in other parts of the country, during the early British rule, *lineage* as the basis of status was replaced by formal–legal proprietorship. Status was defined in terms of the legal categories of owner and tenant, and proprietary rights were vested clearly and unequivocally in individuals (Nazir 1981: 281–85).

Therefore, lineage, descent and caste became less effective institutions in determining social status. Barring some exceptions a landlord generally belonged to a 'superior' caste and an agricultural worker came from a downtrodden community (which would include lower castes and Muslims). In areas where the caste hierarchy was rigid, it coincided with the landholding hierarchy thereby both social and economic statuses determined power and privileges in Indian society.

There were many caste categories and occupational groupings. In areas where caste was not a rigid system, caste and landholding hierarchy did not correspond (see Dasgupta 1984: A-129–A-148). Dasgupta's study of four districts in Bengal in the British period shows the following trends:

1. An increase in the proportion of tenant–cultivators, labourers, and traders.
2. A decline in the proportions of artisans.
3. The absorption of a section of the higher castes and artisans (as also some of the semi-Hinduized tribes) into full-time agriculture.
4. The absorption of a section of the artisans in the trading activities.
5. The absorption of the majority of the semi-Hinduized tribes as labourers and agriculturists, and a part in personal services.

These trends not only indicate flexibility of the caste system and its weak correspondence with occupational and income hierarchies, but also indicate towards considerable upward/downward social mobility in Bengal during the British period. By the end of the nineteenth century there were enclaves of capitalist production which surrounded the ocean of pre-capitalist agriculture (Chua 1986: 2092–99). The pre-capitalist exploitation of the peasants was accomplished by means of capitalist market relations, hence semi-feudalism. While agreeing with Jairus Banaji (1977: 1375–1404) regarding the role of capitalism in Gujarat and parts of western India, Cathy Chua reports that a process of proletarianization was occurring in the countryside, and the lower strata of the peasantry were being separated from the means of production. Such a process weakened the control of the dominant landholders over the peasants. For example, in Surat the ascending capitalists were the Bathelas Brahmins replacing the Anavil Brahmins during the 1800s. In Ahmedabad and in Kaira Kunbis ascended, and in Thana the small landholders were driven out by rich peasants. All these changes were possible due to commoditization of land and accumulation of surplus by 1860s. Improved means of transport and communications made farming an extremely profitable enterprise. Class contradictions got crystallized as traditional bonds got dissolved and dependency withered away as the capitalists were against landholders and landlords were against tenants.

Contributors to a volume edited by Peter Robb (1986) highlight the nature and direction of social change in rural India under British rule in terms of the *nexus between land, power and society*. There is no opposition between the town and the country, and the townsman and the peasant. A village is not static, and it is not dominated by the powers which are distinct from it. Villagers always have/had relations with rulers, merchants and craftsmen. There were changes in the relations between the countryside and a wider world.

A study of the agrarian Bengal from 1919 to 1947 (Bose 1986) provides a typology of agrarian social structure. The study explodes the *'jotedar* thesis' as it finds significant differences in land relations, credit and market patterns between north, east and west Bengal. In north Bengal the *jotedar* class was socially supreme; in east Bengal a predominantly peasant small holding structure was overlaid by various rentier and creditor groups. In west and central Bengal there was the existence of considerable personal demands of the landlords (revenue collectors), small peasants (tenants) and landless people who cultivated land in this part of Bengal. Such a system was different from the village landlord/rich farmer-share-cropper system of north Bengal. Thus it was a highly polarized agrarian structure, and there were several layers of variation and complexity.

Since there were three distinct regions reflecting variations in land relations, the credit and market also affected them differently. Whether a region produces for subsistence or for market determines the role of credit and world economy. In east Bengal's export-oriented jute economy, the control of zamindars and *talukdars* over land was weak. The landlords became money-lenders or *bhuswami mahajans*. A similar situation also existed in Gujarat and western India. Bose observes that such a complex situation had implications for peasant mobilization and politics. He also finds that the classification of peasantry into rich, middle and poor categories is inadequate even as a heuristic device.

The upper middle castes hailing from the former *ryotwari* areas have sprung up as a dominant peasantry. These include Marathas and Tellis, Bhumihars and Rajputs, Jats and Ahirs, Mahishyas and Sadgops, Nayars and Tillanis, Lingayats and Nadars, Kammas and Reddis and so on. They are both rich peasants and dominant castes, not *dominant* in the Srinivasian sense of the term. Green revolution was effective mainly in the *ryotwari* areas, and it has benefited largely families of these castes. However, simply on the basis of landholdings, in many studies all agricultural castes/families have been classified as (*a*) top, (*b*) middle, and (*c*) lowest peasants (Patnaik 1976: A-82–A-101; Swamy 1976: 1933–39). All these classes also belong to corresponding caste ranks (Banaji 1977: 1375–1404; Gough 1980: 338). And caste has never been reducible to ritual status alone. Hence, the caste–class nexus assumes considerable significance as a conceptual device.

In addition to land, there are some other criteria of status determination such as age and sex, social strata and the nature of work. Tenancy systems and the tenant's background (Sharma 1983: 1796–1802; 1851–55) largely determined the status of a peasant in agrarian hierarchy. Several non-economic factors (Béteille 1974: 26–27) and economic factors (Saith and Tanakha 1972: 1069–76) stratified the peasantry.

In a study of interlinkage of land, labour and credit relations in east India covering 276 villages (110 from West Bengal, 101 from Bihar and 65 from east Uttar Pradesh), Bardhan and Rudra

(1978: 367–84) find a close connection between tenancy, wage labour and credit system. The villages are categorized as (*a*) highly advanced, (*b*) moderately advanced, and (*c*) not advanced areas. This classification is based on the use of chemical fertilizers and high yielding variety (HYV) seeds. Agrarian relations vary in these villages but also depend upon the fact whether the landlords are self-cultivators or have some other activities as their main source of livelihood. Whether loan is for consumption and whether the loan is with interest or without it, also determine relations between landlord and his tenants. However, Rudra (1978: 916–23) observes that classes are defined by contradictions of interests arising out of their relations with the means of production. There are only two classes: (*a*) class of big landowners (including rich peasants), and (*b*) class of agricultural labourers (including landless labourers). But the middle peasants as a class category have acquired considerable significance. The studies of agrarian relations in Rajasthan (Sharma 1977), Madhya Pradesh (Jain 1979: 946–50) and Gujarat (Hardiman 1981) bring out the fact that a highly differentiated peasantry existed during the British period and even earlier.

Thus differentiation of landowners and peasantry had been quite elaborate in the Mughal and the British periods. Tenancy systems such as *zamindari*, *mahalbari* and *ryotwari* brought about very basic changes in the agrarian hierarchy in the British period. The real question in the post-independence period is that of distributive justice vis-à-vis land reforms, green revolution and programmes of rural development.

The non-Brahmin movement in the former princely state of Mysore (Dushkin 1979: 661–66) is analyzed in terms of benefits for the elites, middle classes and lower classes from among the Scheduled Castes. The traditional agrarian stratification in Punjab (Mukherjee 1980: A-46–A-58) was characterized by debtors and money-lenders on the one hand and landlords, peasants and share-croppers on the other. John MacDougall (1979: 625–34) examines the theories of dominant castes and rich peasants, and suggests that keeping in view a series of secular changes in the post-independence period the rich-peasantry theory can account for the capitalist mode of production and relations, rural conflicts and class-based power relations. However, the dominant caste theory can provide useful insights and hypotheses for analyzing persistence of socio-cultural inequalities in the changed situation of today.

Rural class structure and class relations can be seen in terms of the mode of production, indebtedness and asset structure (Sivakumar 1978: 762–70; 812–20; 846–51). Sivakumar based on the agricultural assets including ploughs, levellers, sickles, spades, wells, pump sets and carts in two villages of Tamil Nadu classifies the peasantry into (*a*) big, (*b*) medium, (*c*) petty, (*d*) landless peasants, and (*e*) landlords. Besides implements Sivakumar takes into account in his analysis the livestock, crops, inputs, yields, marketing, etc. The assets include gold and silver, real estates, agricultural land, wells and pumps, loans advanced, cash and bank balances, agricultural and non-agricultural stock and livestock.

Distribution of assets corroborates class stratification. Out of 227 households in two villages of Chengalpattu district, 104 are landless peasants, and they own only 3 per cent of the gold and silver, 3 per cent of the real estates and 0.2 per cent of the cash on hand (Sivakumar 1978: 346). The petty peasants are little better. Mortgaging of gold and silver ornaments and land for meeting expenses on marriages and on development of land has become quite common. The Marwari money-lender controls 48.6 per cent of the total credit (ibid.: 348). Outside sources including absentee landlords and banks account for 29.7 per cent. The big peasants advance credit upto 8.8 per cent. Of the total borrowings 62.5 per cent is used on rituals, for clearing old debts and purchase and repair of fixed capital including land. On purchase of food and seasonal expenses for agriculture, 29.4 per cent of the total loans account for. Only 8.1 per cent is meant for education, healthcare and purchase of durable consumer goods.

Stratification of peasants is understood mainly in terms of the mode of production in agriculture (Bhaduri 1973; Bhardwaj and Das 1975: 222–23; Patnaik 1976: A-82–A-101; Prasad 1979; Rudra 1978: 916–23; Swamy 1976: 1933–39) despite its imprecise definition and ideological underpinnings for constructing a hierarchical arrangement of peasantry. Based on the landholding and resources the agrarian hierarchy comprises: (*a*) landless agricultural labourers, (*b*) small peasants, (*c*) middle peasants, (*d*) rich peasants, and (*e*) landlords (mainly absentee). Laxminarain and Tyagi (1977: A-77–A-82) and Saith and Tanakha (1972: 712–23) using both landholdings and resources also emphasize on the need for using attributes and interaction both as the basis of agrarian hierarchy. Sharma (1983: 1796–1802; 1851–55) examines agrarian stratification in terms of the old issues and new explanation and new issues and old explanation.

Patterns of Change in the Rural–Agrarian Stratification System

The pre-independence rural–agrarian system of stratification has changed particularly due to the effectiveness of peasant movements and the abolition of landlordism. N. Krishnaji (1979: 515–22) analyzes the role of the Left movement in Kerala in changing agrarian relations. He (ibid.: 515) observes: 'The abolition of tenancy is widely believed to be an accomplished fact in Kerala. The effective implementation of the law was possible largely due to the organized strength of the Left movement in the state and the related fact that land reforms in Kerala were implemented by the Left-oriented governments. Successful struggle for higher wages for agricultural labourers, espousal of the demand for "fair" prices for farm peasants and struggle for land have brought about enduring changes in agrarian relations with enhanced socio-economic equality.

However, a different picture is presented in regard to *leader–landlord nexus* (ibid.: fn.33: 521). Many of the local-level leaders are now landowners. The contradiction is that the leaders of the labourers are also employers of labour. Some of the leaders have therefore deserted the CPI (M). The leaders-landowners come from a high social stratum, and the agricultural labourers from the lowest stratum. Ronald J. Herring (1990: A-59–A-69) observes that the beneficiaries of the abolition of landlordism are mainly rich peasants, and not poor peasants or agricultural labourers.

The emergence of agricultural class structure depends upon the historicity of a given region/sub-region and effective implementation of land reforms. Dutta (1968) finds six agrarian classes in Goalpara district of Assam. These are: (*a*) cultivating owners, (*b*) cultivating tenants, (*c*) cultivating owners and tenants, (*d*) cultivating owners and rent receivers, (*e*) rent receivers, and (*f*) agricultural labourers. R. K. Bhadra (1979: 166) observes that socio-economic ties between these agricultural groups exhibit four patterns: (*a*) between absentee landlords and tenants, (*b*) between non-absentee but non-cultivators and agricultural labourers and tenants, (*c*) between petty land-owning cultivators and agricultural labourers and tenants, and (*d*) between tenants and agricultural labourers. All these class categories are further internally stratified. None of these are monolithic. For example, there are forms of unfree labour varying

from least unfree to the most unfree (Nagesh 1981: A-109–A-115).
Nagesh provides the following classification:

(1) Most unfree : Slavery
Bonded labour
Agrestic tenurial labour

(2) Mixed (1) : Punitive labour
Prerogative labour
Fiscal labour

(3) Mixed (2) : *Jajmani* labour
Caste obligatory labour
Communal labour
Customary labour

(4) Least unfree: Contractual labour
Exchange labour
Casual/day labour

However, such a pattern of *economic stratification* having im-
plication for hierarchized social ties has not emerged in Bihar and
some other states of India. Today Bihar is divided (Blair
1980: 64–74) into (*a*) forwards or twice-born, (*b*) upper backwards,
(*c*) lower backwards, and (*d*) others (including Muslims, Bengalis,
Scheduled Castes and Scheduled Tribes). Since the late 1970s the
backward castes are emerging as the dominant stratum in the state
of Bihar replacing the 'forwards' who dominated in the state for
centuries. The traditional agrarian hierarchy constituted of (*a*) inter-
mediaries, (*b*) large owners, (*c*) small and middle owners, (*d*) tenants-
at-will, and (*e*) landless workers. Abolition of the *zamindari* system,
tenancy reforms, ceiling on agricultural holdings, consolidation of
landholdings and other reform measures have brought about considerable change in the traditional system (Das 1983; Radhakrishnan 1990: 2617–21) not only in Bihar but also in other parts of
India.

The debate regarding the nature of rural (agrarian) class structure
and its transformation in the Indian context has crystallized in the
recent years. The volume *Peasants in History: Essays in Honour
of Daniel Thorner* (Hobsbawm et al. 1980) has a section on Indian
peasantry incorporating contributions by André Béteille, K. N. Raj,
Jacques Pouchepadass, Elizabeth Whitecombe, V. S. Vyas and
A. K. Sen. Limits on *shifts* and *movements* by the traditional system

of hierarchical values (Béteille 1980: 107–20), importance of *political economy* framework (Raj 1980: 121–35), emphasis on the notion of a *dominant peasantry* (Pouchepadass 1980: 136–55), *landownership* as the main basis of class position (Sen 1980: 194–220; Vyas 1980: 181–93; Whitecombe 1980: 156–80) are some of the main highlights of this volume. Thus, Indian peasantry in addition to its internal differentiation needs to be seen in relation of macro-structural policies and changes.

A study of the Tumkur district in south India by V. M. Rao (1981: 1655) shows that 'understanding rural economic process means, to a large extent, understanding the mechanisms giving rise to and sustaining the stratification of the rural society'. In the Tumkur district the rural–agrarian stratification comprises (*a*) landless workers, (*b*) small cultivators, (*c*) medium cultivators, and (*d*) non-cultivating owners or large capitalist farmers. A major part of land still remains in the hands of the medium and the small cultivators. Rao observes that a broad view of mode of production and of rural classes is not enough; it is also important to develop detailed pictures of specific conditions and circumstances underlying the stratification at the micro level. Though Omvedt (1981: A-140–A-159) generally supports the view that there is *capitalist* agriculture in India and rural classes are formed out of it, yet her analysis offers a critical assessment of the debate on the mode of production and highlights the structure and characteristics of the main rural classes in terms of (*a*) capitalist farmers, (*b*) middle peasants, and (*c*) semi-proletarianized poor peasants and labourers. Omvedt stresses the dominance of *semi-feudalism* and related forces holding back agricultural development. Her analysis resembles with the analyses given by Amit Bhaduri and Pradhan H. Prasad to a considerable extent.

Omvedt's observation regarding *caste and rural classes* (ibid.: A-156) seems to be a definite departure from classical Marxist position regarding social stratification in India. She writes: 'No analysis of class in rural India can be complete without taking caste into account; for not only did Indian feudalism have the specific feature of being structured and shaped through caste, but caste—though in a somewhat different form—remains equally viable and virulent today'. With the emergence of capitalism in agriculture the *'feudal form of caste'* has received a decisive blow, but still a correlation between caste and class persists to a large extent. The 'twice-born' castes are landlords, money-lender-merchants, and bureaucrats and professionals, and middle and low castes constitute the toiling masses. Omvedt observes: 'Today, the development of capitalist agriculture in India has broken down this old correlation between class and caste and reconstituted a new and more complex relationship between the two'. However, the two are no longer absolutely correlated. Economic differentiation has affected almost every caste and differentially to a large extent various families belonging to a particular caste.

A study by P. Radhakrishnan of a village in Kerala (1983: A-143–A-150) shows that the loss of land, status and power by the traditionally dominant caste due to the abolition of landlordism has been the gain of the traditionally dependent and subservient groups in terms of higher socio-economic status and emancipation from the clutches of the upper castes. This has altered considerably the traditional hierarchical socio-economic relations into egalitarian relations. The Namboodiris have lost the status, power and authority, and the Ambalavasis, Nayars, Maniyanis and the Tiyyas have shown a marked improvement in their economic condition. The traditional patron–client system, reciprocal and redistributive relationships have changed. However, the Mavaris, artisan and service castes, Harijans and Mappilas have not been benefited much by the redistribution of land.

Jan Breman (1979) finds the division of village community into landowners, small farmers and agricultural labourers quite inadequate as it does not provide an account of the artisan and service castes. Breman (ibid.: xiv) writes: 'The relations between Anavil Brahmins, the principal local landowners, and Dublas, a tribal caste of landless labourers, still contain many elements of the form of service which existed in earlier times and which is generally known as the *hali* system'. Jan Breman (1985) brings out more sharply the emergence of a new socio-economic formation in rural south Gujarat in a more recent study of agrarian relations and caste–class nexus. The village community has inherited the worst elements of both *feudalism* and *capitalism* in south Gujarat. It has aggravated the exploitation and alienation of labour. Labour mobility or immobility are two sides of the process of transformation. Breman's analysis revolves around the triangular relationship between migrants, local landless, and dominant landowners who are principal employers. He further mentions that class oppositions are articulated along caste lines. Traditional reciprocal relationship is being replaced by a contractual one. Jobbers and middlemen have emerged as new categories of people. Farmers and labourers are mobilizing against the State.

The Caste–Class Nexus

Significance of both caste and class has been highlighted in several studies of peasant movements and organizations. For example, Alexander's study of peasant organizations in south India (1981) brings out the following points:

1. The most conducive areas to radical mobilization of the rural power are rice areas with a high degree of proletarianization and with a high percentage of the Scheduled Caste agricultural labourers.
2. Caste and other conservative forces have limited the scope of mobilization in some parts.
3. Mobilization across caste lines is not quite clear even among the Communist-led movements.
4. Peasantry is highly differentiated in south India as elsewhere.

In an economically advanced state like Punjab, the gap between the rich and the poor is widening, and politics is articulated more along religious than class lines. The root cause of the communal tension in Punjab lies in the challenging of economic growth through the existing inegalitarian social structure, and hence economic growth reinforces it. The well-off castes of the two communities (Hindus and Sikhs) using their respective religious affinity control economy and prevent the have-nots from improving their position (D'Souza 1982: 783–92).

A study of a village in the North Arcot district of Tamil Nadu by John Harris (1982) also shows that there are: (a) big capitalist farmers and rich peasants, (b) dependent middle peasants, and (c) the poor peasants and labourers. The main source of contradiction between the first two categories lies in the first being independent and the second being dependent households in the context of agricultural production. Caste exists as an ideological phenomenon, but it is not a mere epiphenomenon. Caste affects the people by constraining them to accept lower positions and conditions of oppression and exploitation. However, caste has provided a ground in the past for movements to emancipate the oppressed. Caste involves not only an ideological system but also a differential access to and control over resources, and differential access to power. Through caste, class relations have been manifested. Thus caste is more of a historical reality and an infrastructure rather than merely an ideological or ritualistic institution. Caste-based movements and mobilizations have been more effective and intense compared to the ones involving inter-caste involvement and class-based participation.

However, the poor as a social stratum distinguishable from other strata has been taken as a datum for analyzing social stratification (Rao and Vivekananda 1982: 1107–12). Caste, land and occupational groups are analyzed by V. M. Rao (1983: 1177–90) in the context of rural development. As reported by Rao castes/communities are Hindus, SCs, STs and Muslims. The broad categories of landholdings are dry, wet and garden lands, and occupational groups include labourers, artisans, marginal, small, medium and large cultivators and business and trade professionals and salaried groups. Here the poor are treated as a category rather than an entity of interaction across caste and religion.

Following Alice Thorner's scheme of analysis (1982: 1993–99) regarding rural class structure, one can infer that agricultural production, agrarian mobilizations and peasant movements have varied from region to region, and the regional variations are reflected in the agrarian hierarchy. Role of caste and other non-class forces also varies in different regions of India. Mencher (1959: 1495–1503) emphasizes on land relations and a six-fold socio-economic classification stressing upon the overlap between caste and class hierarchies. 'Income' (Chandra: 1975); 'concentration of the means of production' (Patnaik 1976: 82–101), 'class contradictions' (Rudra 1978: 916–23, 963–68, 998–1003), *advantages of class* (Athreya et al. 1986: A-2–A-14; Goran and Lindberg 1975, 1976), *caste–class nexus* (Bose 1984; Harriss 1982a; Pathy 1975: 893–901; Prasad 1973: 481–84) are taken in as the main criteria in working out classifications of agrarian hierarchy. Formations such as feudalism, semi-feudalism, colonialism and capitalism/dependent capitalism and the Indian State have contributed to the emergence of the present agrarian stratification along with its ramifications and regional variations.

The Emerging Pattern

It is argued that peasant stratification or polarization has resulted from a variety of structural and institutional changes in India. Peasant stratification implies a continuum of agrarian classes ranging from landless labourers to the non-cultivating landlords. Peasant polarization, however, refers to differentiation of peasantry into large capitalist farmers and landless proletariat (Hayami and Kikuchi 1981). Because of green revolution and other institutional changes, peasant stratification becomes an inevitable social production, but this does not necessarily accentuate rural inequalities and the process of polarization. Hayami and Masao make this observation regarding the rural communities of South-East Asia. In parts of south India, landlords (belonging to high castes) formed a collective union which governed the village and controlled the village land through its ownership of the *mirasi* shares. The collectivity of the high caste landlords was evident in the management of the village affairs, in the collective obligation to pay land revenue, allocation of village land, etc. The collectivity could interfere with the rights of the mirasidars including transfer of the *kaniatchi* right and even divesting of the right of being a landlord (Shah 1985: PE-65–PE-78). Thus capitalist development in Indian agriculture and differentiation of peasantry have varied from region to region, and the situation described by Shah in Tamil Nadu certainly discouraged the capitalist trend in agriculture.

A study of the process of transformation of peasants and tribesmen to plantation workers (Dasgupta 1986: PE-2–PE-10) shows that the plantation workforce is characterized by the multi-tribe, multi-caste, and multi-lingual composition with the persistence of the primordial (tribal/caste/linguistic) ties. The question is therefore: Can we view and identify the plantation labour force as a working class or a segment of Indian working class? Dasgupta observes that under the existing conditions the capitalist sector emerges and grows, but the capitalist relations are not sufficiently generalized in the economy as a whole. Even in a relatively more economically developed state like Punjab growth with *equity* has not been achieved.

Increasing role of capitalism in Indian economy, particularly in the agricultural production, despite regional variations the use of nativistic categories like *mazdoor*, *kisan* and *malik* in the analysis of agrarian hierarchy implies the persistence of *paternalism* along with the general capitalist categories like rich, middle and poor peasants and share-croppers and agricultural labourers.

The class question, however, remains central in several studies of agrarian structure and change. Thus, it is a *mixed situation* characterized by the forces of caste and feudalism on the one hand and capitalism on the other. Praveen K. Chaudhary's analysis of agrarian unrest in Patna district in Bihar from 1960 to 1984 (1988: 51–56) brings out the role of class structure in the peasant revolt as follows:

1. big landlords versus cultivating tenants;
2. owner-cultivators versus money-lenders; and
3. landless poor peasants versus landlords and owner-cultivators.

Thus there are (*a*) landlords, (*b*) owner-cultivators, (*c*) money-lenders, (*d*) cultivating tenants, and (*e*) landless poor peasants. Despite differentiation of peasantry, the peasant question is a class question (Omvedt and Gala 1988: 1394–96). Utsa Patnaik (1986: 781–91) argues that the application of the concept of *mode of production* should not remain confined to India's agriculture alone, but its relevance should be seen in analyzing India's entire path of development.

The farmer-capitalists of coastal Andhra Pradesh (Upadhyaya 1988: 1376–82; 1433–42) have taken up entrepreneurship in the neighbouring towns and cities. Upadhyaya discusses their social origins in the pre- and the post-green revolution periods, investment of agricultural surplus, the emergence of new rural elite, new urban business class, patterns of migration, social organization of business firm and the households, rural–urban connections, rural–urban flow of resources and ties between caste and business. The rise of a new class of businessmen out of the class of capitalist farmers negates the *landholding* thesis as the basis of *peasant stratification*. The emergence of this class is explained through convergence of several following historical processes:

1. The development of a productive and commercialized agrarian economy in the late nineteenth century and the emergence of a *rich peasant* class;
2. the integration of town and countryside;
3. an early interest in education on the part of the rural elite;

4. the politicization of caste identity; and
5. the green revolution and land reforms.

Upadhyaya observes: 'Furthermore, the development of an entrepreneurial class is not a function merely of economic forces, but also of social, political and cultural processes.' Kalpana Bardhan (1989: A-22–A-23) explains that how the vertical ties between landowners and labourers have not disappeared in India. The enterprising farmers have blocked the organization of landless labourers using these ties. However, the traditional forms of patron–client relations anchored in social hierarchy, and enforced by extra-economic sanctions, are replaced by extra-economic sanctions and market-based labour transactions. Today the asymmetry of wealth, market, power and organization between employers and labourers is quite distinctly visible and this is further reinforced by lack of access to the means of production, education skills and job opportunities. Thus everything remains *stratified*.

Rajendra Singh's study (1988) of relationship between land, power and people in Basti district of Uttar Pradesh also marks a departure from the conventional approaches because (*a*) it establishes the relationship between the rural elite and the agrarian power structure in a historical evolutionary setting; (*b*) it brings out the link between the institutional and social structural factors; (*c*) it explains elite structure in its various aspects, phases and ramifications, and clearly distinguishes elites from leaders; and (*d*) it uses the categories of space, time and social actors as both analytical tools and empirical variables. Singh classifies elites into two categories: (*a*) the established elites; and (*b*) the emerging elites. The established elites refer to the traditionally established rural influentials. The main sources of power and authority of the established elites have been ascriptive statuses drawn from caste, rulership, privileges and honours and control over land. Singh observes that besides these sources, the established elites derive power from the post-feudal and colonial forces of which it is the product. It continues to enjoy power even today. The emerging elites are above the rural leaders, and they are new entrants into the elite sector. They are a product of post-independence political, legal and administrative measures. It tends to outcross the established elites drawn from the upper castes, aristocratic families and priestly classes.

Another trend is reported by Rudolph and Rudolph (1987: 50) as they observe that polarization based on left and right class politics in the agricultural sector and rural society is as unlikely as it is in the industrial economy and society. There are classes of quasi-feudal landlords and of tractor-capitalists which have become a basis for viable conservative politics in India. The emergence of Bharatiya Kranti Dal (BKD), Swatantra Party, Lok Dal, Janata Dal, Bharatiya Kisan Union (BKU) Shetkari Sanghatan, etc. have no doubt brought about a shift in India's socio-political formation, but the benefits of change have not gone beyond bullock capitalists and backward (upper) classes. Rudolph and Rudolph (ibid.: 333–92) consider 'agrarian producers as a demand group', and differentiate them by operational holding size and relate this to their interests and political influence. Thus class-based politics, power alignments and mobilizations as reported by several other scholars are not visualized by Rudolphs in foreseeable future in rural India.

Rural–agrarian stratification is a complex social reality. Not only extra-caste but also extra-class and extra-political factors and forces have entrenched into the rural society. New norms of status-evaluation signifying change in the traditional 'composite status' system have acquired legitimacy and acceptance. Caste has become *weak* and yet it has revitalized giving the impression of its entrenchment in new spheres of social life. Class, occupation, income, power, mobilization capacity and networks are accepted today as the effective channels of upward social mobility.

References

Adnan, Shapan, 1985, 'Classical and Contemporary Approach to Agrarian Capitalism', *Economic and Political Weekly*, Vol. XX, No. 30, pp. PE-53–PE-64.

Alavi, Hamza, 1981, 'Structure of Colonial Formations', *Economic and Political Weekly*, Vol. XVI (Annual Number), pp. 475–86.

Alexander, K.C., 1981, *Peasant Organisations in South India*, New Delhi: Indian Social Institute.

Athreya, Venkatesh B. et al., 1986, 'Economics of Scale or Advantages of Class?: Some Results from a South Indian Farm Economy Study', *Economic and Political Weekly*, Vol. XXI, No. 13, pp. A-2–A-14.

Banaji, J., 1977, 'Capitalist Domination and the Small Peasantry: Deccan Districts in the late 19th Century', *Economic and Political Weekly*, Vol. XII, Nos 33 and 34, pp. 1375–1404.

Bardhan, Kalpna, 1989, 'Poverty, Growth and Rural Labour Markets in India', *Economic and Political Weekly*, Vol. XXIV, No. 12, pp. A-21–A-38.

Bardhan, Pranab and **Ashok Rudra**, 1978, 'Interlinkage of Land, Labour and Credit Relations: An Analysis of Village Survey Data in East India', *Economic and Political Weekly*, Vol. XIII (AN), Nos 6 and 7, pp. 367–84.

Basham, A.L., 1954, *The Wonder that Was India*, New York: Grove Press Inc.

Béteille, André, 1974, *Studies in Agrarian Social Structure*, Delhi: Oxford University Press.

———, 1974, *Six Essays in Comparative Sociology*, Delhi: Oxford University Press.

———, 1980, 'The Indian Villages: Past and Present', *in* Hobsbawm, E.J. et al. (eds), *Peasants in History: Essays in Honour of Daniel Thorner*, Delhi: Oxford University Press, pp. 107–20.

———, 1980, *Ideologies and Intellectuals*, Delhi: Oxford University Press.

Bhadra, R.K., 1979, 'Rural Class Structure in Post-independent Assam', *Economic and Political Weekly*, Vol. XIV, No. 4, pp. 165–67.

Bhaduri, Amit, 1973, 'An Analysis of Semi-feudalism in East Indian Agriculture', *Frontier*, 29 September.

Bhardwaj, K., 1980, *On Some Issues of Method in the Analysis of Social Change*, Mysore: Mysore University Press.

Bhardwaj, K. and **P. K. Das**, 1975, 'Tenurial Conditions and Mode of Exploitation: Study of Some Villages in Orissa', *Economic and Political Weekly*, Vol. X, Nos 5–7, pp. 222–33.

Blair, Harry W., 1980, 'Rising Kulaks and Backward Classes in Bihar, Social Change in the late 1970s', *Economic and Political Weekly*, Vol. XV, No. 2, pp. 64–74.

Bose, P.K., 1984, 'Peasant Production and Capitalist Enterprise', *Economic and Political Weekly*, Vol. XIX, No. 40.

———, 1989, 'Dimensions of Agrarian Structure and Change: Issues in Theory', *Sociological Bulletin*, Vol. 38, No. 2, pp. 183–98.

Bose, Sugata, 1986, *Agrarian Bengal: Economy, Social Structure and Politics, 1919–47*, Cambridge: Cambridge University Press.

Breman, Jan, 1979, *Of Peasants, Migrants and Paupers: Rural Labours Circulation and Capitalist Production in West India*, Delhi: Oxford University Press.

Byres, T.J., **Peter Molavi** and **Milton Keynes**, 1976, *Inequality between Nations: India and China Compared, 1950–70*, London: Open University Press.

Chakravarti, Uma, 1985, 'Towards a Historical Sociology of Stratification in Ancient India: Evidence of Buddhist Sources', *Economic and Political Weekly*, Vol. XX, No. 9, pp. 356–60.

Chandra, Satish, 1986, *Medieval India: Society and Jagirdari Crisis and the Village*, Delhi: Macmillan India Ltd.

Chaudhary, P.K., 1988, 'Agrarian unrest in Bihar: A case study of Patna district 1960–1984', *Economic and Political Weekly*, Vol. XXIII, No. 1, pp. 51–56.

Chua, Cathy, 1986, 'Development of Capitalism in Indian Agriculture: Gujarat, 1850–1900', *Economic and Political Weekly*, Vol. XXI, No. 48, pp. 2092–99.

Cohn, Bernard S., 1969, 'Structural changes in Indian rural society—1596–1885', *in* Frykenberg, Robert E. (ed.), *Land Control and Social Structure in Indian History*, Madison: Wisconsin University Press.

Das, Arvind N., 1983, *Agrarian Unrest and Socio-Economic Change in Bihar, 1900–1980*, Delhi: Manohar Publications.

Dasgupta, Biplab, 1975, 'A Typology of Village Socio-economic Systems from Indian Village Studies', *Economic and Political Weekly*, Vol. X, No. 25, pp. 1395–1414.

———, 1984, 'Agricultural Labour under Colonial, Semi-capitalist and Capitalist Conditions: A Case Study of West Bengal', *Economic and Political Weekly*, Vol. XIX, No. 39, pp. A-129–A-148.

Dasgupta, Ranjit, 1986, 'From Peasants and Tribesmen to Plantation Workers', *Economic and Political Weekly*, Vol. XXI, No. 4, pp. 2–10.

Deva, Indra and **Shrirama**, 1986, *Traditional Values and Institutions in Indian Society*, New Delhi: S. Chand and Co.

D'Souza, V.S., 1982, 'Economy, Caste, Religion and Population Distribution: An Analysis of Communal Tensions in Punjab', *Economic and Political Weekly*, Vol. XVII, No. 19, pp. 783–92.

Dushkin, Lelah, 1979, 'Backward Class Benefits and Social Class in India', *Economic and Political Weekly*, Vol. XIV, No. 14, pp. 661–66.

Dutta, N.C., 1968, *Land Problem and Land Reform in Assam*, New Delhi: S. Chand and Co.

Gough, E. Kathleen, 1980, 'Modes of Production in Southern India', *Economic and Political Weekly*, Vol. XV (AN), Nos 5, 6 and 7, pp. 334–64.

Goran, D. and **S. Lindberg**, 1975, *Behind Poverty: The Social Formation of a Tamil Village*, London: Curzon Press.

———, 1976, *Pills Against Poverty*, London: Curzon Press.

Gupta, Dipankar, 1988, 'Country–Town Nexus and Agrarian Mobilisation: Bharatiya Kisan Union as an Instance', *Economic and Political Weekly*, Vol. XXIII, No. 51, pp. 2688–96.

Gupta, S.P., 1986, *The Agrarian System of Eastern Rajasthan, c.1650–c.1750*, Delhi: Manohar Publications.

Hanumantha Rao, C.H., 1978, 'Urban vs rural or rich vs poor?', *Economic and Political Weekly*, Vol. XIII, No. 40, pp. 1699–1702.

Hardiman, David, 1981, *Peasant Nationalists of Gujarat: Kheda District, 1917–1934*, Delhi: Oxford University Press.

Harriss, John, 1982(a), *Capitalism and Peasant Farming: Agrarian Structure and Ideology in Northern Tamil Nadu*, Delhi: Oxford University Press.

———, 1982(b), *Rural Development Theories of Peasant Economy and Agrarian Change*, London: Hutchinson University Library.

Hasan, Nurul, 1969, 'Zamindars under the Mughals', *in* Frykenberg, Robert E. (ed.), *Land Control and Social Structure in Indian History*, Madison: University of Wisconsin Press.

Hayami, Yujre and **Kikuchi Masao**, 1981, *An Economic Approach to Institutional Change*, Tokyo: University of Tokyo Press.

Herring, Ronald J., 1990, 'Abolition of Landlordism in Kerala: A Redistribution of Privilege', *Economic and Political Weekly*, Vol. XXV, No. 26, pp. A-59–A-69.

Hobsbawm, E.J. et al. (eds), 1980, *Peasants in History: Essays in Honour of Daniel Thorner*, Calcutta: Oxford University Press.

Jain, R.K., 1979, 'Kingship, Territory and Property in Pre-British Bundelkhand', *Economic and Political Weekly*, Vol. XIV, No. 22, pp. 946–50.

Jha, Vivekanand, 1990, 'Social Stratification in Ancient India', Presidential Address, Ancient India, New Delhi: ICHR.

Karashima, Noboru, 1984, 'South Indian History and Society: Studies from Inscription, AD 850–1800', Delhi: Oxford University Press.

Krishnaji, N., 1979, 'Agrarian Relations and the Left Movement in Kerala: A Note on Recent Trends', *Economic and Political Weekly*, Vol. XIV, Nos 7 and 8, pp. 515–21.

Kurien, C.T., 1980, 'Dynamics of Rural Transformation: A Case Study of Tamil Nadu', *Economic and Political Weekly*, Vol. XV, Nos 5, 6, and 7, pp. 365–90.

Laxminarayan, H. and **S.S. Tyagi**, 1977, 'Inter-state variations in types of tenancy', *Economic and Political Weekly*, Vol. XII, No. 39, pp. A-77–A-82.

Lipton, Michael, 1977, *Why Poor People Stay Poor: Urban Bias in World Development*, London: Temple Smith.

MacDougall, John Douglas, 1979, 'Dominant Castes or Rich Peasants', *Economic and Political Weekly*, Vol. XIV, Nos 12 and 13, pp. 625–34.

Mencher, Joan P., 1978, *Agriculture and Social Structure in Tamil Nadu*, New Delhi: Allied Publishers.

———, 1978, 'Why Grow More Food? An Analysis of Some Contradictions in the "Green Revolution" in Kerala', *Economic and Political Weekly*, Vol. XIII, Nos 51 and 52, pp. A-98–A-104.

———, 1980, 'The lessons and non-lessons of Kerala: Agricultural labourers and poverty', *Economic and Political Weekly*, Vol. XV (SN), Nos 41, 42, and 43, pp. 1781–1802.

Mukherjee, Aditya, 1978, 'Indian Capitalist Class and Congress on National Planning and Public Sector, 1930–47', *Economic and Political Weekly*, Vol. XIII, No. 35, pp. 1516–28.

Mukherjee, Ramkrishna, 1957, *The Dynamics of Rural Society*, Berlin: Academie Verlag.

———, 1981, 'Realities of Agrarian Relations in India', *Economic and Political Weekly*, Vol. XVI, No. 4, pp. 109–16.

Mukerji, D.P., 1958, *Diversities*, New Delhi: Peoples Pub. House.

Nagesh, H.V., 1981, 'Forms of Unfree Labour in Indian Agriculture', *Economic and Political Weekly*, Vol. XVII, No. 39, pp. A-109–A-115.

Nazir, Pervaiz, 1981, 'Transformation of Property Relations in the Punjab', *Economic and Political Weekly*, Vol. XVI, No. 8, pp. 281–85.

Omvedt, Gail, 1981, 'Capitalist Agriculture and Rural Classes in India', *Economic and Political Weekly*, Vol. XVI, No. 51, A-140–A-159.

Omvedt, Gail and **Chetna Gala**, 1988, 'Peasant Question is a Class Question', *Economic and Political Weekly*, Vol. XXIII, No. 27, pp. 1394–96.

Patnaik, U., 1976, 'Class Differentiation within the Peasantry', *Economic and Political Weekly*, Vol. IX, No. 39, pp. A-82–A-101.

———, 1986, 'The Agrarian Question and Development of Capitalism in India', *Economic and Political Weekly*, Vol. XXI, No. 18, pp. 781–93.

Pathy, Jaganath, 1975, 'Social Stratification in an Orissa Village', *Economic and Political Weekly*, Vol. X, No. 23, pp. 893–901.

Prasad, Pradhan H., 1973, 'Production Relations: Achille's Heel of Indian Planning', *Economic and Political Weekly*, Vol. VIII, No. 19, pp. 869–72.

———, 1979, 'Caste and Class in Bihar', *Economic and Political Weekly*, Vol. XIV (Annual Number), Nos 7 and 8, pp. 481–84.

———, 1980, 'Rising Middle Peasantry in North India', *Economic and Political Weekly*, Vol. XV, No. 4, pp. 215–19.

Pouchepadass, J., 1980, 'Peasant Classes in Twentieth Century Agrarian Movements in India', *in* Hobsbawm, E.J. et al. (eds), *Peasants in History*, Calcutta: Oxford University Press, pp. 136–55.

Radhakrishnan, P., 1980, 'Peasant Struggles and Land Reforms in Malabar', *Economic and Political Weekly*, Vol. XV, No. 50, pp. 2095–2102.

———, 1981, 'Land Reforms in Theory and Practice: The Kerala experience', *Economic and Political Weekly*, Vol. XVI, No. 51, pp. A-129–A-137.

———, 1982, 'Land Reforms and Change in Land System: Study of a Kerala village', *Economic and Political Weekly*, Vol. XVIII, Nos 52 and 53, pp. A-107–A-119.

———, 1983, 'Land Reforms and Social Change: Study of a Kerala village', Review of Agriculture, *Economic and Political Weekly*, Vol. XVIII, Nos 52 and 53, pp. A-143–A-150.

———, 1990, 'Backward Classes in Tamil Nadu: 1872–1988', *Economic and Political Weekly*, Vol. XXV, No. 10, pp. 509–20.

———, 1990, 'Karnataka Backward Classes', *Economic and Political Weekly*, Vol. XXV, No. 32, pp. 1749–54.

Raj, K.N., 1980, 'Village India and its Political Economy', *in* Hobsbawm, E.J. et al. (eds), *Peasants in History: Essays in Honour of Daniel Thorner*, Calcutta: Oxford University Press.

Rao, V.M., 1981, 'Nature of Rural Under-development: A Field View', *Economic and Political Weekly*, Vol. XVI, No. 41, pp. 1655–66.

———, 1983, 'Barriers in Rural Development', *Economic and Political Weekly*, Vol. XVIII, No. 27, pp. 1177–90.

Rao, V.M. and **M. Vivekananda**, 1982, 'The Poor as a Social Stratum', *Economic and Political Weekly*, Vol. XVIII, No. 27, pp. 1107–12.

Robb, Peter (ed.), 1986, *Rural India*, New Delhi: Segment Book Distributors.

Rudolph, S.H. and **L. I. Rudolph**, 1987, *In Pursuit of Lakshmi: The Political Economy of the Indian State*, Delhi: Orient Longman.

Rudra, A., 1978, 'Class Relations in Indian Agriculture', *Economic and Political Weekly*, Vol. VIII, Nos 22, 23 and 24, pp. 916–23, 963–68, 998–1003.

Saith, Ashwani and **Ajay Tanakha**, 1972, 'Agrarian Transition and the Differentiation of the Peasantry: A Study of a West U.P. Village', *Economic and Political Weekly*, Vol. VII, No. 14, pp. 1069–76.

Sen, A.K., 1980, 'Famine Mortality: A Study of the Bengal Famine of 1943', *in* Hobsbawm, E.J. et al. (eds), *Peasants in History*, Calcutta: Oxford University Press, pp. 194–220.

Shah, Mihir, 1985, 'The Kaniatchi Form of Labour', *Economic and Political Weekly*, Vol. XX, No. 30, pp. PE-65–PE-78.

Sharma, G.D., 1977, *Rajput Polity: A Study of Politics and Administration of the State of Mewar: 1638–1749 AD*, Delhi: Manohar Publications.

Sharma, K.L., 1983, 'Agrarian Stratification: Old Issues, New Explanations and New Issues, Old Explanations', *Economic and Political Weekly*, Vol. XVIII, Nos 42 and 43, pp. 1796–1802, 1851–55.

———— (ed.), 1986, *Social Stratification in India*, Delhi: Manohar Publications.

Singh, Hira, 1981, 'Decline of Feudalism: Marwar from 1870 to 1940s', Ph.D. thesis, University of Delhi.

Singh, Rajendra, 1988, *Land, Power and People: Rural Elite in Transition, 1801–1970*, New Delhi: Sage Publications.

Sivakumar, S.S., 1978, 'Aspects of Agrarian Economy in Tamil Nadu: A Study of Two Villages', *Economic and Political Weekly*, Vol. XIII, Nos 18, 19 and 20, pp. 762–70; 812–20; 846–51.

Srinivas, M.N., 1975, 'Village Studies, Participant Observation and Social Science Research in India', *Economic and Political Weekly*, Vol. X (SN), Nos 22–25, pp. 1387–94.

Stein, Burton, 1969, 'Integration of the Agrarian System of South India', *in* Frykenberg, Robert E. (ed.), *Land Control and Social Structure in Indian History*, Madison: University of Wisconsin Press.

————, 1980, *Peasant, State and Society in Medieval South India*, Delhi: Oxford University Press.

Swamy, Dalip S., 1976, 'Differentiation of Peasantry in India', *Economic and Political Weekly*, Vol. XI, No. 50, pp. 1933–39.

Thorner, Daniel, 1976, *The Agrarian Prospect in India*, Delhi: Allied Publishers.

Vyas, V.S., 1980, 'Changes in Land Ownership Pattern: Structural Change in Indian Agriculture', *in* Hobsbawm, E.J. et al. (eds), *Peasants in History*, Calcutta: Oxford University Press, pp. 181–93.

Whitecombe, Elizabeth, 1980, 'Whatever Happened to the Zamindars?', *in* Hobsbawm, E.J. et al. (eds), *Peasants in History*, Calcutta: Oxford University Press, pp. 156–80.

Upadhya, Carol Boyack, 1988, 'The Farmer-capitalists of Coastal Andhra Pradesh', *Economic and Political Weekly*, Vol. XXIII, Nos 27, 28, pp. 1376–82, 1433–42.

Thorner, Alice, 1982, 'Semi-feudalism or Capitalism? Contemporary Debate on Classes and Modes of Production in India', *Economic and Political Weekly*, Vol. XVIII, Nos 49, 50 and 51, pp. 1961–68, 1993–99, 2061–66.

Four

Social Stratification in Urban–Industrial Setting

The two main criteria for understanding urban–industrial social structure and stratification are the extent of closure or openness, and the nature of deprivations and gratifications of members of a society. Other important criteria include: (*a*) the motivational structure, (*b*) the opportunity structure, and (*c*) the communication structure or the extent of visibility of opportunity. Based on these criteria multiple references for an individual emerge since a person is evaluated in terms of his/her education, income, occupation, life-style, etc. These criteria of evaluation are juxtaposed to the rural–agrarian social structure and stratification.

Country–Town Nexus and Urban–Industrial Social Stratification

Rural and urban phenomena are two distinct patterns of life because of the distinctions between the populations of these two settings.

This does not imply two different principles of social stratification. It becomes, however, difficult to draw a strict line of demarcation between rural and urban and individual and group rankings. Because the rich and the poor are basically similar in both the settings, the difference is a contextual one. An individual is a part of his family, and a family is linked with a group, and therefore individual does exist as part of a collective entity to a considerable extent. Similarly, a village is part of its region, and the region is linked with civilization, hence village is part of a wider society and civilization.

A lot of changes are taking place in the countryside particularly in the caste stratification, agrarian relations and power structure, but rural social stratification has not transformed itself into an urban stratification system. There are several common features of social stratification in both rural–agrarian and urban–industrial settings as the same principles determine social relations in the two situations. The difference between the two settings is that of the extent of operation of a particular principle or a set of criteria/ attributes. Caste, class and power are common to both the settings, but they differ operationally because of the structural and cultural differences.

Urban–industrial social stratification is characterized by the professional and the working classes to a large extent. Professionalism requires training to acquire skills for performing specific roles. It imparts values of rationality, objectivity and pragmatism. Professional classes reflect social and structural differentiation or changes from tradition to modernity in the fields of occupation, industry and economy. Emergence of professional classes becomes a measure of social mobility. Suren Navlakha (1971) observes that in comparison to other Asian countries the professional classes in India constitute a less significant proportion of all workers. Navlakha highlights the uneven growth of professions revealing the pattern of recruitment process heavily biased in favour of the upper castes, urban dwelling groups and the metropolitan population. It is evident from several other accounts as well that caste is not merely a rural phenomenon and class is not confined to urban India (see, for example, D'Souza [1968], Saberwal [1976], Singer [1972], Singer [ed] [1973]). Both these have coexisted in rural–agrarian and urban– industrial formations though in different forms and proportions.

Urban–industrial social stratification consists of the following classes: (a) upper class, (b) upper-middle class, (c) lower-middle class, and (*d*) working class. These classes are generally formed on the basis of income and occupation. However, it may be quite difficult to know the real income from the apparent occupational status. Victor S. D'Souza (1968: 26–64) analyzes the bases of social organization in the city of Chandigarh taking into consideration kinship, caste, class, religion and displaced or non-placed condition of the inhabitants. D'Souza discovers that the educational, occupational and income hierarchies are significantly correlated with each other. But the correlation of each of them with the operational caste hierarchy is not significant. In a recent study, Sanjay Kumar Mishra (1991) observes that the local institutions such as caste and kinship play a significant role in recasting the relationship between man and machine, without dislocating the traditional social structure and at the same time, not affecting the process of industrialization adversely.

Thus, industrial society can be characterized by a very open view of status, role and power allocation. Open relationships, competition, radicalism, innovation and utilitarianism–rationalism are the main features of an industrial society. Relevant questions regarding social stratification in an industrial society are as follows:

1. What is the social background of the entrepreneurs and managers?
2. Does the hierarchy of the industrial elite correspond with the caste hierarchy?
3. Do the values of the pre-industrial society coexist with those of the industrial society?
4. What is the relationship between the internal structure of the factories, and the caste and class structure of the workers?
5. Do the industrial employers, municipal councillors, the benefactors and controllers of the educational and religious institutions belong to the families which have become prominent in recent decades?

Studies of the urban–industrial social stratification in India may be viewed as a consequence of macro-structural processes of change, migration from rural to urban areas, social mobility and increase in the number of urban–industrial towns. Studies by Akbar (1990), Bala (1986), Berna (1960), D'Souza (1968), Lambert (1963), Navlakha (1971), Saberwal (1976), Sharma (1981, 1986), Sheth

(1968), Sheth and Patel (1979), Singer (1972), Singh (1985), Philips (1990) impress upon the need to go beyond the village, and see how the urban–industrial society and its components are constituted. Studies on urban–industrial social stratification have concentrated on the themes such as class and caste, occupation, income, education and class, social mobility and elite formation, professionals and working classes, middle classes, processes of social change and status-crystallization, dissonance and inconsistency, professional associations and trade unions.

An annotated biography and analysis of the trends in industrial sociology in India by Sheth and Patel (1979), and by Patel (1985) examine the impact of society on industrialization and the effects of industrialization on society. Sociology of industrialization studies workers, supervisors and managers as the major human components along with trade unions, informal groups and owners of industry. M. N. Panini (1986: 255–71) hypothesizes that industrialization has economically fragmented the Indian society into classes by weakening the caste system. The economic fragmentation created by industrialization has brought about both vertical and horizontal changes, thereby a change is being registered in the persisting criteria of status-evaluation. Barnett R. Rubin (1986: 69) lends strength to Panini's hypothesis. He writes: 'And industrialization can produce the professional employments and affluent style of life to which urban middle and upper classes aspire.' Hence, the question is: Are urban–industrial and rural–agrarian settings poles apart or they can be located on a continuum?

Historicity of Urban–Industrial Stratification System

The process of urbanization and industrialization though not necessarily unrelated are also not essentially concomitant in entirety. In the pre-industrial period, urbanization was not an exclusive phenomenon; it was quite pronounced and was an ideal reference for a desired living. Based on the study of *Arthashastra* (*c.* 300–200 BC) and *Varna Ratnakara* (early fourteenth century AD), Hetukar Jha (1988: 46–55) explains urbanism as a way of life in ancient Bihar. According to the *Arthashastra*, besides provisions for water, roads, grounds, defence and other civic amenities, there was a developed system of social ranking in the urban settlements. The head of the city was called *nagarka* (mayor). Next in the rung were *sthanikas* and the latter had *gopas* as their subordinates. There were other functionaries and officials to look after various essential services.

The administrative hierarchy was constituted independent of varna/caste ranking. Non-agricultural occupations, formal groups and impersonal relationships were the main features of urban social life. *Varna Ratnakara* also provides a vivid account of the lower castes, market–activities, cultural and artistic endeavours, and ascetics. It also provides a description of predominant non-agricultural occupations, the complexity and heterogeneity of the population and the preference for personalized relationships. These two valuable classical sources reveal the dynamics of urbanization, explaining at the same time, structural and cultural indices of urban life.

There are several towns which acquired a place of cultural and religious significance in ancient India (Rao 1991: 21–41). Many of these towns became known as centres of administrative and political activities. Naqvi (1968: 266) classifies towns in medieval India into four categories: (*a*) capital cities (centres of administration, industry and trade), (*b*) administrative centres with trading activities, (*c*) pilgrimage centres, and (*d*) specific-economy towns. Such a classification of towns indicates the criteria on the basis of which people were ranked differentially high and low. However, a study of a north Indian *qasba* (small town) in the nineteenth century (Pandey 1984: 231–70) shows that community consciousness centered around religious fraternity, class *qasba* and *mohalla*. This consciousness cannot be explained in terms of today's social science vocabulary, for example, Muslim/Hindu, working class/rentier, urban/rural. Self-respect and human dignity were the main determinants of the community consciousness. Despite the rootedness of community consciousness into a certain perception of honour and dignity, people were *socially* differentiated as zamindars, weavers, trader-money-lenders, cultivating tenants, labourers and others (*halwais*, *pansaris*, beggars, etc.). Fragmentation of society and community was not the overarching feature of urban life in medieval and British India. Meera Kosambi's comparative study of Bombay and Poona between 1650 and 1900 provides details regarding occupational structure, ethnic composition, languages, religious composition and age–sex structure. It clearly brings out community-based consciousness and social life in these two major towns of western India (1991: 142–78).

Michael Lipton (1977: 66–81) adds a new dimension to our understanding of urban–industrial stratification. He argues: 'Inequalities *within* rural areas also owe much to the urban-biased nature of the development policy'. Rural-born doctors, teachers, engineers and administrators serve the urban population. Surpluses from rural areas are extracted for the urban populace. In India the urban–rural balance is not as disappointing as is implied in Lipton's formulation. Green revolution has brought about a considerable change in agrarian stratification, thereby having implications for urban social structure. Urban social stratification in terms of capital/ labour relation can be characterized by capitalists, administrators, professionals, labour aristocracy and large landowners. On the contrary, there are small farmers and tenants, landless agricultural workers and members of the informal sector in the countryside (Griffin 1977: 109). Byres (1979: 210–44) contradicts Lipton's hypothesis by pinpointing rural bias as the main hindrance in India's industrialization.

Two recent studies of the sugar industry (Chithelen 1985: 604–12; Commander 1985: 505–16) provide enough evidence to show the emergence of a new pattern of social stratification. Commander writes about the sugar industry in north India:

> The hub of the system was clearly agricultural and the divorce from the means of production characteristic of the factory system proper was never wholly engendered. Instead, the controls exercised by the zamindar-khandasari over labour, land and credit, which provided the basis of the system, were in many respects antagonistic to a model of pure capitalism.

The assimilation of the non-capitalist features of economy with the capitalist system of production (Chithelen 1985: 604) has produced social stratification system different from both the rural–agrarian and the urban–industrial systems. The growth of regional markets and the development of modern transportation networks initially provided the requisite stimulus for the rise of sugar industry. The main factors for this development were ample reservoir of cheap, unorganized labour, and money-lending–debt linkages which generated significantly high profit margins. However, the emergence of a rich peasant strata in the early twentieth century, and the spread of canal irrigation, coupled with financial support from a co-operative credit infrastructure, facilitated the cultivation of sugar-cane in the Ahmednagar district of Maharashtra.

In 1902, in the Upper Doab, Rohilkhand and eastern UP (Gorakhpur and Azamgarh) (Commander 1985: 507) besides the owners, other functionaries of the sugar mills, there were: (*a*) *munshi*, (*b*) *darogah*, (*c*) *halwai*, (*d*) *bhishti*, and (*e*) *shukia/jhorkia*. Of these the *munshi* was the highest paid functionary. A remarkable change is noticed in 1935. Rosa Sugar Mill in the Shahjehanpur district of Rohilkhand had: (*a*) managerial grades, (*b*) supervisory staff, (*c*) clerks, (*d*) skilled labour, and (*e*) unskilled labour. However, the sugar industry has remained in the informal sector despite its rapid proliferation and enhanced technical and management skills.

Changes in the stratification system of the Deccan peasantry in early twentieth century contributed to the emergence of a rich peasant stratum placing them in a commanding position (Chithelen 1985: 604–5). By the middle of the first decade of the twentieth century, the distinction between rich peasants and the mass of poor peasants had become distinctly clear. A rich peasant had control and ownership of land as well as ownership and mastery of agricultural implements and techniques. The rich peasants also enjoyed independence and autonomy in the credit relationship. They were also money-lenders and suppliers of credit to the small peasants. By having control over the debtor's crop as well as his lands, the rich peasants expanded their commercial links. These rich peasants belonged to the non-Brahmin upper castes of Maharashtra, who were part of the traditional cultivating elites, or sometimes were members of former royal families or were *inamdars* and other office-holders. A few low-status caste groups like *malis* also rose to become rich peasants. Several factors including the spread of canal irrigation, cooperatives, legislations, favourable political milieu brought about socio-economic and political transformation of the peasantry having implications for change in the rural as well as the urban social stratification. The rise of the peasantry could exemplify the shaping and reshaping of the country–town nexus.

The Indian Bourgeoisie/Capitalist Class

The bourgeoisie/capitalist class can be characterized (Hamilton and Hirszowicz 1987: 106–27) as follows:

1. Concentration and private ownership of the means of production;
2. A free market for the sale and purchase of commodities and services;
3. Formally free labour sold in the market as commodity;
4. The pursuit of profits by entrepreneurs for wages; and
5. The division of society into two opposed and antagonistic classes as a consequence of the exploitation and alienation of the labour from the means of production.

The property-owning, entrepreneurial, capitalist-employer has emerged from a variety of sources including the decline of the feudal system. Along with the bourgeoisie, the capitalist system has produced a *working class*. Marx's theory of the capitalist society is the theory of the commodity-producing society. The worker is treated as a *commodity* (Bottomore 1985: 4–21). Though Marx refers to the bourgeoisie and the proletariat as the main antagonistic classes, he realizes the transition of society and the emergent role of the intermediate strata, situated between the workers and the industrial capitalists. He also realizes the increasing role of the managerial and ministerial classes, and trade unions as a result of the transition from capitalism to socialism.

There is differentiation between and within the bourgeoisie, the petty bourgeoisie and the working class. Class inequality is not simply economistic. However, economic groupings in the form of classes and domination of one class over the other are found in all societies irrespective of the level of their industrialization (Giddens 1987: 35–45; Godelier 1978: 77–102). Capitalist society has undergone vast changes over a period of its long journey (Hamilton and Hirszowicz 1987) as stated below:

1. Capital and industry are today controlled by professional salaried management due to growth of large joint-stock enterprises.

2. The class structure has diversified. Middle classes have grown enormously particularly in the developing countries like India due to the new state apparatus.
3. The material standards of workers have improved considerably all over the world.
4. Power of the working class has enhanced greatly due to trade unions, civil liberty movements and democratization.

Planning in India prior to independence was aimed at overthrowing the colonial state structure and its replacement by an independent indigenous capitalist state structure (Mukherjee 1978: 1516–28). The big capitalists, a large number of small traders and merchants actively supported the national movement opposing thereby the colonialist mercantalism and capitalism (Chandra et al. 1988: 375–85). The Indian capitalist class had the following features:

1. The Indian capitalists had largely an independent capital base and did not act as junior partners of foreign capital or as compradors;
2. The capitalist class on the whole was not tied up in a subservient position—either economically or politically—with pre-imperialist feudal interests; and
3. It grew rapidly between 1914 and 1947, a period close to independence.

Rudolph and Rudolph (1987: 19–59) state 'the marginality of class politics' as a major development in the post-1947 period. Capital and labour play a marginal role in Indian politics and policy because of the centrality of a 'third factor', the *state*. The Indian state has acquired the role of a defender and protector of the interests of the poor and the working class. There are also strong unions and organizations of the white-collar groups which in turn weaken both the bourgeoisie and the proletariat. Big business has exercised some influence on the government but it has not been able to control it directly or indirectly.

The Industrial Policy Resolution of 1956 reasserts the constitutional position that the common good of the people and distributive justice would remain the central concerns, though the role of big industrial houses and multinationals remains unaffected to a large extent (Siddharthan 1979: 1197–1203). Associations formed by the capitalists have been used to promote economic as well as political interests (Mukherjee 1978; Sharma 1981). But A. R. Desai (1984) considers the Indian state as an agent of the bourgeoisie pursuing the capitalist path of development. According to Desai, the state has been repressive and oppressive in nature.

Whether the Indian big bourgeoisie, like the big landlords, was a product of colonial rule or not is not a relevant question. What is important here is that the Indian bourgeoisie was never a monolith, and its character was partly determined by the colonial rule and partly by the class character of the Indian National Congress, the movements launched by it and the fact of India's freedom and partition. The bourgeoisie comprises two categories: (*a*) big comprador, and (*b*) small and medium national bourgeoisie (Ghosh 1985: 2445–58). The comprador character of the big bourgeoisie and a similar though latent tendency of the national bourgeoisie resulted in guided industrialization.

The Entrepreneurs and Entrepreneurship

Changes in social dynamics present new opportunities for economic activities. These are perceived as opportunities to enhance one's economic and social standing. While presenting 'an integrated view of entrepreneurship', Dwijendra Tripathi (1985: M-163–M-168) analyzes the entrepreneurial process by accounting for (*a*) the constellation of forces, (*b*) the entrepreneurial initiative, and (*c*) changes in the constellation of forces. An entrepreneur is a person who finds a constellation of socio-political and economic forces favourable for venturing into one or other enterprise, and if he succeeds, he comes socially and economically distinct from those who remain out of such activities and from those who prove to be a failure.

Recent studies have shown that money-lending and trading were taken up even by the landlords and substantial cultivating families in many parts of the country prior to independence. Today entrepreneurial area is wide open for castes and communities which were earlier engaged in non-mercantile pursuits. There were *peasant entrepreneurs*, and there were upper caste manual and agricultural workers. Moreover, entrepreneurship is not confined to agriculture, business and industry alone. It has spread to the domains of medicine, science, government service, teaching, etc.

Interest in the study of entrepreneurs as a significant stratum in the scheme of social stratification is evident in some recent studies (Akbar 1990; Singh 1985; Singh 1985: Trivedi 1991). Sheobahal Singh's study shows that 39 per cent of the total entrepreneurs in a carpet-manufacturing town in eastern Uttar Pradesh were Muslims, whereas 56 per cent were Hindus, 3 per cent Jains and 2 per cent Sikhs. Banias, Muslims and to some extent Rajputs dominated the carpet industry. A close tie was found between landownership, leadership and entrepreneurship by R. S. Singh. However, about 75 per cent of the rural entrepreneurs belong to three upper castes, namely, Brahmins, Rajputs and Bhumihars. In the city of Calcutta, Mahisyas, a peasant caste, have dominated the engineering industry surpassing both Brahmins and Kayasthas, mainly due to historically contingent factor after the Second World War (Owens 1973: 133–66). That entrepreneurship could emerge as a new criterion of status determination is borne out by Madhusudan Trivedi's study of 250 tribal entrepreneurs. Muslim entrepreneurs find no social values obstructing entrepreneurial growth. Thus, despite linkages between caste, religion and entrepreneurship, departures signifying weakening of such linkages are also found as a consequence of entry of some castes and communities in those enterprises which were traditionally forbidden for them.

Middle Classes and Professional Elites

The pre-colonial approximation of middle class comprised the merchant, the artisan and the landed aristocracy having their roots in normative structure of the society. During the British period the structure and complexion of the middle classes transformed due to a variety of factors and policy changes. The new middle classes included the businessmen and entrepreneurs, industrialists, landed people, educated groups, professionals, etc. The middle classes are basically trained service groups, and therefore ideally serve both the upper and lower classes, though not making available their services actually in equal measure. The structure of the middle classes after independence has undergone a considerable change in terms of their size(s), functions and the role mainly due to the nature and character of the Indian state.

In the context of anti-reservation agitations in Gujarat, Ghan-shyam Shah (1987: AN-115–AN-142) writes:

> The middle class has grown in size disproportionately with economic growth in Gujarat. While their aspirations have risen, they are unable to satisfy their needs and maintain the traditional status, and therefore, they experience a strong sense of deprivation. This is specially true of the upper and middle caste members who are jealous of the new entrants from the traditionally low castes.

For Shah, the middle class is a class between labour and capital. The middle classes in India are a product of both capitalist development and the State. The anti-reservation agitations in Gujarat as understood by Shah imply a conflict-situation between the *entrenched* middle classes and the lower classes aspiring for the middle classes status by having access to lucrative white-collar occupations.

Elite formation in India (Navlakha 1989) is largely determined by the traditional social structure (particularly caste), religion, language, networks, income, occupational background, education, family background, etc. The findings of this study indicate that select social positions are usually taken by persons from select social strata. This select group controls the positions of prestige, power and responsibility. Higher education is still under the grip of upper castes, hence it is status-stabilizer (Jayaram 1977) rather than an invader on status-rigidities. Take the example of four of the most prestigious institutions in Bangalore. Despite a long history of reservations, they have 60 per cent Brahmin, 34 per cent Lingayat and Vokkaliga, and only 4 per cent lower caste students in the higher professional and administrative careers bracket.

Navlakha's findings are quite revealing: 81.3 per cent of the Hindu respondents hailed from the upper caste groups (Brahmin, Kayastha, Vaishya and Kshatriya), 6.8 per cent came from the higher cultivating and other intermediate castes, and only 4.6 per cent belonged to lower castes. Further 86.5 per cent of the respondents were of urban origin, 89.3 per cent were educated in modern educational institutions and 79 per cent of the respondents came from the highest advantaged stratum of the society.

A study of lawyers and law students in Pune (Pranjape 1983: 1474–75) reveals that the Brahmins dominate the profession both in terms of quantity and professional success. The proportion of lawyers from the backward classes is quite small, and most of them are recent entrants to the system. They also earn much less. However, there are more women lawyers belonging to the backward classes as compared to those from the upper castes. The main reason given in the study is that it is easier to accept a backward woman lawyer as junior practitioner. Several studies in the field of sociology of law and legal profession provide sketches of stratification among lawyers and relations between lawyers, judges, *munshis*, touts and clients (see Baxi 1982; Gandhi 1982, 1987, 1989; Lal 1988: 337–402; Oommen 1983; Sharma 1980, 1984, 1988; Sharma 1985; Singh 1989: 51–73).

There are not many studies of technocrats, scientists and managers partly because of their considerable distance from administrative–political set-up and partly because of their style of work and way of life. Today, a technocrat or an engineer combines management expertise with scientific know-how. An engineer with a Master of Business Administration (MBA) degree enjoys high status in Indian society. Even an MBA without an engineering degree has more job opportunities than those having skills in several other fields. Higher technical education provides a passport for a high-status lucrative job. Graduates of the Indian Institutes of Technology enjoy more prestige and they are more in demand than the graduates of ordinary engineering colleges. A large number of IIT Bombay graduates have gone abroad for better career prospects and work-conditions (Sukhatme and Mahadevan 1988: 1285–93).

The industrialists, technocrats and managers have to work in India under politicians in particular, and to a considerable extent under administrators (Bhattacharya 1984: M-21–M-31). Managers and officers are organizing themselves through trade unions and associations (Ramaswamy 1985: M-75–M-88). Hardly any literature is available on Indian scientists. Three articles in S. K. Lal (1988) by Sri Chandra (227–33), A. Ramanama and Usha Bambawale (234–59), and A. L. Srivastava and M. Toha (260–68) on India's scientists provide just preliminary sketches and rudimentary profiles. Some early studies of medical profession (Madan 1980; Oommen 1978) have, however, particularly emphasized social structural and organizational aspects of the profession. Madan and his associates while conducting a comparative study of India, Sri Lanka and Malaysia have found a high degree of professionalization among the doctors in terms of their group identity, code of ethics and relationships to society. A few recent studies too put more emphasis on the patterns of relationship between different segments of hospital as a social organization (Advani 1980; Chandani 1985; 1988: 281–90; Mehta 1988: 271–80; Nagla 1988: 291–318; 1988). In these studies, high status of professionals such as managers, technocrats, scientists and medical doctors, is taken for granted; thus instead of probing the actual social status, more emphasis is placed on the formal criteria of social status.

Formal positions like professor, reader and lecturer and non-formal criteria such as academic achievements, reputation as a teacher and scholar, cultural life-style, and family background matter in the academic profession. Since the academic profession is accredited with a high degree of autonomy like the legal profession, informal criteria of status–evaluation are valued in good measure along with the formal criteria like rank, income and office. The recent studies (Bhoite 1987; 1988: 166–76; Khanna 1988) also stress upon the stratificational aspect of the academic community.

A controversial and significant dimension is added by Ashok Rudra (1989: 142–50) who considers the *intelligentsia* as a ruling class in India. This is in addition to the two existing ruling classes: one with base in agriculture, and the other with base in large industry. The intelligentsia has become a member of the ruling coalition. The two traditional ruling classes have co-opted the intelligentsia as a member of their fraternity. The intelligentsia include the following:

1. All white-collar workers in the organized private sector from managers and top executives down to clerical workers.
2. All office workers in administrative services from top bureaucrats right up to lower division clerks.
3. Teachers (from the school to the university levels), doctors and nurses, lawyers and judges, engineers and architects in both private and public sectors.
4. Writers, journalists, artists and other skilled workers.
5. Professionals, politicians, trade union leaders, etc.

One common feature of all these middle classes is that 'they do not themselves produce any values in the material product sense of value' (ibid.: 144). 'Members of this (middle) class therefore depend for their economic gains on the largesse of the other two ruling classes as well as the state' (ibid.: 144). However, there is no homogeneity among its members in terms of income, wealth and level of living. Very high inequality exists within the classes in respect of these criteria. Another commonality is the social nature, that is, they all can be regarded as a babu class, salaried people or the class of people earning equivalent to the salaried class. One more point of commonality among them is found in terms of culture and ideology. The intelligentsia as a class have contradictions and conflict of interests with other classes. The intelligentsia are considered as ally and not as adversary by the traditional ruling class.

André Béteille (1989: 151–55) while generally accepting Rudra's hypothesis regarding intelligentsia as a third co-opted ruling class in India, observes that intellectuals in India would not like to associate themselves with the exploiters of the masses—the workers and the peasants. Béteille suggests for seeking more empirical evidence before drawing conclusions on the status and role of the intelligentsia. Béteille's disagreement to Rudra's hypothesis centres on the concepts of class and contradiction. Béteille writes: 'I maintain that contradiction is an inherent feature of all human societies whereas others believe that it is a feature of some or even most societies, but not necessarily all' (ibid.: 152).

Pranab Bardhan (1989: 155) is also critical of Rudra's understanding of India's middle classes. He writes:

> Ashok Rudra underestimates the power of the professional class vis-à-vis the other two dominant classes. Compared to most western countries the State is considerably more autonomous in India not merely in the political spheres but as a predominant *economic actor*. In some sense the State has captured commanding heights of the economy and sections of the professional class which run this gigantic machinery have thereby acquired powers which are not just of a junior partner in the ruling coalition. Further, because of the increasing social and economic interpenetration among these classes, the conflicts among the classes in the dominant coalition are likely to decline.

The public sector professionals benefit directly from all kinds of state subsidies and indirectly from the rental income earned by the state (Bardhan 1984: 51).

Middle classes are not the direct rulers nor are they economic producers like the industrialists, workers and peasants. There is a marked lack of homogeneity among the middle classes. In fact, structural distinctions are quite marked even between the apparently equal/homogenous classes. Some classes are not so important in people's eyes, yet they enjoy high prestige because of the autonomy of their professions and the networks which they develop simply as a by-product of their professional obligations.

Indian Working Class

For Karl Marx the central issue was the understanding of the productive system in which the interests of the owners of the means of production and the wage-earning working class clashed. Marx always thought of ways and means of organizing the working class into a collective force to transform the capitalist system. Connections between social relations of production, social organization of the exploited classes and state power formed the main basis of Marxian analysis. The growing social power of the organized working class was taken as a challenge to the authority of the state.

Weber, however, always emphasized on the problem of authority and legitimacy. Rational authority was considered as key to the smooth functioning of bureaucracy and modern state. James Petras (1989: 1955–58), however, considers the notion of political legitimacy as irrelevant issue or at best a derivative or subsidiary concern. 'Different electoral regimes derive their legitimacy from different class reference groups and different balance of class forces.' Power creates its own legitimacy. The organized working class itself becomes a power to reckon with, as it is embodiment of the class interests of the poor and the less privileged sections of society. An organized group representing its class interests becomes a political class in its own right.

Studies of the Indian working class consider labour as a commodity, and the value of labour power as the basis of understanding the capitalist appropriation and exploitation of the surplus generated by the proletariat. Thus the working class is highly stratified within and in relation to the capitalist and the middle classes. The factors such as caste, ethnicity and gender create inequalities within the working class structure and therefore obstruct smooth sailing of the working class movement. The distinctions found within the working class structure ranging from the *labour aristocracy* on the one hand and the *pauperized labour* on the other explain the consequences on the workers (Nathan 1987: 805).

The study of textile industry in Ahmedabad by Sujata Patel (1987) locates the genesis of the working class movement in context of the economic crisis in the post-war period and the subsequent mobilization of the workers by Mahatma Gandhi. Gandhian ideology was not class specific. Worker's rights and needs were the crux of Gandhian mobilization. Strike was the most potent weapon. More significant were the multiple factors in the worker's movement including the Ahmedabad tradition, the codes evolved by Gandhi, his connections with the working class and the millowners.

G. K. Lieten's study of workers in multinational companies (1987: 810–22) shows that a segment of the working class is able to command higher wages and can thus divide the class in a distinct manner. Such a structural divide within the working class hampers uniform class consciousness. The consciousness of the jute mill workers of Bengal (Chakrabarty 1984) could not transient their identity as a Hindu or a Muslim to have a solid working class identity. Inevitably, any collective public action by the workers was marked by this inherent duality. The working class in terms of its socio-cultural composition is constituted of the urban poor, living in slums and hutments. They are found working in industries, textile mills, sugar factories, plantations, railways, cottage industry and informal sector. The working class, despite these differences, is constituted of the urban and the rural poor both in the organized and informal sectors of economy. This would mean that the poor are just poor, and therefore, it would be better if one understands them as such without undermining this fact by using rural/urban, caste/class and caste/caste criteria (Joshi 1979: 355–66). Caste is not found as a major principle of social organization among industrial workers (Ramaswamy 1979: 367–76). But Sujata Patel (1987) finds that there was a caste relationship in the recruitment of workers. The members of traditional weaving castes were recruited such as Dhedhs and Waghris as spinners, and Kanbis and Muslims were recruited as weavers. The *mukkadams* played a significant role in recruitment. The jobber commandeered recruitment, training, supervision and control of workers. Indebtedness of the workers increases their dependence on the jobber. The institution of zamandar also serves as jobber for the construction workers in Delhi particularly coming from Rajasthan. Caste-based recruitment in factories has been reported in some other studies as well.

The special number of the *Economic and Political Weekly* (1981) highlights the following aspects of the working class:

1. Structure of the labour market in colonial India;
2. Labour legislation and working class movement, specifically the case of the Bombay labour officer, 1934–37;
3. Some structural features of Kanpur textile labour in the formative years;
4. The growth of trade union consciousness among jute mill workers, 1920–40;
5. Industrial unrest and growth of labour unions in Bengal, 1920–24; and
6. Recruitment and government policy, 1840–80, towards tea labour in Assam.

Labour market, labour legislation, caste and class background of workers, class consciousness, working-class movements and their leadership are some of the issues taken up in these studies of the working class in India.

The industrial man is not a monolith. Mark Holmström (1984) discusses at length that the industry is primarily an inegalitarian system in terms of organized and unorganized labour sectors. Contract labour, labour markets, working class conditions, workers' social worlds, the domineering role of owners, managers, superiors and leadership of trade unions, the distinctions based on gender (Mies 1981: 487–500; 1982) and the nature of industrial or semi-industrial work (Behal 1985: PE-19–PE-26; Bhowmik 1980: 1524–27; Isaac 1982: PE-13–PE-40; Prasanneswari 1984: 956–60), are the mentioned criteria to explain the socio-cultural and economic heterogeneity of the working class particularly in the context of working class consciousness, intra- and inter-working class relations and relations of the working class with the owners and managerial and supervisory cadres of industry.

References

Advani, Mohan, 1980, *Doctor-Patient Relationship in Indian Hospitals*, Jaipur: Singhi Prakashan.

Akbar, M., 1990, *Entrepreneurship and Indian Muslims*, New Delhi: Manak Publications.

Bala, Raj, 1986, *Trends in Urbanization in India*, Jaipur: Rawat Publications.

Bardhan, Kalpana, 1989, 'Poverty, Growth and Rural Labour Markets in India', Review of Agriculture, *Economic and Political Weekly*, Vol. XXIV, No. 12, pp. A-12–A-38.

Bardhan, Pranab, 1989, 'The Third Dominant Class', *Economic and Political Weekly*, Vol. XXIV, No. 3, pp. 155–56.

Baxi, Upendra, 1982, *The Crisis of the Indian Legal System*, New Delhi: Vikas Publishing House.

Behal, Rana Pratap, 1985, 'Forms of Labour Protest in Assam Valley Tea Plantations, 1900–1930', *Economic and Political Weekly*, Vol. XX, No. 4, pp. PE-19–PE-26.

Berna, James, J., 1960, *Industrial Entrepreneurship in Madras State*, London: Asia Publishing House.

Béteille, André, 1989, 'Are the Intelligentsia a Ruling Class?', *Economic and Political Weekly*, Vol. XXIV, No. 3, pp. 151–55.

Bhattacharya, S.K., 1984, 'Managers and Technocrats' Role in the Political Administrative World: Some Current Issues', *Economic and Political Weekly*, Vol. XIX, No. 8, pp. 21–31.

Bhowmik, Sharit K., 1980, 'The Planatation as a Social System', *Economic and Political Weekly*, Vol. XV, No. 36, pp. 1524–27.

Bhoite, U.B., 1987, *Sociology of Indian Intellectuals*, Jaipur: Rawat Publications.

———, 1988, 'Academic Profession and Social Development', *in* Lal, S.K. et al. (eds), *Readings in the Sociology of Professions*, Delhi: Gian Publishing House, pp. 166–76.

Bottomore, T.B., 1985, *Theories of Modern Capitalism*, London: George Allen and Unwin.

Byres, T.J., 1981, 'The New Technology, Class Formation and Class Action in the Indian Countryside', *Journal of Peasant Studies*, Vol. 8, No. 3.

Chakrabarty, Dipesh, 1984, 'Trade Unions in a Hierarchical Culture: The Jute Workers of Calcutta 1920–50', *in* Guha, Ranjit (ed.), *Subaltern Studies III*, Delhi: Oxford University Press.

Chandani, Ambika, 1985, *The Medical Profession: A Sociological Exploration*, New Delhi: Jainsons.

———, 1988, 'Doctors and Doctrine', *in* Lal, S.K. et al. (eds), *Readings in the Sociology of the Professions*, Delhi: Gian Publishing House, pp. 281–90.

Chandra, Bipan, Aditya Mukherjee, Mridula Mukherjee and **Sucheta Mahajan**, 1988, *India's Struggle for Independence, 1857–1947*, New Delhi: Viking Penguin Books India Ltd., pp. 375–85.

Chandra, Sri, 1988, 'Indian Scientists and Social System', *in* Lal, S.K. et al. (eds), *Readings in the Sociology of the Professions*, Delhi: Gian Publishing House, pp. 227–33.

Chithelen, Ignatius, 1985, 'Origins of Cooperative Sugar Industry in Maharashtra', *Economic and Political Weekly*, Vol. XX, No. 14, pp. 604–12.

Commander, Simon, 1985, 'Proto-industrial Production as a Barrier to Industrialization?—Case of North Indian Sugar Industry, 1850–1950', *Economic and Political Weekly*, Vol. XX, No. 12, pp. 505–16.

Desai, A.R., 1984, *India's Path of Development*, Bombay: Popular Prakashan.

D'Souza, V.S., 1968, *Social Structure of a Planned City—Chandigarh*, New Delhi: Orient Longman.

Gandhi, J.S., 1982, *Lawyers and Touts: A Study in the Sociology of the Legal Profession*, Delhi: Hindustan Publishing Corporation.

——— 1987, *Sociology of Legal Profession, Law and Legal System: The Indian Setting*, Delhi: Gian Publishing House.

——— 1989, *Law and Social Change*, Jaipur: Rawat Publications.

Giddens, Anthony and J. H. Jumer (eds), 1987, *Social Theory Today*, Cambridge: Polity Press.

Godelier, Maurice, 1978, *Perspectives in Marxist Anthropology*, Cambridge: Cambridge University Press.

Griffin, K., 1977, 'Review of Lipton's *Why Poor People Stay Poor*', *Journal of Development Studies*, Vol. 14, No. 1.

Guha, Amalendu, 1984, 'More about the Parsi Seths, Their Roots, Entrepreneurship and Comprador Role, 1650–1918', *Economic and Political Weekly*, Vol. XIX, No. 3, pp. 117–32.

Hamilton, Malcolm and Maria Hirszowicz, 1987, *Class and Inequality in Pre-Industrial Capitalist and Communist Societies*, New York: St. Martins Press.

Holmström, Marc, 1984, *Industry and Inequality: The Social Anthropology of Indian Labour*, Cambridge: Cambridge University Press.

Isaac, T.M. Thomas, 1982, 'Class Struggle and Structural Changes: Coir-mat and Matting Industry in Kerala, 1950–80', *Economic and Political Weekly*, Vol. XVIII, No. 31, pp. PE-13–PE-40.

Jayaram, N., 1977, 'Higher Education as a Status Stabiliser: Students in Bangalore', *Contributions to Indian Sociology*, (New Series), Vol. II, No. 1.

Jha, Hetukar, 1988 'Tradition of Urbanism in Bihar: A Sociological Probe', *Explorations*, Vol. 2, pp. 46–55.

Joshi, P.C., 1979, 'Perspectives on Poverty and Social Change: The Emergence of the Poor as a Class', *Economic and Political Weekly*, Vol. XIV, Nos. 7 & 8, pp. 355–66.

Khanna, Kirti, 1988, 'Career Decision-Making: A Case of University Teachers', in Lal, S.K et al. (eds), *Readings in the Sociology of Professions*, Delhi: Gian Publishing House.

Kosambi, Meera, 1991, 'A Socio-Ecological Study of Two Indian Cities: Bombay and Poona (1650–1900)', in Rao, M.S.A., C. Bhatt, L. N. Khandekar (eds), *A Reader in Urban Sociology*, Delhi: Orient Longman, pp. 142–78.

Lambert, R.D., 1963, *Workers, Factories and Social Change in India*, Bombay: Oxford University Press.

Lal, Sheo Kumar (ed.), 1988, *Readings in the Sociology of Professions*, Delhi: Gian Publishing House, pp. 337–402.

Lieten, G.K., 1987, 'Indian Workers in Multinational Companies', *Economic and Political Weekly*, Vol. XXII, No. 18, pp. 810–22.

Lipton, Michael, 1977, *Why Poor People Stay Poor: A Study of Urban Bias in World Development*, London: Temple Smith.

Madan, T.N., 1980, *Doctors and Society*, New Delhi: Vikas Publishing House.

Mehta, S.R., 1988, 'Towards a Profession of Health and Professionalisation of Health Personnel', *in* Lal, S.K. et al. (eds), op cit., pp. 271–80.

Mies, Maria, 1981, 'Dynamics of Sexual Division of Labour and Capital Accumulation: Women Lace-Workers of Narsapur', *Economic and Political Weekly*, Vol. XVI, Nos. 10, 11 & 12, pp. 487–500.

———, 1982, 'Rural Women and the World Market', *in* Beneria, Lourdes (ed.), *Women and Development: The Sexual Division of Labour in Rural Societies*, New York: Praeger Publications.

Mishra, Sanjay, K., 1991, 'Industrialization and Social Structure: A Case Study of Hatia, Ranchi', Ph.D. thesis, Jawaharlal Nehru University, New Delhi.

Mukherjee, Aditya, 1978, 'Indian Capitalist Class and Congress on National Planning and Public Sector, 1930–47', *Economic and Political Weekly*, Vol. XIII, No. 35, pp. 1516–28.

Nagla, Madhu, 1988, *Medical Sociology: A Study of Professionals and their Clients*, Jaipur: Printwell Printers.

———, 1988, 'Professionals and their Clients: A Study of Doctor-Patient Relationship', *in* Lal, Sheo Kumar et al. (eds), op. cit., pp. 291–318.

Naqvi, H.K., 1968, *Urban Centres and Industries in Urban India, 1506–1803*, Bombay: Asia Publishing House.

Nathan, Dev, 1987, 'Structure of Working Class in India', *Economic and Political Weekly*, Vol. XXII, No. 18, pp. 799–809.

Navalkha, Suren, 1971, 'Ethnic Divisiveness in the New States of Asia: A Model for Analysis', *in* Joshi, P.C. and R. Dutta (eds), *Studies in Asian Social Development*, No. 1, New Delhi: Tata-McGraw Hill.

———, 1989, *Elite and Social Change: A Study of Elite Formation in India*, New Delhi: Sage Publications.

Oommen, T.K., 1978, *Doctors and Nurses: A Study in Occupational Role Structures*, Delhi: Macmillan.

———, 1983, *Social Transformation in Rural India: Mobilization and State Intervention*, New Delhi: Vikas Publishing House.

Owens, Raymond L., 1973, 'Peasant Entrepreneurs in a North Indian Industrial City', *in* Singer, Milton (ed.), *Entrepreneurship and Modernization of Occupational Cultures in South Asia*, Durham, NC: Duke University Press, pp. 133–66.

Panini, M.N., 1986, 'Industrialization and Social Stratification in India', *in* Sharma, K.L. (ed.), *Social Stratification in India*, Delhi: Manohar Publications.

Pandey, Gyanendra, 1984, 'Encounters and Calamities: The History of a North Indian Qasba in the 19th Century', *in* Guha, Ranjit (ed.), *Subaltern Studies III*, Delhi: Oxford University Press, pp. 231–70.

Patel, P.J., 1985, 'Industrial Sociology', *in A Survey of Research in Sociology and Social Anthropology*, Vol. III, New Delhi: Satvahan Publications.

Patel, Sujata, 1987, *The Making of Industrial Relations: Ahmedabad Textile Industry, 1918–39*, Delhi: Oxford University Press.

Petras, James, 1989, 'Class Politics, State Power and Legitimacy', *Economic and Political Weekly*, Vol. XXIV, No. 31, pp. 1955–58.

Philips, W.S.K., 1990, *Social Stratification and Mobility in Urban India*, Jaipur: Rawat Publications.

Pranjape, H.K., 1983, 'Legal Profession and Social Change, Review of S. P. Sathe's book—*Legal Profession: Its Contributions to Social Change: A Survey of the Pune City Bar*', *Economic and Political Weekly*, Vol. XVIII, No. 34, pp. 1475–76.

Prasanneswari, 1984, 'Industrial Relations in Tea Plantations: The Deoars Scene', *Economic and Political Weekly*, Vol. XIX, Nos. 24 & 25, pp. 956–60.

Ramanamma, A. and **Usha Bambawale**, 1978, 'Occupational Attitudes of Physicians', *Sociological Bulletin*, Vol. 27, No. 2, pp. 234–59.

Ramaswamy, E.A., 1986, 'Managerial Trade Union', *Economic and Political Weekly*, Vol. XX, No. 21, pp. M-75–M-88.

Ramaswamy, Uma, 1979, 'Tradition and Change among Industrial Workers', *Economic and Political Weekly*, Vol. XIV, Nos. 7 & 8, pp. 367–76.

Rao, M.S.A. (ed.), 1991, *A Reader in Urban Sociology*, Delhi: Orient Longman, pp. 21–41.

Rubin, Barnett R., 1986, 'Journey to the East: Industrialization in India and the Chinese Experience', *in* Basu, Dilip K. and Richard Sisson (eds), *Social and Economic Development in India: A Reassessment*, New Delhi: Sage Publications.

Rudolph, S.H., and **L. I. Rudolph**, 1987, *In Pursuit of Lakshmi: The Political Economy of the Indian State*, New Delhi: Orient Longman.

Rudra, Ashok, 1989, 'Emergence of the Intelligentsia as a Ruling Class in India', *Economic and Political Weekly*, Vol. XXIV, No. 3, pp. 142–50.

Saberwal, Satish, 1976, *Mobile Men: Limits to Social Change in Urban Punjab*, New Delhi: Vikas Publishing House.

Sathe, S.P., 1986, 'Elusive Pursuit of Equality', *Economic and Political Weekly* Vol. XXI, No. 33, pp. 1451–54.

Shah, Ghanshyam, 1987, 'Middle Class Politics: Case of Anti-Reservation Agitation in Gujarat', *Economic and Political Weekly*, Vol. XXII (AN), Nos. 19, 20 & 21, pp. AN-155–AN-172.

Sharma, K.L., 1980, *Essays on Social Stratification*, Jaipur: Rawat Publications.

————, 1981, *Voluntary Business Associations in Organizational Frame*, Jaipur: Rawat Publications.

————, 1984, *Sociology of Law and Legal Profession*, Jaipur: Rawat Publications.

————, 1986, *Caste, Class and Social Movements*, Jaipur: Rawat Publications.

————, 1988, 'Legal Profession and Society: A Case Study of Lawyers and their Clients', *in* Lal, Sheo Kumar et al. (eds), op. cit.

Sharma, S.L., 1985, 'Sociology of Professions in India', *in Survey of Research in Sociology and Social Anthropology, 1969–1979*, Vol. II, New Delhi: Satvahan Publications.

Sheth, N.R., 1968, *The Social Framework of an Indian Factory*, Manchester: Manchester University Press.

Sheth, N.R. and **P. J. Patel**, 1979, *Industrial Sociology in India*, Jaipur: Rawat Publications.

Siddharthan, N.S., 1979, 'Industrial Houses, Multinationals and Industrial Policy', *Economic and Political Weekly*, Vol. XIV, No. 29, pp. 1197–1203.

Singer, Milton, 1972, *When a Great Tradition Modernizes: An Anthropological Approach to Indian Civilization*, New York: Praeger Publishers.

Singh, R.S., 1985, *Rural Elite, Entrepreneurship and Social Change*, Jaipur: Rawat Publications.

Singh, S.B., 1985, *Entrepreneurship and Social Change*, Jaipur: Rawat Publications.

Singh, Yogendra, 1989, 'Law and Social Change in India: A Sociological Perspective', *in* Gandhi, J.S. (ed.), *Law & Social Change*, Jaipur: Rawat Publications, pp. 51–73.

Srivastava, A.L. and **M. Toha**, 1989, 'Professional Obsolescence: A Needed Area of Research', *in* Lal, S.K. et al. (eds), *Readings in the Sociology of Professions*, Delhi: Gian Publishing House, pp. 260–68.

Sukhatme, S.P. and **I. Mahadevan**, 1988, 'Brain-Drain and the IIT Graduates', *Economic and Political Weekly*, Vol. XXIII, No. 25, pp. 1285–93.

Tripathi, Dwijendra, 1985, 'An Integrated View of Entrepreneurship', *Economic and Political Weekly*, Vol. XX, No. 48, M-163–M-168.

Trivedi, Madhusudan, 1991, *Entrepreneurship Among Tribals*, Jaipur: Printwell Printers.

Five

Social Stratification and Weaker Sections of Society

The Scheduled Castes (SCs), the Scheduled Tribes (STs) and the Other Backward Classes (OBCs), have been accorded special treatment in the Constitution, since they are traditionally the weaker sections of society. Articles 14, 15, 16, 29, 38, 46, 334, 335 and 342 of the Constitution guarantee *equality before law*. These sections of Indian society are backward socially, economically, educationally and politically, hence the above *articles* in favour of the SCs, the STs and the OBCs for preferential treatment. The preferential treatment implies *equality* of status and of opportunity to the weaker sections of society.

The role of the state to bring about effective equalization is not only unavoidable, but it has become an essential component of social transformation in the post-independent India. Both *formal* and *substantive* forms of equality (Galanter 1984: 378–93) have become functions of the state apparatus. Galanter also refers to the *horizontal view* and the *vertical view* regarding equality (ibid.: 391–93).

In the horizontal view, emphasis is laid on the present time and equality of opportunity, and not on the opportunity to achieve equality. Only marginal equality is visualized and valued in the horizontal view. In the vertical perspective, the emphasis is put on the long-range goal of redistribution and equalization. The present is seen as a transition from a position of inequality to a desired future of substantive equality. Galanter (ibid.: 41–44, 361–63) also prefers the use of compensatory discrimination rather than protective discrimination as the latter bears a paternalistic tone and refers to static quality of the benefits given to the weaker sections. Thus the main points of discussion are the role of the state in the process of equalization and the emerging patterns of status-mobility among the weaker sections.

The Policy of Protective Discrimination

The policy of compensatory discrimination (Galanter 1984; 1989) has been in vogue for ameliorating the lot of the SCs, the STs and the OBCs with a view to enabling them to compete with the upper castes and classes. In an unequal society, this was considered as the most effective method of providing equality to the depressed sections of Indian society. Extra facilities, reservation of seats in legislatures and educational institutions, provisions for special protection against untouchability, and land alienation, etc., have resulted in the weakening of the traditional rigidity of status–hierarchy. But the question is: How far have such reservations helped the depressed sections? What new forms of inequality have emerged due to the provisions made available for the SCs and the STs?

Consequences of protective discrimination have not led to the emergence of equality as expected in the relevant provisions. What is needed is for the removal of *situational constraints* through an integrated programme for the dispersal of the benefits. Samuel Paul and Ashok Subramaniam (1983: 349–58), after examining the effects of eight development programmes, conclude that benefits of economic progress were not reaching the poor. However, the effects of these programmes were not uniform. The question is: Under what conditions do benefits of development programmes flow to the weaker sections? In a similar study of the people's housing it is found that the scheme appears to have failed as a welfare measure. T. K. Oommen (1984: 45–61) finds that a hierarchy in the structure of deprivations and participations by the Dalits has stratified the Dalits into *dominant* and *dominated jatis*, and the privileged few and a mass of the underprivileged.

The Weaker Sections and Social Movements

What constitutes the weaker sections or Dalits? Broadly speaking, the SCs and the STs who are largely agricultural workers, sharecroppers and marginal farmers may be considered as *weaker sections*. A large number of them do not own land. However, several studies have shown that the SCs and the STs were never monolithic lots before they were scheduled, and due to differential and uneven impact of the developmental processes status-differentiation has further sharpened among them. Today, a significant section from the SCs and STs of the socially mobile and articulate people has emerged, not denying the fact of the majority of the SCs and the STs still remaining backward and poor. Some castes/communities from among the OBCs too remain backward and poor like the SCs and the STs. Besides the depressed sections from among the SCs, STs and OBCs, there are also people who are backward and poor from among other castes and communities in both villages and towns.

The protest movements by the Dalits (Harijans and *adivasis*) have not just sprung up recently; in fact they have a long history and tradition of challenge to the upper caste–class domination characterized by some degree of autonomy and organization. Stephen Henningham (1981: 1153–56) reports that the protests launched by Musahars (Harijans) and Santhals (*adivasis*) in Bihar in the 1930s exhibited the kind of autonomy currently associated with various Harijan and *adivasi* movements.

Most of the movements launched by the weaker sections have challenged the hegemony of Brahmins and other castes in social, political and administrative spheres. S. Chandrasekhar (1985) while highlighting the dimensions of socio-political change in the princely Mysore State during 1918–1940 emphasizes that land was not a source of conflict because of the predominance of the owner-cultivators. The main reason was the ambition of the backward groups for seeking more representation in service in the state. The most well-known of these anti-Brahmin movements in the nineteenth and the early twentieth century is the movement spearheaded by Mahatma Phule. J. R. Shinde (1986: 740) analyzes Phule's revolt against the iniquitous Hindu social structure in terms of his anti-caste struggles and attacks on the oppressive and exploitative ancient institutions and practices. Religious and cultural fervour was used for mobilizing the workers. However in the study of the Santhal agrarian movement in Purnea district during 1938–42, Anand Chakravarti (1986: 1847–65; 1897–1909) observes that the Indian National Congress did not effectively deal with the agrarian issues along with its programme of national struggle. The interests of the *maliks* and not of the *bataidars* (who were sharecroppers, tenure-holders and occupancy tenants and tenants-at-will) dominated the Indian National Congress and the national movement. Thus, all the movements of the weaker sections were against the oppressive socio-economic and political system, but the modus operandi was not uniformly the same in these struggles, and the structural and cultural impediments also varied from movement to movement perhaps because of regional, socio-structural and political differences in the country.

The Scheduled Castes

The ideology of varna and caste and its impact are negated by the educated and the political leaders and yet atrocities on Harijans are committed uninterruptedly. Caste/varna ideology functions in real life more as a means of economic and political domination by the upper caste/class people on the lower castes/classes. Mobilization whether during elections or for some other specific purpose is made possible by evoking caste sentiments and ethnocentric feelings.

Despite socio-cultural and economic disabilities suffered by the lower and untouchable castes, they have been benefited by the constitutional provisions and various developmental schemes launched exclusively for their welfare.

But a small minority and that too really not the needy one has been benefited by these provisions and schemes, hence new imbalances and criteria of social ranking within the ranks of the SCs.

The distributive disparities affecting the SCs are found at three levels: (*a*) between the SCs and the rest of the population, (*b*) between the SCs, and (*c*) within the SCs (Sharma 1980: 183–92; 169–81). For example, the peasantry and all the lower castes including the Shudras and *ati*-Shudras were benefited by Phule's attacks on the Brahminical hegemony. Phule's movement was known as the Satya Shodhak Samaj. His fight was against casteism which was being perpetuated under the intellectualism of Brahmins. However, Phule's movement not only united the lower and peasant castes, it also promoted casteism while attacking the caste system itself.

M. S. Gore (1989: 928–36) proposes with reference to the non-Brahmin movement in Maharashtra a paradigm of functional analysis of social movements. Stratificatory differentiations in terms of differential access to wealth, social status and political power are found as the basis of identity formations in social movements. Groups formed as such 'give the individual his sense of identity and often serve to give him a preferential access to special opportunities of upward mobility, material gain or political clout' (ibid.: 930). These identities, in fact, are transformed into interest groups in practice. Ethnic and other socio-cultural identities are evoked by literary activities. The Dalit Sahitya Movement in Maharashtra (Bhoite and Bhoite 1977: 60–75) highlights the principle of equality as a dominant element. The Dalit idiom is projected as an attack on the Brahminic cognitive system.

Ranjit Dasgupta (1989: 2197–2202) finds that though the agitation of the Oraon tea plantation workers in the Jalpaiguri district in 1915–16 had an anti-colonial content, and was aimed against the exploitation by zamindars and *mahajans*, yet its origins were in the Tana Bhagat Movement in Chhotanagpur. Hence, culture and social movements are intrinsically inter-related phenomena.

Some of the studies have raised the question: how close to social equality are the SCs in relation to the traditionally privileged castes? Bernard S. Cohn's narrative (1987: 255–308) of the untouchables of Madhopur, a north Indian village, highlights continuity and change over a period of time in the context of wider changes in Indian society. Despite the implementation of protective and promotional measures for more than four decades, the SCs still lag far behind compared to the upper and middle castes. Education has not filtered down to the lowest SCs as expected and equal access is mere rhetoric for the unequal groups. However, social consciousness and political mobilization have emerged as the most visible consequences of the measures taken for the SCs and the STs.

In a comprehensive analysis of the untouchables in contemporary India, Mendelsohn and Vicziany (1994) show that the circumstances of their living have undergone no comparable transformation. They look at the untouchables as a social and political category and have transformed recently into a bureaucratic and welfare category. In this process of transformation, the untouchables have remained a subordinated people. They remain subordinated on the grounds of poverty, discrimination, and low-level of consciousness (ibid.: 78–94). Policies relating to the untouchables have failed. Anti-poverty measures, land reforms, and compensatory discrimination have not proved quite effective.

James Freeman (1986: 153–71) poses the following questions: Do untouchables accept their oppression? Can they be made to believe that they deserve such treatment? Have the higher castes used or threatened force to suppress untouchables? Do untouchables resist to their oppression? Did open revolts by untouchables occur in the past? Did untouchables historically accept the moral authority of their oppressors? Berreman (1979) observes that the untouchables have never accepted their low status in society. Moffatt (1979: 304) writes that they are also among the truest believers in the system that so oppresses them. Freeman (1986: 154) observes:

> My aim in this essay is (*a*) to assess the adequacy of these conflicting views about the *compliancy* of Indian untouchables; and (*b*) to show the significance of these views in the struggle for social equality by the untouchables since India's independence.

The desire for freedom from oppression has been part of the experience of the untouchables for over 2,000 years. The untouchables have lacked a means of adequate expression of these desires. Today, the untouchables are conscious about the creation of a fundamentally new society through a new vision of freedom. The Indian State has, despite several limitations, heightened consciousness and resistance of untouchables to oppression.

To understand the status–dynamics of the SCs, it may be neces-sary to acquaint with the changes in the discourse on caste. Pauline Kolenda (1989: 1831–38) states that in the mid-fifties the issues were educational and occupational access for low castes and un-touchable people and other practices of untouchability. The villag-ers could not conceive of a society that was not organized on caste lines, and equal treatment was a foreign and urban issue, something that was of interest only to the Congress party. She poses the question: 'Has the discourse about caste changed in the last gen-eration? If so, how?'

The discourse on caste has changed a great deal. Instead of talking about untouchability, pollution–purity and accessibility to educa-tional and occupational opportunities, caste is being used as a re-source for mobilization to reach all the possible corners of social life. Caste-based demands are being made as assertions of rights of the people. Certainly man on the street is not doing it. A leader of some standing from a particular caste is turning his caste into an instrument of mobilization for his community, but quite often he uses it for self-aggrandizement.

Kolenda observes that:

> the caste ideology of an ordinary person is not coherent, consistent set of ideas, but is composed of thoughts from here and there heard over the years in the discourse on the caste, as well as of observations of events going on around him, or those in which he was himself involved (1989: 833).

Quoting Geertz (1973: 201) she mentions two kinds of theories of ideology, namely, (*a*) *interest* theories, and (*b*) *strain* theories, and states that the first are applicable to the high caste men, and the ideologies of low caste men are more likely to be strain theories. But the recent expressions and articulations of ideology and practice of caste show that the high caste men are generally evasive whereas the other backward castes and the SCs are behaving more as aggres-sive interest groups. Kolenda also observes that ideas about equal etiquette and equal rights are becoming ideology in Khalapur.

A stratified economic system is the most significant factor in a stratified social system in Kerala (Saradamoni 1981). People in Kerala are not socially handicapped, yet the SCs are the lowest in the class hierarchy. Despite radical land reforms, there are still agrestic slave castes in Kerala. The only visible change in their status is from slave-labour to wage-labour. Saradamoni (ibid.: 11) finds that 64 per cent of the Pulaya households are agricultural labourers, whereas they are 21 per cent from the OBCs, and only 6 per cent from among the forward castes. Most of the SCs are landless, and 40 per cent of them own less than 10 per cent of the whole land. They depend upon labour and meagre land, whereas the bigger landowners have also regular non-agricultural income. Education is also eluding employment for the Pulaya youth. She points out that the most advanced SC community in Kerala consists of a few primary school teachers and peons.

Uma Ramaswamy's study of the SCs, namely, Malas and Madigas in Andhra Pradesh (1986: 399–403) also confirms Saradamoni's findings on·the Pulayas of Kerala. The Malas and Madigas are internally differentiated in terms of occupation, numerical strength, geographical spread and ritual status (see also Guhan and Mencher 1983: 1013–22; 1063–74; Jain 1981: 325-32; Nagesh 1981: A-109–A-115). The mass of SC people are not benefited by the welfare measures. Those few who are benefited join the ranks of the SC and ST elites. G. Narain's study (1978) shows that the SC members had become as part of a single Indian political elite. However, in general, 'the reservation has failed to alter the relative prosperity between high or middle castes and untouchables or tribals and has therefore not engendered the resentment that a more successful scheme would have' (Mendelsohn 1986: 501–9). Marginal effects on alleviation of mass poverty on the one hand and on creation of leadership from among the SCs on the other are the useful gains of the welfare measures including the policy of reservation.

Dalitism as an expression of the consciousness of the downtrodden has been a notable feature since the beginning of the eighties. Dalit protests, Dalit writers, critics and literature have become an instrument of the educated middle class from·among the Dalits. Despite sharpening of contradictions and changes in values in the countryside, violence and massacres have remained unabated (Chaudhary 1988: 51–56; Prasad 1987: 847–52). Violence against the SCs by the dominant upper caste/class families in Bihar, Maharashtra, Andhra Pradesh, Uttar Pradesh, Gujarat and some other states has increased, corresponding with the increased consciousness among the weaker sections (Bose 1981: 713–16; Desai 1981: 819–23; Kalathil 1985: 265–66; Yagnik 1981: 553–55).

The most significant structural consequences of the welfare measures for the SCs are in the nature of their education and employment in government services and public sector enterprises. Another logical corollary of these changes is social mobility and mobilization of the SC masses. A brief reference of these trends in regard to the SCs may be made here. A small sub-elite among the SCs and STs has been benefiting from protective discrimination. Education has contributed more to *individual mobility rather than group mobility*. A. R. Kamat (1981: 1279–84) discusses some features of social change associated with the advance of education among the SCs and STs during the post-independence period. As a result of the educational advance, there emerged a new elite and allowing for greater politicization. The tribal poor have become more conscious, more organized and militant. The educated SCs and STs are finding it difficult to withstand competition in jobs. The vested interests from the caste Hindus are on the offensive to frustrate the efforts of the educated SCs and STs.

A comparative study of 48 SC and ST, 42 non-SC and non-ST students of IIT Bombay highlights a host of social and educational problems of the SC and ST students (Kripal et al. 1985: 1238–48). 'None of the SC/ST students has very good performance and none of the non-SC/ST students has bad performance' (ibid.: 1239). Only 3 SC/ST students have good performance, 33 have average performance, and 12 have performed badly. On the contrary 10 non-SC/ST students have very good performance, 13 have good performance, 21 have average performance, and none has performed badly. Certainly the IIT trained technocrats from among the SCs and STs would add further to the existing pool of the SC and ST elite, but nevertheless its impact on the SC and ST masses cannot be underrated. Uma Ramaswamy (1985: 1523–28) in her study of the impact of education on the inequality among the SCs in Andhra Pradesh observes that despite new status–distinctions and continuing social divisions between the Malas and the Madigas (both SCs), the protectionist policy could eventually make them occupationally and economically quite indistinguishable from any other caste.

Focusing on the multi-dimensional nature of the issues relating to socio-economic background of SCs, their social mobility in the context of caste and class structures, social interaction and social relations and status identification, Nandu Ram (1989) observes that as a result of social mobility among the SCs, a *new class* has emerged in the city of Kanpur in Uttar Pradesh. Ram finds that the most important indicator of mobility is the social perception of individuals belonging to the group about their own social status and social mobility. Perception of others is also important. About 98 per cent of the respondents in Ram's study were found upwardly mobile compared to their fathers. The new middle class arising out of social mobility among the SCs is not in a position to identify either with the middle class in general or with the SC masses. Thus the SC middle class is seeking for a new identity.

The Scheduled Tribes

The tribal society in India has been analyzed in terms of two perspectives, namely, (*a*) the isolationist, and (*b*) the assimilationist (Chattopadhyay and De 1969: 1985–94; Singh 1978: 1221–32). According to the isolationist view tribal communities are treated as isolates and distinct socio-cultural entities, hence an emic view is necessitated. The emphasis in the assimilationist perspective is on the tribal society as an inseparable part of wider Indian society, hence their integration in the mainstream of Indian social life becomes inevitable. K. S. Singh (ibid.: 1227) observes: 'There always existed within a tribe a measure of distinction between the high and the low in terms of social and physical distance, notion of purity and pollution, prestige and status, habits and customs, etc.' These distinctions have emerged mainly due to the process of sanskritization and the impact of Christianity among the tribal people. The colonial system, according to K. S. Singh, created and strengthened a three-fold division comprising (*a*) the feudatory chiefs/zamindars at the top; (*b*) the well-to-do headmen in the middle; and (*c*) the general masses at the bottom. There were a class of middlemen, merchants and money-lenders who could be either caste Hindus or tribal.

A study of the *adivasis* of the Thane district by Ashok K. Upadhyaya (1980: A-134–A-146) shows that the introduction of the *ryotwari* system transformed the tribals into peasant-tenants and agricultural labourers. Tribals who depended upon natural and forest economy became a part of the class structure which comprised (*a*) rent-receiving landowners, (*b*) cultivating-owners,

(c) cultivating-tenants, (d) unclassified cultivators, (e) farm servants and field labourers, and (f) indentured labour. Land alienation (Dubey and Murdia 1977) provides a vivid account of this problem in different parts of the country. A study of the Chaudhri tribe in the Surat district (Shah 1979: 459–69) shows four economic strata on the basis of occupation and ownership of land. These are:

1. Agricultural labourers and poor cultivators.
2. Middle cultivators.
3. Rich cultivators.
4. White-collar employees.

Such a system of economic stratification in a tribal community resembles with socio-economic differentiations found in the non-tribal communities and castes.

The question of class in the tribal society is more pervasive than the caste-tribal approach. Class interests do not obey caste or tribal boundaries (Kulkarni 1979: 465–68). The tribal revolts of the 19th century centered against the outsiders because they were also the exploiters of the *adivasis*. In the Jharkhand area (Sengupta 1980: 664–71) the question of class in the form of land-alienation and exploitation was transformed into the demand for an autonomous state of Jharkhand. According to a study of the Bhils of Rajasthan (Jain 1989) there are elites among the Bhils, but they are more a replica of their society which continues to be socially and economically backward. Despite their social origin the tribal elites are more akin to the non-tribal elites and the non-tribal masses than to the tribal masses. Sachchidananda (1990: 279–317) reports that even in the pre-colonial and colonial India stratification among tribes had emerged in the form of a quasi-feudal agrarian exploitative system. There were (a) the upper classes, and (b) the commoners. The upper class controlled more land, occupied leadership positions and enjoyed higher status. With the coming of money-lenders on the tribal scene the system of social stratification became further distinct and elaborate. Jaganath Pathy (1984: 147–60) also reports *five classes* among the tribes of Orissa.

Social stratification among tribes in India is not significantly different from the system of stratification in general in Indian society. Based on his study of Gujarat, Pradip Kumar Bose (1981: 191–96) reports that the tribes in Gujarat today are equally affected by the processes of planned and unplanned change and by the continuous structural and institutional shifts in rural India. They are stratified in terms of control over resources. Four distinct classes of peasants have emerged among the tribes, namely, rich peasant, middle peasant, poor peasant and agricultural labourer. This class hierarchy is reflected in all aspects of tribal life including education and political power. However, K. S. Singh (1982: 1318–25; 1376–84) while commenting on the view held by Ghanshyam Shah and Pradip Kumar Bose, observes that there are also contrary pulls in the opposite direction. The bonds of ethnicity and the appreciation of the political advantages of the tribes as an ethnic minority are still strong. The tribals remain aloof from the non-tribals. The *diku* (outside exploiter) is also a middleman, trader and money-lender. This class has survived despite several movements and legislative measures against its role in the tribal society. Thus there are two views regarding social stratification, namely, (1) the class perspective, and (2) the ethnicity perspective. B. K. Roy-Burman (1989: 693–97) too outlines that the problems and prospects of tribal development may be considered along two axes: (*a*) as ethnic entities, and (*b*) as status-class. R. K. Bhadra and S. R. Mandal (1991) discuss the role of class and ethnicity as the main bases of social stratification in north-east India.

Several studies and reports about the tribes in Bihar (Devi 1981: 1595–97; 1983: 329–330; 1984: 663–66; Dhar 1980: 1299–1300; 1984: 1139; Dogra 1985: 1775; Sengupta 1982; Singh 1985: op. cit; Sinha 1978: 1544–46; 1979: 648–50; Weiner 1978: 145–216) have highlighted mainly the conflicts arising out of control over resources in terms of landownership, money-lending, political power, social status and employment opportunities. Some of the earlier studies (MacDougall 1974; Prasad 1961; Sachchidananda 1965; Sharma 1976; Singh 1972; Vidyarthi 1967; 1969; 1970) discuss the impact of the measures initiated in India after independence. The studies of the Jharkhand movement in particular have highlighted the problems of exploitation, oppression, unemployment and hegemony of north Bihar in the tribal belt of south Bihar (Bharti 1989: 183–84; 1385–87; 1503–5; Chaudhuri 1982: 99–232; Das 1990: 1624–26; DN 1988: 1726–29; Gupta, Banerji and Guleria 1981; Sengupta: 1988: 943–45; 1003–5; 1054–55; 1153–54; Sharma 1993: 463–73; Singh 1985: 119–54; 155–73;

Sinha 1987: 1887–89; 2051–53; 2087–88). These studies discuss not only the problems of the tribals in Bihar, but also emphasize on the *tribal question* in terms of elite formation, political leadership, factionalism, ethnicization of politics and on the issue of class versus ethnicity in particular. Guha (1983: 1882–96; 1940–47) highlights the *class interests* behind the formation and execution of forest policy in India as it serves the capitalists rather than the poor. Ramchandra Guha (1985: 1939–52) emphasizes on protest movements, changing land use patterns, alienation of man from nature, etc. as notable social changes emanating from scientific forestry in Uttarakhand in Uttar Pradesh. The social and forestry aspects have been neglected and commercial tree farming has been accepted as social forestry (Ramaswamy 1988: 1314–16).

Besides the forest question and the question of development, the problems of tribal identity and poverty remain central problems to the tribals of Tripura and some other parts of the north-east India (Dasgupta 1985: 38–40). What Ghanshyam Shah (1995: 23–46) writes in the context of the multiple character and issues of Dalit movements in India seems to be quite significant as they exhibit concerns for identity and quest for equality, dignity and eradication of untouchability. The questions of poverty and exploitation are not so important as are the questions of opposition to the dominant caste ideology, establishing a new identity, and continuity of reservations as a measure of social justice.

Uneven structures of landholdings, wage-rates, literacy and participation in economic activities have kept some parts of tribal Kerala backward (Kunhaman 1985: 466–74). Anti-alienation movements (Kulkarni 1985: 1171–74; 1987: 2143–48) have been on the increase in Maharashtra because most of the *adivasis* are small farmers and agricultural labourers. R. V. Bhuskute (1989: 2355–58) provides an account quite contrary to Sharad Patil's view about the positive role performed by law and the state in Maharashtra. Bhuskute writes:

> The process of driving off dalits, *adivasis* and nomadic tribes from their rightful land has been going on for the last century.... At times *generosity* and at other times muscle power have rendered thousands of dalits and *adivasis* landless.

The SCs and the STs have been reported to be the victims of systematic exploitation by the state and its anti-poor laws. In the 29th Report of the Commissioner for Scheduled Castes and Scheduled Tribes (1988–89) various questions regarding role of the state, material issues, command over resources, displacement, etc. have been dealt with in a forthright manner. The state has been tightening its grip legally over the tribals to take complete control of forests and their lands. Class and ethnicity, though apparently in contravention to each other, have been found as the main criteria of social stratification among the tribes of India (Badgaiyan 1986: 293–308; Doshi 1989: 309–24; Jain 1989; Kothari 1985). However, class-based status distinctions are largely a consequence of state's policy of tribal development whereas ethnicity, besides being a perennial phenomenon, is also affected and at times even strengthened by reform and conversion movements among the tribal people. Differentiation within same tribal communities (Singh 1995: 71–84) in terms of ecology, occupation, status, degrees of exposure, etc. is reported in different parts of India. A class structure due to impact of colonialism also surfaced among the tribes in India more or less corresponding with the pattern in general in the country. Singh notes that a tribal middle class consisting of professionals, lower level administrators, and entrepreneurs is emerging. However, such an ethnic differentiation has not put a check on the emergence of a new class of the poor among the tribals of India.

Some articles in the *Subaltern Studies* (Arnold 1982: 88–142; Dasgupta 1985: 101–35; Guha 1985: 1939–52; Hardiman 1987: 1–54; Sarkar 1985: 135–64) have highlighted the dynamics of tribal economic formation vis-à-vis socio-cultural and ethnic dimensions. Thus unlike the non-tribal society, absence of caste or caste-like status-system in the tribal society is not incongruent with ethnicity and class as the main bases of social stratification. But like the non-tribal society, in the tribal society too power and privilege become the most crucial concerns of the people, and these are largely an offshoot of the state's policy of tribal development.

The Other Backward Castes

The category of the Other Backward Castes (OBCs) comprises the non-untouchable lower and intermediate castes who were traditionally engaged in agriculture, animal husbandry, handicrafts and functional services. A great deal of social change and mobility has occurred in regard to their traditional occupation and socio-political and economic standing. Despite this the OBCs have remained weak and backward socially and educationally. The position of the OBCs is, however, far better than the SCs and the STs.

The OBCs are not a monolith. A study of a village in the East Godavari district in Andhra Pradesh (Reddy and Murthy 1978: 1061–76) shows that the backward castes have a highly differentiated land tenure system corresponding to their economic status and caste rank. The pure tenant category essentially comprises low castes from the backward castes. In terms of size of landholdings they are divided into small, medium and big categories and in terms of tenurial category there are (*a*) pure-tenant cultivators, (*b*) owner-cum-tenant cultivators, (*c*) pure-rent receivers, and (*d*) owner-cum-rent receivers. All these categories are seen in relation to caste whether it belongs to a backward caste among the OBCs.

There is no provision for reservation of seats in legislatures and Parliament for the OBCs. Reservation for seats in educational institutions and government jobs exists though not on a uniform pattern throughout the country. Historically as well as in today's context, the OBCs are in much superior position than the SCs and STs. It was this structural reality which had been a bone of contention regarding the implementation of the recommendations of the B. P. Mandal Commission (1978–80). The OBCs are not only superior and stronger socially, materially and politically than the SCs and STs, also their overall position has improved more than even some of the upper castes and classes particularly in economic and political spheres.

Caste rank and occupation are the main criteria by which the intermediate castes (not all) are considered backward. They depend mainly upon agriculture, traditional crafts and other non-agricultural occupations. The OBCs, however, continue to be peasant castes. In education, professions and white-collar jobs they lag behind the upper castes. Since they are clean castes, they are superior to the SCs, and their superiority over the STs is mainly in terms of their better economic and political status. Certainly the OBCs are not forward groups like the upper castes. But there are forwards of the OBCs and some of whom are even more forward than the forwards of the upper castes. Recent writings on backwardness and reservation have thrown up the following questions:

1. Who is a backward?
2. What are the criteria of backwardness?
3. Is there a correspondence between different criteria of backwardness?
4. Do all the OBCs suffer the same form of backwardness?
5. Can there be a uniform provision for the upliftment of the OBCs as a whole?
6. Can reservation be based on caste?

The systems of preferential treatment for the weaker sections of Indian society both before and after independence have been used to lift them up close to the traditionally privileged upper castes and communities. Reducing inequality and ensuring equality are its twofold inseparable objectives. However, the preferential treatment in the form of protective discrimination or compensatory discrimination has been questioned as a suitable method to address the problems of the SCs, the STs and the OBCs. It has generated hatred among different sections of society, at times leading to violence. It is considered against the very spirit of India's Constitution. Lelah Dushkin (1979: 661–67) raises the following questions:

1. Who really benefits?
2. What price is paid and who pays it?
3. Is there any better way to address the problems?

Two more questions may be added here:

1. Are the provisions for preferential treatment not creating a new form of socio-economic and political inequality?
2. Are the traditionally privileged groups not able to explore new domains for re-establishing their superiority?

Dushkin refers to *levels of benefits* in terms of (*a*) elite benefits, (*b*) middle class benefits, and (*c*) lower class benefits. Besides the persisting social and economic divides between the upper castes and backward castes, the differential benefits occurring from the systems of preferential treatment have further divided the backward castes in economic and political spheres. Harry W. Blair (1980: 64–75) observes that the Karpoori Thakur's reservation policy changed Bihar's political economy, and initiated the process of replacing the forwards or twice-born caste groups by the backward castes as the dominant stratum in the system of social stratification. The forwards as twice-born comprise (*a*) Brahmin, (*b*) Bhumihar, (*c*) Rajput, and (*d*) Kayastha. The upper backwards include (*a*) Bania, (*b*) Yadava, (*c*) Kurmi and (*d*) Kahar, Kandu, Kumhar, Mallah, Tatwa, Teli, others (Shudras, Muslims, Bengalis), SCs and STs are other social categories in Bihar's population. The upper castes are 13 per cent, the upper backwards 19.3 per cent and the lower backwards 32.0 per cent of the total population in Bihar. The SCs constitute 14.4, STs 9.1, Muslims 12.5 and Bengalis 2.4 per cent of the total population of this state (ibid. 1980: 65).

Some of the expected conclusions of Blair's study (ibid.: 71–72) were: (*a*) the transfer of power to the upper backwards might be expected to continue at the local level along political lines; (*b*) there would be a noticeable transfer of economic power in the country-side to the backwards as the forwards would not be able to face the fury and aggressiveness of the upper backwards; (*c*) there would be a continuing struggle between the forwards and the backwards; and (*d*) the condition of landless agricultural labour would weaken further because of inroads of capitalism in Bihar's economy. The decline in semi-feudal production relations (Prasad 1980: 215–19) has been noted in north India in favour of the middle peasantry hailing from the backward castes.

How can we determine backwardness of the backwards? This question has been central to the debate on reservation policy for a long time. 'Should *caste* be the basis for recognizing backwardness?' (Desai 1984: 1106–16). I. P. Desai discusses in detail ascribed and achieved status, social mobility movements, occupations in historical perspective, rural and urban situations, homo hierarchicus, interest conscious unities, trends in self-perception groups, new activities, caste and class and some other related issues. He comes to the conclusion that *family*, and not caste, should be accepted as the beneficiary unit of the secular basis of reservation. Desai also suggests a scheme of dereservation of those who have extracted advantages for a certain period of time.

Extra-legal measures, namely social movements have been quite effective in bringing about social mobility. Occupational diversification and change in people's orientations, new rural–urban nexus, absence of homo hierarchicus, pre-eminence of interests and high degree of differentiation within the OBCs would not warrant *caste* as the basis of reservation policy. On the contrary, Ghanshyam Shah (1985: 135–36) states that there is casteism in jobs as appointments are made by the upper castes, and they are doing so because of their advantageous position historically and culturally. Shah's advocacy is for reservation for the poor strata of the low castes/social groups of different religions. Status of caste/social group needs to be seen in the sub-regional context. Rescheduling should be built into the reservation scheme itself. In defence of I. P. Desai's viewpoint, Upendra Baxi (1985: 426–28) writes that future *society* in India must necessarily be casteless, and in Baxi's opinion Shah's critique of Desai reinforces caste by accepting social groups as the units of reservation policy. Shah (1987: AN-155–AN-172) observes that the lumpens have a strong sense of deprivation particularly amongst those upper and middle caste members who dominate the middle class. 'They are jealous of the new entrants from the traditionally low castes in the middle class' (ibid.: AN-172). The anti-reservation agitations in Gujarat were, essentially as perceived by Shah, struggle within the middle class. The class background of the agitators was not uniform or homogeneous either within the upper and middle classes or within the newly aspiring class of the SCs, STs and the OBCs to join the ranks of the middle class.

Since some social groups and families are socially and educationally backward, pursuing equality for them through the policy of reservation or protective or compensatory discrimination has become both a value and practice for the Indian State (Frankel and Rao 1989; 1990; Galanter 1984; 1986: 129–52; Mehta and Patel 1985; Rao 1979; Rudolph and Rudolph 1987; Shah and Agrawal 1986). The role of state and its policy of protective discrimination to bring about social equality has become a focal point of debate in recent years.

Galanter (1986: 130–31) mentions three basic types of *preference*, namely, (*a*) reservations, (*b*) programmes, and (*c*) special protections. These preferences have been implemented on communal basis by accepting caste as a unit for distributing benefits. As such these preferences entail a violation of the vision of a *secular society* as envisaged in the Indian Constitution. The contradiction here is that India has embraced equality as its cherished goal, and it is being achieved by the policy of protective discrimination. At the same time the implementation of this policy distorts its value of achievement of a caste-free secular society by accepting caste as a unit of distributing benefits. Compensatory discrimination policies have produced substantial redistributive effects. All the three measures (Galanter 1986: op. cit.) have brought about for the weaker sections what the upper castes traditionally had in terms of power and prestige. Galanter (ibid.: 547–67) speaks volumes in praise of the compensatory discrimination policies. Advocacy of caste to gain power on the number and to mobilize its members against the attacks of other castes and groups is forcefully argued in K. C. Yadav (1994) who considers the OBCs as India's unequal citizens. S. P. Sathe (1986: 1451–54) considers Marc Galanter's perspective as an elusive pursuit of equality and raises questions regarding identification of beneficiaries, parameters of merit, and socio-cultural environment.

The upper castes and some middle castes not covered under the category of Backward Classes by the Mandal Commission or the state level commissions have opposed continuation of the policy of reservation for the SCs and STs and its extension to the OBCs as recommended in the Mandal Commission Report. Support to the reservation policy has come besides the SCs and STs from the OBCs (the new beneficiaries) and the left political parties, Janata Dal and some regional parties like Telugu Desam, D.M.K. and B.S.P.

Politicization of the reservation policy particularly from 1984 onwards has divided the Indian society and polity in terms of caste-based politics (Balagopal 1986: 1571–74; Balagopal 1990: 2231–34; Bharti: 1990: 309–10; Bharti 1990: 2407; Chalam 1990: 2333–39; Chaudhary 1990: 1929–35; Kundu 1990: 2477–78; Ilaiah 1990: 2307–10; Nigam 1990: 2652–53; Pandian 1990: 1938–39; Patil 1990: 2733–44; Radhakrishnan 1990: 509–20; Radhakrishnan 1990: 1749–54; Shatrugna 1988: 237; Sheth 1987: 1957–62; Vidyasagar and Suresh 1990: 822–23). The announcement by the government in August 1990 regarding the implementation of the Mandal Commission's recommendations for reserving 27 per cent jobs in central government jobs for the OBCs created a nationwide stir resulting in arson, violence, police firing and killing of students.

Several students and youth committed self-immolation and suicide against this decision of the government. The situation looked as if the whole country was absolutely divided into two strata, namely, those who supported the anti-Mandal agitation and those who supported the announcement by the Government. Public debate was so intense that for nearly two months newspapers and magazines were full of pro- and anti-Mandal views. Finally, the recommendations of the Commission were accepted and implemented as directed by the Supreme Court of India.

The weaker sections have been differentially benefited by the constitutional provisions for their upliftment as it is evident from the class-like distinctions within the SCs, STs and OBCs that have emerged in the post-independence period. Social movements have brought about a great deal of consciousness among the weaker sections about their low socio-economic status vis-à-vis the upper and middle castes. *Caste* continues to occupy the central place in regard to the policy of reservation despite the fact that it has lost its traditional sanctions and functions.

References

Arnold, David, 1982, 'Rebellious Hillmen: The Guden Rampa Risings, 1839–1924', in Guha, Ranjit (ed.), *Subaltern Studies I*, Delhi: Oxford University Press, pp. 88–142.

Badgaiyan, S.D., 1986, 'Class and Ethnicity: Chota Nagpur in the 19th Century', in Sharma, K.L. (ed.), *Social Stratification in India*, Delhi: Manohar Publications, pp. 293–308.

Bakhru, Mira, 1984, 'Distribution of Welfare: People's Housing Scheme in Karnataka', *Economic and Political Weekly*, Vol. XIX, No. 10, pp. 427–36.

Balagopal, K., 1986, 'Andhra Pradesh: Anti-Reservation, Yet Once More', *Economic and Political Weekly*, Vol. XXI, No. 36, pp. 1573–74.

———, 1990, 'This Anti-Mandal Mania', *Economic and Political Weekly*, Vol. XXV, No. 40, pp. 2231–34.

Baxi, Upendra, 1985, 'Caste, Class and Reservations', *Economic and Political Weekly*, Vol. XX, No. 10, pp. 426–28.

Berreman, G.D., 1979, *Caste and Other Inequalities*, Meerut: Folkore Institute.

Bhadra, R.K. and **S.R. Mandal** (eds), 1991, *Stratification, Hierarchy and Ethnicity in North-East India*, Delhi: Daya Publishing House.

Bharti, Indu, 1989, 'Differences in Jharkhand Movement', *Economic and Political Weekly*, Vol. XXIV, No. 4, pp. 183–84.

———, 1989, 'Paharia tribals' plight and government's indifference', *Economic and Political Weekly*, Vol. XXIV, No. 27, pp. 1503–6.

Bharti, Indu, 1989, 'Jharkhand Movement: Caught in the Electoral Morass', *Economic and Political Weekly*, Vol. XXIV, No. 25, pp. 1385–87.

————, 1990, 'Politics of anti-reservation stir', *Economic and Political Weekly*, Vol. XXV, No. 6, pp. 309–10.

————, 1990, 'Bihar ballot: Expected outcome', *Economic and Political Weekly*, Vol. XXV, No. 12, pp. 595–97.

————, 1990, 'The Bihar formula', *Economic and Political Weekly*, Vol. XXV, No. 44, p. 2407.

Bhoite, Uttam and **Anuradha Bhoite**, 'The Dalit Sahitya Movement in Maharashtra: A sociological analysis', *Sociological Bulletin*, Vol. 26, No. 1, pp. 60–75.

Bhuskute, R.V., 1989, 'Tribals, Dalits and government lands', *Economic and Political Weekly*, Vol. XXVI, No. 42, pp. 2355–58.

Blair, Harry W., 1980, 'Rising Kulaks and backward classes in Bihar, social change in the late 1970s', *Economic and Political Weekly*, Vol. XV, No. 2, pp. 64–74.

Bose, P.K., 1981, 'Stratification among tribals in Gujarat', *Economic and Political Weekly*, Vol. XVI, No. 6, pp. 191–96.

————, 1981, 'Social mobility and caste violence: A study of Gujarat riots', *Economic and Political Weekly*, Vol. XVI, No. 16, pp. 713–16.

Chakravarti, Anand, 1986, 'The unfinished struggle of Santhal Bataidars in Purnea District, 1938–42', *Economic and Political Weekly*, Vol. XXI, No. 42, pp. 1847–65.

Chalam, K.S., 1990, 'Caste reservations and equality of opportunity in education', *Economic and Political Weekly*, Vol. XXV, No. 41, pp. 2333–49.

Chandrashekhar, S., 1985, *Dimensions of Socio-Political Change in Mysore, 1918–1940*, New Delhi: Ashish Publishing House.

Chaudhuri, Budhadeb (ed.), 1982, *Tribal Development in India: Problems and Prospects*, New Delhi: Inter-India Publications.

Chaudhary, Kameshwar, 1990, 'Reservation for OBCs: Hardly an abrupt decision', *Economic and Political Weekly*, Vol. XXV, Nos 35 & 36, pp. 1929–35.

Chaudhary, P.K, 1988, 'Agrarian unrest in Bihar: A case study of Patna district 1960–1984', *Economic and Political Weekly*, Vol. XIX, No. 1, pp. 51–56.

Chattopadhyay, G. and **Barun De**, 1989, 'Problem of tribal integration to urban industrial society: A theoretical approach', *Economic and Political Weekly*, Vol. IV, No. 52, pp. 1985–94.

Cohn, Bernard S., 1987, *An Anthropologist among the Historians and Other Essays*, Delhi: Oxford University Press.

Das, Victor, 1990, 'Jharkhand movement: From realism to mystification', *Economic and Political Weekly*, Vol. XXV, No. 30, pp. 1624–26.

Dasgupta, Ranjit, 1986, 'From peasants and tribesmen to plantation workers', *Economic and Political Weekly*, Vol. XXI, No. 4, pp. 2–10.

————, 1989, 'Oraon labour agitation, Duars in Jalpaiguri district, 1915–16', *Economic and Political Weekly*, Vol. XXIV, No. 30, pp. 2197–2202.

Dasgupta, Malabika, 1985, 'Tribal Unrest in Tripura, An Alternative View', *Economic and Political Weekly*, Vol. XX, No. 1, pp. 38–40.

Dasgupta, Swapan, 1985, 'Adivasi Politics in Midnapur (1760–1924)', *in* Guha, Ranjit (ed.), *Subaltern Studies IV*, Delhi: Oxford University Press.

Desai, I.P., 1981, 'Anti-reservation agitation and structure of Gujarat society', *Economic and Political Weekly*, Vol. XVI, No. 18, pp. 819–23.

———, 1984, 'Western educated elites and social change in India', *Economic and Political Weekly*, Vol. XIX, No. 15, pp. 1106–16.

Devi, Mahasveta, 1981, 'Witch-Sabbath at Singhbhum', *Economic and Political Weekly*, Vol. XVI, No. 40, pp. 1595–97.

———, 1983, 'A countryside slowly dying', *Economic and Political Weekly*, Vol. XVIII, No. 10, pp. 329–30.

———, 1984, 'Palamau in bondage: For ever?', *Economic and Political Weekly*, Vol. XIX, No. 16, pp. 663–66.

Dhar, Hiranmay, 1980, 'Split in Jharkhand Mukti Morcha', *Economic and Political Weekly*, Vol. XV, No. 31, pp. 1299–1300.

———, 1984, 'Split in Jharkhand movement', *Economic and Political Weekly*, Vol. XIX, No. 29, p. 1139.

DN, 1988, 'Agrarian movement in Palamu', *Economic and Political Weekly*, Vol. XXIII, No. 34, pp. 1726–29.

Dogra, Bharat, 1985, 'First stirrings and repression: A report from Palamu', *Economic and Political Weekly*, Vol. XX, No. 42, p. 1775.

Doshi, S.L., 1986, 'Ethnicity and class among the Bhils of Rajasthan', *in* Sharma, K.L. (ed.), *Social Stratification in India*, Delhi: Manohar Publications.

Dubey, S.N. and **R. Murdia**, 1977, *Land Alienation and Restoration in Tribal Communities in India*, New Delhi: Himalaya Publishing House.

Dushkin, Lelah, 1979, 'Backward class benefits and social class in India', *Economic and Political Weekly*, Vol. XIV, No. 14, pp. 661–67.

Frankel, Francine R. and **M. S. A. Rao** (eds), 1989, *Dominance and State Power in Modern India: Decline of a Social Order, Vol. I & Vol. II*, 1990, Delhi: Oxford University Press.

Freeman, James M., 1986, 'The consciousness of freedom among India's untouchables', *in* Basu, Dilip K. and Richard Sisson (eds), *Social and Economic Development in India: A Reassessment*, New Delhi: Sage Publications.

Galanter, Marc, 1984, *Competing Equalities*, Delhi: Oxford University Press.

———, 1986, 'Pursuing equality: An assessment of India's policy of compensatory discrimination for disadvantaged groups', *in* Basu, Dilip K. and Richard Sisson (eds), *Social and Economic Development in India: A Reassessment*, New Delhi: Sage Publications.

———, 1989, *Law and Society in Modern India*, Oxford: Oxford University Press.

Geertz, C., 1973, *The Interpretation of Cultures*, New York: Basic Books.

Gore, M.S., 1989, 'Social movements and the paradigm of functional analysis with reference to the non-Brahman movement in Maharashtra', *Economic and Political Weekly*, Vol. XXIV, No. 17, pp. 928–36.

Guha, Ranjit, 1983, 'Forestry in British and post-British India: A historical analysis', *Economic and Political Weekly*, Vol. XVIII, No. 44, pp. 1882–96, No. 45, pp. 1940–47.

———, 1985, 'How social is social forestry?', *Economic and Political Weekly*, Vol. XX, No. 14, pp. 1939–52.

——— (ed.), 1985, *Subaltern Studies, Vol. IV*, Delhi: Oxford University Press.

Guhan, S. and **Joan P. Mencher**, 1983, 'Iruvelpattu revisited-I', *Economic and Political Weekly*, Vol. XVIII, No. 23, pp. 1013–22 and No. 24, pp. 1063–74.

Gupta, Ranjit, Prabha Banerji and **A. Guleria**, 1981, *Tribal Unrest and Forest Management in Bihar*, Ahmedabad: Indian Institute of Management.

Hardiman, David, 1987, 'The Bhils and Shahukars of eastern Gujarat', *in* Guha, Ranjit (ed.), *Subaltern Studies V*, Delhi: Oxford University Press.

Henningam, Stephen, 1981, 'Autonomy and Organisation: Harijan and Adivasi Protest Movements', *Economic and Political Weekly*, Vol. XVI, No. 27, pp. 1153–56.

Ilaiah, Kancha, 1990, 'Reservations: Experience as framework of debate', *Economic and Political Weekly*, Vol. XXV, No. 41, pp. 2307–10.

Jain, L.C., 1981, 'Emancipation of Scheduled Castes and Tribes: Some Suggestions', *Economic and Political Weekly*, Vol. XVI, No. 9, pp. 325–32.

Jain, P.C., 1989, *Tribal Agrarian Movement*, Udaipur: Himanshu Publications.

Kalathil, Mathew, 1985, 'Repression of Scheduled Castes and Tribes in Breach', *Economic and Political Weekly*, Vol. XX, No. 7, pp. 265–66.

Kamat, A.R., 1981, 'Education and Social Change amongst the Scheduled Castes and Scheduled Tribes', *Economic and Political Weekly*, Vol. XV, No. 31, pp. 1279–84.

Kolenda, P., 1989, 'Micro-ideology and Micro-utopia in Khalapur: Changes in the discourse on caste over thirty years', *Economic and Political Weekly*, Vol. XXIV, No. 32, pp. 1831–38.

Kothari, K.L., 1985, *Tribal Social Change in India*, Udaipur: Himanshu Publications.

Kripal, Vinay, 1985, 'Scheduled Caste and Tribe students in higher education: A study of an IIT', *Economic and Political Weekly*, Vol. XX, No. 29, pp. 1238–48.

Kulkarni, S.D., 1979, 'Class and Caste in Tribal Movement', *Economic and Political Weekly*, Vol. XIV, Nos. 7 & 8, pp. 465–68.

Kulkarni, Sharad, 1987, 'Forest legislation and tribals: Comments on forest policy resolution', *Economic and Political Weekly*, Vol. XXII, No. 50, pp. 2143–48.

Kundu, Amitabh, 1990, 'Reservationists, anti-reservationists and democracy', *Economic and Political Weekly*, Vol. XXV, No. 45, pp. 2477–78.

Kunhaman, M., 1985, 'The tribal economy of Kerala: An intra-regional analysis', *Economic and Political Weekly*, Vol. XV, Nos. 5, 6 & 7, pp. 466–74.

Mandal, B.P., 1978–80, *The Backward Classes Commission*, New Delhi: Government of India.

Mehta, H. and **H. Patel** (eds), 1985, *Dynamics of Reservation Policy*, New Delhi: Patriot Publishers.

Mendelsohn, Oliver, 1986, 'A Harijan elite?—The lives of some untouchable politicians', *Economic and Political Weekly*, Vol. XXI, No. 12, pp. 501–9.

Mendelsohn, Oliver and **Marika Vicziany**, 1994, 'The Untouchables', *in* Mendelsohn, Oliver and Upendra Baxi (eds), *The Rights of Subordinated Peoples*, Delhi: Oxford University Press, pp. 64–116.

Moffatt, Michael, 1979, *An Untouchable Community in South India: Structure and Consensus*, Princeton: Princeton University Press.

Nagesh, H.V., 1981, 'Forms of un-free labour in Indian agriculture', Economic and Political Weekly, Vol. XVI, No. 39, pp. A-109–A-115.

Narayan, G., 1978, 'Social background of Scheduled Caste Lok Sabha members, 1962–71'. Economic and Political Weekly, Vol. XIII, No. 37, pp. 1603–1608.

Nigam, Aditya, 1990, 'Mandal Commission and the Left', Economic and Political Weekly, Vol. XXV, Nos. 48 & 49, pp. 2652–53.

Oommen, T.K., 1984, Social Structure and Politics: Studies in Independent India, Delhi: Hindustan Publishing Corporation.

Pandian, M.S.S., 1990, 'From exclusion to inclusion: Brahminism's new face in Tamil Nadu', Economic and Political Weekly, Vol. XXV, Nos. 35 & 36, pp. 1938–39.

Pathy, Jaganath, 1984, Tribal Peasantry: Dynamics of Development, New Delhi: Inter-India Publications.

Patil, Sharad, 1990, 'Should class be the basis for recognising backwardness?', Economic and Political Weekly, Vol. XXV, No. 50, pp. 2733–44.

Paul, Samuel and Ashok Subramaniam, 1983, 'Development Programmes for the Poor: Do Strategies Make a Difference?', Economic and Political Weekly, Vol. XVIII, No. 10, pp. 349–58.

Prasad, Narmadeswar, 1961, Land and People of Tribal Bihar, Ranchi: Bihar Tribal Research Institute.

Prasad, Pradhan H., 1980, 'Rising middle peasantry in north India', Economic and Political Weekly, Vol. XV, No. 4, pp. 215–19.

————, 1987, 'Towards a theory of transformation of semi-feudal agriculture', Economic and Political Weekly, Vol. XXII, No. 31, pp. 847–52.

Radhakrishnan, P., 1990, 'Backward classes in Tamil Nadu: 1872–1988', Economic and Political Weekly, Vol. XXV, No. 10, pp. 509–20.

————, 1990, 'Karnataka backward classes', Economic and Political Weekly, Vol. XXV, No. 32, pp. 1749–54.

Ram, N., 1989, Mobile Scheduled Castes: Rise of a Middle Class, Hindustan Pub. Corporation.

Ramaswamy, S.R., 1988, 'Social costs of social forestry', Economic and Political Weekly, Vol. XXIII, No. 26, pp. 1314–16.

Ramaswamy, U., 1985, 'Education and inequality', Economic and Political Weekly, Vol. XX, No. 36, pp. 1523–28.

————, 1986, 'Protection and inequality among backward groups', Economic and Political Weekly, Vol. XXI, No. 9, pp. 399–403.

Rao, M.S.A., 1979, Social Movement and Social Transformation, Delhi: Macmillian Co.

Reddy, V.N., and C.S. Murthy, 1978, 'Backward castes and tenancy: A village study', Economic and Political Weekly, Vol. XIII, No. 26, pp. 1061–76.

Roy, Burman, 1989, 'Problems and prospects of tribal development in North-East India', Economic and Political Weekly, Vol. XXIV, No. 13, pp. 693–97.

Rudolph, S.H. and L.I. Rudolph, 1987, In Pursuit of Lakshmi: The Political Economy of the Indian State, Chicago: University Press of Chicago.

Sachchidanand, 1965, Profiles of Tribal Culture in Bihar, Calcutta: K. L. Mukhopadhyay.

————, 1990, 'Patterns of politico-economic change among tribals in middle India', in Frankel, F.R., and M. S. A. Rao (eds), Dominance and State Power in Modern India, Vol. II, Delhi: Oxford University Press.

Saradamoni, K., 1981, *Divided Poor: Study of a Kerala Village*, New Delhi: Ajanta Publications.

Sarkar, Tanika, 1985, 'Jitu Santhal's movement in Malda, 1924–1932', *in* Guha, Ranjit (ed.), *Subaltern Studies IV*, Delhi: Oxford University Press.

Sathe, S.P., 1986, 'Elusive pursuit of equality', *Economic and Political Weekly*, Vol. XXI, No. 33, pp. 1451–54.

Sengupta, Nirmal, 1980, 'Class and tribe in Jharkhand', *Economic and Political Weekly*, Vol. XV, No. 14, pp. 664–71.

———— (ed.), 1982, *Fourth World Dynamics: Jharkhand*, Delhi: Authors Guild.

————, 1988, 'Reappraising tribal movements: A myth in the making', *Economic and Political Weekly*, Vol. XXIII, No. 19, pp. 943–45. See also on Jharkhand Nirmal Sengupta, *Economic and Political Weekly*, Vol. XXIII, No. 20, pp. 1003–5, No. 21, pp. 1054–55, No. 22, pp. 1153–54.

Shah, Ghanshyam, 1979, 'Tribal identity of class differentations: A case study of the Chauduri Tribe', *Economic and Political Weekly* (AN), Vol. XIV, Nos. 7 & 8, pp. 459–69.

————, 1985, 'Caste, Class and Reservation', *Economic and Political Weekly*, Vol. XX, No. 3, pp. 135–36.

————, 1987, 'Middle Class Politics: Case of Anti-reservation Agitation in Gujarat', *Economic and Political Weekly*, Vol. XXII (AN), Nos. 19, 20 & 21, pp. AN-155–AN-172.

Shah, Vimal P. and **Binod C. Agrawal** (eds), 1986, *Reservation: Policy, Programmes and Issues*, Jaipur: Rawat Publications.

Sharma, K.L., 1976, 'Jharkhand Movement in Bihar', *Economic and Political Weekly*, Vol. XI, No. 1, pp. 37–43.

————, 1980, *Essays on Social Stratification*, Jaipur: Rawat Publications.

————, 1993, 'The questions of identity and sub-nationality: A case of Jharkhand Movement in Bihar', *in* Miri, Mrinal (ed.), *Continuity and Change in Tribal Society*, Simla: Indian Institute of Advanced Study, pp. 463–73.

Shatrugna, M., 1988, 'Backward class support for Telugu Desam intact', *Economic and Political Weekly*, Vol. XXIII, No. 6, p. 237.

Sheth, D.L. 1987, 'Reservations policy revisited', *Economic and Political Weekly*, Vol. XXII, No. 46, pp. 1957–62.

Shinde, J.R., 1986, *Dynamics of cultural revolution: 19th century Maharashtra*, Delhi: Ajanta Publications, quoted from *Economic and Political Weekly*, Vol. XXI, No. 17, p. 740.

Sinha, Arun, 1978, 'Resurgent adivasis', *Economic and Political Weekly*, Vol. XIII, No. 36, pp. 1544–46.

————, 1979, 'Containing the Jharkhand Movement', *Economic and Political Weekly*, Vol. XIV, No. 14, pp. 648–50.

————, 1987, 'Recurrent pattern of Jharkhand politics', *Economic and Political Weekly*, Vol. XXII, No. 45, pp. 1887–89.

————, 1987, 'The plains man's burden', *Economic and Political Weekly*, Vol. XXII, No. 48, pp. 2051–53.

————, 1987, 'Jharkhand: Straining to be heard in Delhi', *Economic and Political Weekly*, Vol. XXII, No. 49, pp. 2087–88.

Singh, K.S. (ed.), 1972, *Tribal Situation in India*, Simla: Indian Institute of Advanced Study.

Singh K.S., 1978, 'Colonial transformation of tribal society in Middle India', *Economic and Political Weekly*, Vol. XIII, No. 30, pp. 1221–32.

———, 1982, 'Transformation of tribal society: Integration v/s assimilation', *Economic and Political Weekly*, Vol. XVII, No. 34, pp. 1318–25 and No. 35, pp. 1376–84.

——— (ed.), 1983, *Tribal Movements in India* (2 Vols.), Delhi: Manohar Publications.

———, 1985, *Tribal Society in India: An Anthropo-Historical Perspective*, Delhi: Manohar Publications.

———, 1995, 'Inequality in Tribal Society: The Emerging Trends', *in* Savur, Manorama and Indra Munshi (eds), *Contradictions in Indian Society*, Jaipur: Rawat Publications.

Vidyarthi, L.P. (ed.), 1967, *Leadership in India*, Delhi: Asia Publishing House.

——— (ed.), 1969, *Conflict, Tension and Cultural Trends in India*, Calcutta: Punthi Pustak.

———, 1970, *Socio-Cultural Implications of Industrialisation in India: A case study of tribal Bihar*, Ranchi: University of Ranchi.

Yadav, K.C., 1994, *India's Unequal Citizens, A Study of Other Backward Classes*, Delhi: Manohar Publications.

Yagnik, Achyut, 1981, 'Spectre of Caste War', *Economic and Political Weekly*, Vol. XVI, No. 13, pp. 553–55.

Six

Gender and Social Stratification

Patriarchy legitimizes culturally-backed bio-physiological differences between men and women as the basis of unequal access to resources, opportunities and rewards and to rights. Status-inequality between men and women is an age-old phenomenon reinforced through patriarchy and its institutions, gendered division of labour, and social institutions like marriage, dowry, property and inheritance, and subordination. Sylvia Walby (1994: 22–28) observes that patriarchy is not just a matter of the differential distribution of power; it is built into the very mechanics of production. There is the existence of a 'patriarchal mode of production'. In *Persistent Inequalities* (Tinker 1990) the contributors ask the question: Why do inequalities persist? Male–female relationships are discussed in terms of the economic development theory, and it is observed that inequalities persist in the face of development. Vina Mazumdar and Kumud Sharma (1990: 185–97) show how new forms of subordination and gender asymmetry have superseded the old, leaving patriarchal control undisturbed in India. Industries, like the textile industry, which were the exclusive (or near exclusive) domain of women, have been taken over by men strengthening patriarchy and existing hierarchies. Some aspects of women's lives can be gauged by studying women in history, and by analyzing their social customs and attitudes, idealization of their domestic roles which in turn determine the state of their health and nutrition. The status of women has changed due to their improved health and nutrition. The improvement is also due to better education and participation in wider societal activities. Legislations, movements, spread of education and employment among women have helped in alleviating inequality between men and women. However, such statements will have to be qualified, as inequality between men and women, and between women (of different castes and classes or even within the family) persists.

Gender and Stratification Theory

The omission of *gender* (Mann 1986: 40–56) as a basis of social stratification—just like class, power, caste, and ethnicity—has created a crisis in the stratification theory. The gendered aspect has been emphasized as an essential component in the theory of social stratification (Crompton and Mann 1986). Michael Mann (1994: 177–94) pleads for the integration of gender divisions into the core of the stratification theory. Five main areas of stratification have influenced and have been influenced by gender. These are: the individual, the family and household, the division of labour between the sexes, social classes, and nation-states. The relations between gender and stratification are mediated by each of these different 'nuclei'. Further, Mann argues that gender and stratification can no longer be kept in separate compartments, as stratification is gendered and gender is stratified.

Leela Dube, Eleanor Leacock and Shirley Ardener (1986) provide a cross-cultural perspective, focusing upon the insignificance and passivity of women, and the primacy of men in understanding human behaviour and thought, structures and processes of human societies. This primacy finds expression in the study of social sciences. Leela Dube (ibid.: xi) observes that making women invisible despite their obvious preference and effective visibility is the root cause of their low status in society. Women suffer from many disadvantages in social life. This extends to controlled access to essential domains of life such as education, mobility, employment, property, income and decision-making. This happens because the value system perceives woman as a social category inferior to man in all aspects of social life. This value system holds for all castes and communities besides the matriarchal and matrilineal societies. A woman, as such, derives her status from the position of her family and her husband. Her status within the family is in effect lower than the family's status as perceived by outsiders as she is inferior to her husband and other adult members (both male and female) of the family. Rajni Palriwala and Carla Risseeuw (1996) also emphasize on contextualization of kinship and gender in South Asia and Sub-Saharan Africa.

Inequalities of gender can be explained by 'gender regimes' (Cornell 1994: 29–40). Gender regimes refer to a complex of institutions (family, work, state) that create and substantiate gender inequalities; gender is reproduced within these institutions through 'male reason' and the dichotomy of 'maleness' and 'femaleness'.

> A gender regime is a cluster of practices, ideological and material, which in a given social context, acts to construct various images of masculinity and femininity and thereby to consolidate forms of gender inequality (ibid.).

The 'femino-phobic' character of society has been highlighted in several cross-cultural studies of gender and inequality. Gender forms a basis in all forms of social inequalities (Kabeer 1995). The exclusion of women in its various manifestations persists; this would even include development thought. Kabeer advocates the application of Marxist analyses to the study of gender hierarchies as she observes that gendered inequalities have implications for the production of knowledge and the allocation of resources. Hence, she argues for the 'deconstruction' of conventional concepts.

Kabeer argues that it is in the socially differentiated arrangements of gender that we must seek an explanation for the very different ways in which men and women experience the world. She says that 'biology is gendered as well as sexed' (ibid.: 37). Male and female are translated as man and woman based on mutually exclusive traits of masculinity and feminity. People in history have resisted, though not always successfully, this translation of biological categories into social roles. Kabeer is clearly of the view that class mediates the way in which biological difference is translated into gender inequality. She argues that the sexually-based system of human thought has to be deconstructed. All these explanations help to understand the gendered nature of social relations and make sufficient grounds for the addition of the gender factor in the stratification theory.

But all women are not equally unequal in their families and communities. Women in fact are attached to a two-fold stratification, namely, in relation to men, and in relation to other women. After all, such status distinctions imply a differential distributive process for women in terms of access to resources and positions of power and authority. Gender as the basis of social inequality is structured into female and male spheres. Likewise, the differentiation within the family is structured and complex. There is no equitable sharing of status among members of the family.

Margaret Stacey (1986: 214–23) discusses the following questions in the context of Western society:

1. What are the core characteristics of the social order in the Western society in the late twentieth century?
2. Do these relate crucially to the market-place, to the ownership and control of the means of production? If so, are they gendered?
3. Is gender of any consequence?
4. Is the familial and kinship system marginal nowadays or does it remain of central importance to structural and social inequalities?
5. How can one (or does one need to?) relate social inequalities associated with paid work and the mode of production to the differential position of women and men in the familial and kinship system?

These questions are also relevant to the Indian situation. In contemporary Western society, inequality between men and women is a feature, which needs to be taken into account. The existing theories of stratification have so far ignored this (Walby 1986: 23–29). Status which women derive from their own achievements such as education and salaried jobs is not fully recognized and even such individualistic gains are attributed to the husbands and their families or to the parents of the upwardly women. Thus, it implies that ultimately women have only derived status. Rehana Ghadially (1988) highlights the multi-faceted problems of women in terms of depiction and reality of their life-situations.

Status of Women in Indian Society

In the Indian scenario, the need for a gendered basis in studying stratification is highlighted by Kalpana Bardhan (1986: 94). She points out:

> Although the family is the salient unit of analysis for stratification studies, whether based on class or caste analysis, it is not quite sufficient. Situated within the broader framework, the divisions by sex and status affect its properties of stability and dynamics.

In Indian society the following questions may be asked:

1. Is the family the basic unit of stratification?
2. How do kinship, family and the everyday relations structure gender?
3. Does the male head of the household determine social position of the family?
4. Within families is the status of women equivalent to that of men?
5. Can women determine their status independent of their relationship with men?
6. How does the inequality between men and women affect the structure of stratification?

Michael Mann (1986: 40–56) while attempting to answer these questions, discusses patriarchy, economy and class structure. The traditional patriarchy might have become weak, but neo-patriarchy and femininity have emerged in the public realms of employment. Women can no longer be kept in separate sociological compartments. However, compartmentalization of women persists despite involvement of women in politics, developmental programmes and processes, feminism, and even in the challenge to patriarchy (Tinker 1990).

The question 'Is there any such category as women?' is posed by Nita Kumar (1994: 211–31). In her reply to this rhetorical question she states that 'women worked within a categorization that represented them through negation, repression and opposition' (ibid.: 228). Indian society has been divided into *purush jati* and *stree jati*. Women could use their agency and their actions could be radical, but their representations were at best merely liberal, more typically the representations were conservative. 'How do we conceptualize women (or any subject) and write about them?' (ibid.: 4). Nita Kumar suggests four ways to deal with this question: (*a*) to make women the object of human 'gaze' (borrowing the concept of 'gaze' from Michel Foucault), (*b*) to see women as actors and subjects, to give them the prerogative of males, (*c*) to focus on the patriarchal, ideological, discursive structures within which women exist and which seemingly control them without a chance to get out of them, and (*d*) to look at the hidden, subversive ways in which women exercise their agency, even while outwardly forming a part of a repressive normative order (ibid.: 4).

Following the post-modernist discourse analysis, Kumar adheres to the fourth perspective while incorporating the third one within it for understanding 'women as subjects'. She herself raises the question 'whether it is desirable to have women as subjects' (ibid.: 5). 'Is it desirable to replace the masculine, rational, free subject with a feminine one?' The question is important as it refers to the nature of power itself. The very dichotomy between subject and object needs to be dissolved. The Foucauldian approach dispenses with the subject in favour of a 'genealogy' of knowledges, discourses, domains of objects, etc. (Foucault 1980: 117). Knowledge and power are fused in history in terms of practices. Individuals and groups can comprehend their 'subjection' to a plurality of discourses. Women's status can be defined in terms of such a diversity of knowledge.

In the Indian context we now have reliable data on rural and urban women both employed and housewives, educated and illiterate. Women's movements and their identities of selfhood, their involvement in development programmes and politics, and awareness regarding their problems relating to health, conjugal rights, dowry, violence (domestic/against women), exploitation and discrimination are questions that have been addressed. If women are seen as independent members, social inequality becomes quite obvious. If they are seen as the attached members, their unequal existence remains hidden. All these aspects have a bearing on women's status in the family and wider society. Differential status within the family or outside it implies differential access to resources and opportunities. Women compared to men suffer from differential access in society in general, hence their inferior status becomes the basis of a structured social inequality. Patriarchy becomes the dominant value in shaping such differences between men and women.

Monisha Behal's account of the women's perceptions (1984: 1775–77) in a village in the Mainpuri district of west Uttar Pradesh is an eye-opener about women's status. Inside their *angan* (courtyard) women would work on the grain stone, prepare food, rear children, sweep/wash and plaster house walls or floors. Their work outside the house would include preparing fodder for animals, collecting cow-dung for the field, making and mounting cow-dung cakes, fetching water, and winnowing and cleaning of the agricultural yields. Behal finds women's lives in the village full of gloom and sadness because of work overload, bad health, drudgery and poverty. There is no escape from work and there is no freedom to move out of the house and from their menfolk. The limited mobility (in terms of village exogamy) which women have, isolates, deprives and narrows women's outlook and aspirations. Marriage, in fact, further binds women to men and patriarchy. Deviation from these two is taken as a social evil and invites stigma.

Madhu Kishwar and Ruth Vanita (1984) pose the women's question by highlighting the value system, the incompatibility of our Constitution and law, and violence, aggression and crimes against women. Kishwar and Vanita besides analyzing the common problems discuss suppression of women by women and the modes of struggle against this in towns and cities.

Gandhi's notions of womanhood, particularly Indian womanhood, have also been studied in an effort to understand societal set-ups. His view that a woman has 'infinite capacity for sufferings' because she is the mother of man has also been critically examined (Banerji 1985: 997–99; Kishwar 1985: 1691–1702; 1753–58). Gandhi's view regarding the *dress* worn by modern girls is also disapproved by several feminist critics.

The studies on the oppressive nature of dowry, the preference for sons and the deprivation of the female infant/child do not provide adequate answers to the women's everyday questions which centre around the gendered nature of work, remuneration, options and opportunities, and power and control (Bardhan 1985: 2207–20; 2261–69). Bardhan observes that 'the central question is how patriarchy combines with the caste-and-class hierarchy to sustain the segmentation of the labour market and the iniquities in access to the means and resources for work' (ibid.: 2207). How gender division, based on control over women's sexuality and economic resources was integral to the formation of a social structure is the focal theme of Joanna Liddle and Rama Joshi's study of Indian women (1986) in the context of interconnections between gender, caste and class. They write:

> The patriarchal upper castes tightened both caste and gen-der divisions as they consolidated their economic suprem-acy and defended challenges to that supremacy. These processes reveal the link between female sexuality and the economic position of the community, where female property is removed from the family at marriage but is contained within the caste group by controls on the women's sexu-ality. One result of the high caste male supremacy is the persistent association between ideas opposed to caste and ideas opposed to the subordination of women within all the social reform movements over the centuries (ibid.: 233).

Differentials in work participation affect other aspects of women's status and welfare, and the quality of female life. 'Gender and caste are important aspects of class exploitation' (ibid.: 2209). Kalpana Bardhan (ibid.: 2210) writes about the status of women:

> In a society as divided by economic inequality, and as permeated by the ideology of hierarchy, women hardly constitute a collectivity with shared interests and needs. They are stratified, as men are, by enormous differences in material resources, by the options that are available to them, and by the norms of status-appropriate work closely linked with their class-and-class-locations. Women, par-ticularly those from the Dalit sections, suffer from triple oppression—caste, class, gender (Omvedt 1995: 175–87).

Work is the prime mover of women's status because there is a correspondence between economic stratification, social hierarchy and differentiation of female work pattern and employment modes. Productive labour by women over a period of time can bridge status-hiatus between men and women. Though caste oppression and class exploitation are stark realities of our social fabric, gender iniquities are not only more stable and durable, they are also more insidious because they are generally practised within the family. Women have remained largely invisible inspite of the fact that many are employed and enjoy a degree of economic independence. To make women visible they have to be brought into the fold of the planning process. There is also a need to make them a special target group especially in terms of development (Dube and Palriwala 1990; Jain 1990: 1454–55; Shiva 1988).

Dynamics of Status of Women

Regarding the changing status of women, Indra Deva and Shrirama (1986: 148) observe that 'the status a society assigns to woman largely depends upon the basis of the structure of that society itself'. They write:

> The womenfolk belonging to a stock which was racially and culturally different were regarded' inimical and given a low position. Due to extraneous origin of womenfolk a feeling of suspicion against them was deeply ingrained in the society.

Somehow women's low status because of radical admixture and intermarriage accompanied with suspicion became an integral feature of traditional Indian thought and social structure. However, the position of women was not very low in the beginning (ibid.: 164) as it became later with the invasion by Aryans. The patriarchal ethos of Indian society became stronger with the passage of time and this resulted in the subjugation of women.

The Mietei society in Manipur and other parts of the North-East have experienced a feminist social structure. Chaki Sircar attributes this to a remarkable absence of social evils like *sati*, child-marriage, infanticide, the dowry system and the social persecution of widows in this region. Women of the Manipur valley have been able to preserve their collective identity as a powerful social force partly because of economic independence and integration with the wider society. However, Tilottoma Misra and Malini Bhattacharya (1986: WS-54–WS-58) have questioned this brand of feminism in Manipuri society. Uneven distribution of work and uneven participation in remunerated work within the household produce family-status production work, and this pattern is the main cause of gender hierarchy in Indian society (Papanek 1989: 97–116). The concept of family status production work highlights the role that women of middle and upper classes play in families and in strategies of social mobility. This facilitates the increased control over women's labour and mobility, but increases the competitive advantage of households as women's work contributes to family status rather than their own development. In this way, women indirectly support activities for the paid work of other members, for the future paid work and status aspirations of children, for establishing political linkages, performance of religious acts and rituals, etc. Even withdrawal of women from work among the middle class families adds to the social status of the family. Thus, women re-strengthen patriarchy and the welfare of the family undermines their personal status.

After independence, some effort was made to promote equality of status between men and women. A. M. Shah (1989: 513–16) finds that the real impetus came with the United Nations Decade (1975–85) for Women (1974) and the inclusion of a chapter on 'Women and Development' in the Sixth Five Year Plan (1980–85). He feels that the recognition of women as a target group in the Seventh Plan has brought about consciousness among women and promoted several studies on the women's question.

The constitution of the National Commission for Women may be understood as a significant step in the right direction. Traditional patriarchal controls over women, especially within the family, have become considerably weak. However, on the contrary the increased state-sponsored religious fundamentalism has curbed equal rights for women. Both capitalist and patriarchal interests aim at the control of women's labour, fertility and sexuality (Chhachhi 1989: 567–78). Gender inequality is built into the state's seemingly progressive policies. This is highlighted by Padmini Swaminathan

(1987: WS-34–WS-39), who observes that subordination of women is reflected in the Minimum Wages Act and the Equal Remuneration Act as well as in the policies for women's education and the Hindu law of succession. One could debate the questions of capitalist development and patriarchy and their happy conjunction, but the fact remains that even in ideal conditions women are subordinate to men. General statements such as the one made previously always need some qualifying clauses (Jayant and Rothermund 1989: 1722–23).

Women's movements against their oppression and exploitation and for equality in family and society have created a high level of consciousness. There has also been a visible reduction in injustices and atrocities committed on women by their family members, employers and the toughs and bullies but these apparent improvements are embedded in caste and class privileges. Besides articulation of quest for equality in general, specific demands have been made for equal wages, for recognition of women's work in the family and for special provision for women to facilitate their participation in decision making in all walks of life. Some schools of history would claim that prior to independence, women struggled against the British and their liberation from the rigid moorings of Indian society and culture, the latter was a common cause with the Indian freedom struggle. Today women's struggle is largely for emancipation from rigid cultural bonds which define their existence.

Sujata Ghotoskar, Rohini Banaji and Neelam Chaturvedi (1983: 339–44) outline four major forms of the struggle of women: (*a*) autonomous organizations and movements, (*b*) trade unions, (*c*) housewives associations, and (*d*) general social movements. The main issues taken up through these fora are: rape, family planning, suffrage, oppression in the family, pornography, improvements in the standard of living, conditions of work, social recognition of housewives and remuneration for their work, political repression, price-rise and so on. It is argued time and again that women have fought against the society to get out of their inhuman subordinate existential conditions. Padma Prakash (1984: 1656) writes:

> Women's struggles have encompassed, through history, a gamut of issues ranging from the right to vote to the fight against oppression and exploitation in all aspects of their lives. Whatever their theoretical framework, women's

struggles have challenged the existing social relations in society which have forced women into the fragmented, dichotomised, oppressed lives they lead.

It is through such a struggle that people's science movement can demystify science as a means of capitalist control over women and weaker sections of Indian society. The structural bases of male's domination over females are discussed in Lerner (1986), Dube, Leacock and Archer (1986), Saradamoni (1985), and Liddle and Joshi (1986). The main issues related to the origin of patriarchy are the visibility/invisibility of women and their power and authority, work and status, and class and gender. Leela Dube discusses the relationship between man and woman through the metaphoric use of the *seed* and the *earth*. In all these writings it is admitted that patriarchy, stratification system and status of women are closely inter-related, and any kind of positive change in women's status would be an attack on patriarchy and stratificatory systems like caste and class.

During the nineteenth century women's enclosed space of domesticity was under attack urging the transformation of the man–woman relationship. This development is reflected in several literary and other writings (Alexander 1985: WS-68–WS-71; Bagchi 1985: WS-58–WS-62). Joanna Liddle and Rama Joshi (1985: WS-72–WS-78) in their article 'Gender and Imperialism in British India' note that 'the British used the particular form which gender divisions took in India as a vehicle for proving their liberality as a demonstration of their superiority, and as a legitimation of their rule'. They reinforced aspects of male oppression within Indian culture. The women's movement in India attacked both male supremacy and foreign domination as the two together were the cause of women's low status. It could be said that the British rulers did not address the issues of women's welfare and progress substantially. The same could be said of the national movement; many resisted women's demands in the family and wider society as it threatened men's hegemony over them. A 'Review of Women Studies' (1986: WS-2–WS-52) brought out articles which dealt with the role of missionary women (Forbes 1986: WS-2–WS-8), the contribution of the Arya Samaj in women's education (Kishwar 1986: WS-9–WS-24), debate on women's education in Bengal (Karlekar 1986: WS-25–WS-31), discourse on sati (Mani 1986: WS-

32–WS-40), and the role of tribal women in the Warli Revolt (Saldhana 1986: WS-41–WS-52).

The concern over issues such as consciousness, education, social practices and class is not a recent one; the issues, too, are as old as time. The constraints created by new technology and aspirations for affluence and luxurious/improved life-style have resulted in a renewed and covert form of women's oppression and exploitation in the form of dowry and extortions from the girl's parents. The spread of education and an educated reaction to some of these injustices and cruelties have helped feminists to rise as a strong and expressive voice.

However, the structure of society itself largely determined social position of women. In Haryana in the colonial period the dominant peasant cultural ethos and the Arya Samaj upheld women in high position, almost equal to men (Chowdhry 1987: 2060–66). Women were highly visible being full working partners with men but only in a *ghunghat* (veil). Women in Haryana, simultaneously enjoyed high and low status. *Purda*, sexual exploitation, and exclusion/seclusion from decision making were indices of women's low status. The indices of high status included bride price, widow remarriage, equal economic work partnership and liberal sexual climate. In reality the peasants' socio-economic system was such that there was hardly any scope for women to share the fruits of their remunerative work.

Thus, the seclusion of women's work is nearly an impossibility in a peasant community. This is also true about *purda* observance in north India (Mandelbaum 1986: 1999–2004). 'A family can properly observe *purda* only if its members can afford to do so.' If the family cannot afford to forego earnings of its female members, it has to ignore observance of *purda*. As soon as the family's economic/financial standing improves it may withdraw its women-folk from remunerative work and impose socio-cultural restrictions such as the observance of *purda*. The neo-rich and middle class in rural India have opted for enhanced domesticity for women considering it as an indicator of high status. With a sense of pride they often mention that their women do not work in the fields and farms and they do not depend upon the earnings of their women-folk. Mandelbaum (ibid.: 2002) calls it 'Men's Honour and Women's Seclusion'. Women are active agricultural producers in Himachal Pradesh and yet they suffer segregation and seclusion

(Sethi 1984). Despite the day-to-day sufferings of rural women (Omvedt 1995: 175–88), through struggles and movements they have challenged the Western capitalist model of development adopted by the Indian state. Green earth, women's power and human liberation are being rigorously demanded with some degree of success by women's organizations in Maharashtra. Some other success stories have been reported from other parts of rural India as well.

Discrimination against Women

Women have been projected in literary writings from a conservative point of view. They have been denied employment, any voice in decision making, and have been oppressed through social moves like sati. Women are poor in spite of belonging to relatively well off families. They suffer in the family because dowry is arranged for them. Their identity is not of theirs but of their parents before marriage and of the husbands and their families after the marriage. Women's drudgery is fathomless. Conjugal rights are unknown to them. Poor women are exploited sexually and some are even dragged into prostitution. Violence and crime against women (Ahuja 1987) are understood to be a man's privilege.

The list of injustices is in fact an endless one. Despite these inhuman acts of oppression, exploitation and discrimination, women have become conscious of their position in modern India. Women's education has become a desirable activity. Preference for an educated bride is expressed even by the village-folk. Women have been opting for employment. They have been seeking employment outside their homes. They also participate in politics and other extra-familial activities. Urban educated women could be seen today as teachers, doctors, nurses, artists, social workers, writers, airhostesses, clerks, typists, stenographers and personal secretaries, etc. Their work is being recognized in various walks of life including ecology, technology, mass media, industry, health care and development programmes. It would not be possible to have a detailed discussion here, though a brief discussion on rural–agrarian and urban–industrial situation vis-à-vis women may not be out of context.

Rural women have much more acute unemployment than men. The female labour market is also somewhat different from that of men. Leela Gulati (1978: A-27–A-35) asks two questions: (*a*) who are the working women of India? and (*b*) what is the value of their labour? Gulati based on her case study on the women of a Scheduled Caste in Kerala finds answers to these questions by exploring the difference between male and female employment. Pushpa Sundar (1981: 863–71) observes that employment does not ipso facto mean improvement in the status of women. However, K. Saradamoni (1982: 155–62) observes that in Palghat district of Kerala the changes brought about in the lives and status of women are mainly due to changes in the agrarian structure.

The abolition of landlordism and the breakdown of its sociocultural milieus have affected women of the stratified agrarian community in a positive manner. The abolition of feudalism has certainly given a new *izzat* (honour) to women as it has eliminated sexual oppression by feudal lords.

In a survey of female agricultural labour in rice production Mencher and Saradamoni (1982: A-149–A-167) find that female income was essential for households below the poverty line. Women are engaged in three types of work: (*a*) participation in the traditionally defined labour force, (*b*) domestic work plus activities like fuel collection and animal care, and (*c*) domestic work alone (Sen and Sen 1985: WS-49–WS-56). Women participate in the traditionally defined labour force in response to their economic need. Women's status in society is enhanced when they take up jobs irrespective of their class position.

Even then, women are handicapped in shouldering responsibility in managing their households due to their class position and gender. In their efforts to sustain themselves and their families, women are victimized because of their sex and poor economic background. Because women struggle for survival in their everyday lives, they become more militant than men in movements for the betterment of their own position. Improvement in their economic conditions certainly reduces their subordination in the society (Agarwal 1986, 1988, 1989: WS-46–WS-75). Even in rural areas, tribal women have gained considerable consciousness about their status and role, education, employment and decision making.

Education, Employment and Status of Women

Education and employment among women of the urban middle classes have raised their socio-economic status. It is otherwise with rural women who work hard within their households and on farms, yet they do not enjoy higher status (Ahmad 1979: 1435–40). Ahmad finds five trends in women's employment: (*a*) clustering of women in a few occupations, (*b*) clustering either in low status occupations or in the lower rungs of the prestigious professions, (*c*) women receive lower salaries than men, (*d*) decline in the representation of women in certain occupations, and (*e*) high proportion of highly educated and professionally trained unemployed women.

In a study of working women living in the *chawls* and *jhopad-pattis*, Alice Thorner and Jyoti Ranadive (1985: WS-9–WS-14) mention that working women are operationally defined as those currently employed or engaged in income-earning occupations. Some women had gainful occupations within their own homes while others were devoted exclusively to their domestic duties. The working-class women pursued an array of occupations and enjoyed some degree of autonomy. But the lives of these women seemed to be determined by their husbands and by the position of their households in the society. Hilary Standing (1985: WS-23–WS-38) reports that with the emergence of gender-segregated industries in Calcutta the participation of women in the labour increased alongwith high male unemployment. For semi-skilled or unskilled employment, women workers were preferred as they could be paid much less than the male workers. Relations between husband and wife depend upon the fact whether the former is the main bread-winner or not. In case the wife remains secondary wage-earner, gender hierarchy persists more than if the situation is in the reverse order. Class differentials are found in the work–time allocation of men and women (Sen 1988: 1702–6).

It has been briefly mentioned earlier that more and more women are demanding autonomy by seeking their identity as persons/members of society equal to male members. They demanded the reservation of 30 per cent of jobs and seats in panchayats and other civic bodies. This demand has been accepted for one-third reservation in the local-self government bodies under the Seventy-second and Seventy-third Constitutional amendments. An increased consciousness of their rights forces women to denounce patriarchal institutions of control and oppression. As a result of this awareness women are trying to counter gender bias, malnutrition, under/low-paid employment. They are now seeking equal remuneration for equal work vis-à-vis men, better health care and a say in decision making both in the family and in society. Women's identity is being reconstructed in history. Today, a woman is seen in terms of her own perceptions rather than that of others including man/husband/son. The ideology of motherhood and woman's commercial exhibition are being problematized.

According to the National Alliance of Young Entrepreneurs (NAYE) there are 50,000 women entrepreneurs in the country today. They are managing hotels, computer enterprises, garment manufacturing and establishments dealing with processed foods, chemicals, electronics and engineering goods. According to 1981 Census about 21 per cent of women are main workers as against 53 per cent men. University enrolment figures for 1982–83 demonstrate that every year 32,000 women opt to study medicine, 6,000 for engineering, 1,800 for agricultural and veterinary sciences, and 14,000 for law. A sociological analysis of these women could reveal their caste and class and family backgrounds. May be that it is changing slowly, but the old order is under strain and has been showing clearly cracks in its structure and functioning. However, the openings are quite limited for women because of slow economic growth and traditional stereotypes and perceptions. In most cases even women in professions remain *secondary earners*, hence the low status accorded to them (Ahmad 1984: 75–90). Raj Mohini Sethi (1976) on the basis of a comparative analysis, arrives at two conclusions regarding the effects of the employment of women: (*a*) it does not necessarily lead to a change in the work patterns at home; and (*b*) their contribution to the family finances does not bring about a change in the persisting status–role nexus and power relations within the family. In a collection of interesting studies by Noeleen Heyzer and Gita Sen (1994) issues relating to interconnections between gender, economic growth and poverty in the countries of Asia-Pacific region such as in India, Korea, Sri Lanka, Pakistan, Thailand, Vietnam and Papua New Guinea, have been discussed at length. Noeleen Heyzer (1994: 4) makes the following points:

1. What kind of market growth, state-led development and interventions would effectively reduce poverty and improve gender equity?
2. What key lessons can be learned from the relationship between market growth, poverty, poverty alleviation programmes and gender equity?

3. How can states and markets be transformed to strengthen the entitlements of poor women and treat them as people in their own right, not merely as dependents, targets and instruments?
4. How can this empowerment of people be made central to the framing of development alternatives?

The situation in the above-mentioned countries is not uniform with regard to types of market and state-led development. Differences are also found with regard to different policy environments, role of the NGOs and people's participation. The interaction of these issues with gender equity is complex. Women today have more income earning opportunities and bargaining power within households, but they are not able to compete with men on equal terms due to their gendered limitations. Hence, women continue to be relatively powerless and marginalized. Alternatives suggested by Heyzer (ibid.: 25) are: economic growth with social equity, sustainable livelihoods, social justice, and ecological sustainability. Heyzer also places emphasis on developing women's empowerment (ibid.: 26).

A contextual analysis is required to assess the status and power enjoyed by working women in their families and in the wider society. A wife's economic status is an important factor in domestic decision making (Ramu 1988: 49–69). The non-working women either use covert influence to share power or subordinate themselves to their husband's domination. Marital and family life also determines sharing of power in the domestic affairs. A study of working women in Jawaharlal Nehru University (Sood 1988) suggests that women of all the categories in the hierarchy of the University reflect their position in society in terms of caste and class backgrounds and educational achievements. However, problems of adjustment and role–conflict are more in the case of the upper and middle categories of women than the women of the lower categories. Women of the lower categories earn equal to their husbands and yet do not specifically ask for their participation in decision making in the family. However, perhaps due to the assertion of this right there are more problems of adjustment in the families of the two upper categories.

Perceptions regarding status (Kazi and Ghadially 1979: 59–70) are shaped by modern education than the traditional values regarding marriage and family. Based on a comparative study of 200 women in the Delhi metropolis Renuka Singh (1990) finds status–experiences of women as the central concern than the objectively determined status. Status is a relative and contextual phenomenon, and therefore, it cannot always be determined by objective indices like property, income, occupation and education. It is more a matter of experiential awareness, subjectively realized and inter-subjectively objectivized.

It may be stated that education for girls even in villages has become a desirable qualification. People are also seeking educated brides, and certainly in case of the educated employed girls, dowry is not insisted upon though it is rarely denied. Thus, the issue of the status of women is very complex and it is fractured along the structured social inequalities in Indian society. Education and employment have been found as the most effective mechanisms in reducing iniquitous relations between men and women and between women and women.

A critique of the developmental approach to the study of women is well orchestrated in Bina Agarwal's study of gender and land rights in South Asia (1994). Employment, education and health care for women imply a top-down manner to analyze their problems projecting 'statization' and patronage and not right of women in property. Agarwal investigates the central importance of women's lack of effective property rights, especially land, in explaining their economic, social and political subordination in South Asia. She recognizes that it is critical for women to 'win' land/property rights for establishing more equal gender relations. A resource theory rather than the reform theory is Agarwal's main contention. Land is a critical resource for well-being and empowerment of women. Not just property ownership but property (land) control is of crucial significance (ibid.: xv). While explaining a multiplicity of factors which constrain women a subordinate group, Bina Agarwal points to the interactive effect of economic factors, cultural norms, gender ideologies and politics, in determining women's property position.

Through acquiring of land rights empowerment of women is important, but the end result of this is also quite important. 'Land defines social status and political power in the village, and it structures relationships both within and outside the household' (ibid.: 2). Development, according to Agarwal, is not gender-neutral (ibid.: 4). Effective rights in land alone can empower women. Household is not a unit of congruent interests; it implies conflict/ power relations. She discusses at length (ibid.: 11–45) household property status, women's property status, ownership and control of property, land as property, rights in land, non-land-based households, etc., in the context of gender relations. Equality and empowerment are interrelated aspects of gender relations. Gender disadvantages and gender inequalities can be challenged if rights in land are actualized because they become a facilitator for women's equality with men by empowering them in economic, social and political spheres.

Indu Agnihotri expressing her preference for the Marxist analysis of land rights for women in her critique of Bina Agarwal's study observes: 'A number of questions which would have a bearing on gender relations, however, get obfuscated in the absence of any discussion of the production process, the organization of produc- tion and relations of production' (1996: 527). The question of land rights has to be addressed beyond arguing for the rights of women from the standpoint of ownership alone. The rights of Dalits, rural masses (including women) to land-ownership would demand wid- ening of the framework of analysis beyond patriarchy. The issue regarding women's class position also remains problematic. Agni- hotri raises two questions: (*a*) Is class a descriptive category which can be interchanged/substituted with status or even wealth? (*b*) What role does social location play in determining this and where would ideology figure in all this? (ibid.: 527). Agarwal's view is more of a judicial nature and is based on land as a means of security. Her viewpoint does not go, in fact, beyond the 'welfare' argument and it counterposes to 'empowerment' (ibid.: 527).

While Agarwal studies land-ownership, the construction of women and womanhood has been studied by Rajeswari Sunder Rajan (1993: 129) who talks of two faces of women—real and imagined. The construction of women in terms of recognizable roles, images, models, and labels occurs in discourse in response to specific social imperatives. In a similar view Sangari and Vaid (1986: 17) observe that womanhood is often part of an asserted or desired, not an actual, cultural continuity. Sangari (1991: 57) also argues that fe- maleness is constantly made, and redistributed. One has to see its formation in terms of space and time, composition and correlates and ideological potentials and freedoms. There is a politics and/or representation of real and imagined women.

Dynamics of the status of women bring out the above contradictory character signifying *mutatis mutandis* the cultural production. Despite the metaphor of reforms and individuation of women, emphasis on chastity, patriarchy, division of labour, sacredness of marriage, seclusion within the household has persisted. The ideals of *stree dharma*, asceticism for widows, self-denial, self-control, model for others have blurred the developmental metaphor giving way to more and new contradictions in everyday life. Male dominance within aboriginal culture(s), which is somewhat autonomous and segmentary in nature, represents as an 'enduring, non-negotiable and timeless reality' (Bell 1994: 221–50), and needs to be seen as an expression of gendered power reflected through rape, violence, etc.

Why are women considered to be 'subordinated peoples'? Is the law not meant for them?

References

Agarwal, Bina, 1986, 'Women, Poverty and Agricultural Growth in India', *The Journal of Peasant Studies*, Vol. 13, No. 3.

———, 1988, 'Who Sows, Who Reaps? Women's Land Rights in India', *The Journal of Peasant Studies*, Vol. 15, No. 4.

———, 1989, 'Rural Women, Poverty and National Resources: Sustenance, Sustainability and Struggle for Change', *Economic and Political Weekly*, Vol. XXIV, No. 43, pp. WS-46–WS-75.

———, 1994, *A Field of One's Own, Gender and Land Rights in South Asia*, Cambridge: Cambridge University Press and New Delhi: Foundation Books.

Agnihotri, Indu, 1996, 'Bringing Land Rights Centre-State', *Economic and Political Weekly*, Vol. XXXI, No. 9, pp. 526–29.

Ahmad, Karuna, 1979, 'Studies of Educated Working Women in India: Trends and Issues', *Economic and Political Weekly*, Vol. XIV, No. 33, pp. 1435–40.

———, 1984, 'The Trishankus: Women in the Professions in India', *Sociological Bulletin*, Vol. 33, Nos 1 and 2, pp. 75–90.

Ahuja, Ram, 1987, *Crime Against Women*, Jaipur: Rawat Publications.

Alexander, Meena, 1985, 'Sarojini Naidu: Romanticism and Resistance', *Economic and Political Weekly*, Vol. XX, No. 43, pp. WS-68–WS-71.

Bagchi, Jasodhara, 1985, 'Positivism and Nationalism—Womanhood and Crisis in Nationalist Fiction: Bankim Chandra's *Anandmath*', *Economic and Political Weekly*, Vol. XX, No. 42, pp. WS-58–WS-62.

Banerjee, Sumanta, 1985, 'Reporting to Each Other', *Economic and Political Weekly*, Vol. XX, No. 28, pp. 997–99.

Bardhan, Kalpana, 1985, 'Women's Work, Welfare and Status: Forces of Tradition and Change in India', *Economic and Political Weekly*, Vol. XX, Nos 51 and 52, pp. 2207–20 and pp. 2261–69.

Behal, Monisha, 1984, 'Within and Outside the Courtyard: Glimpses into Women's Perceptions', *Economic and Political Weekly*, Vol. XIX, No. 41, pp. 1775–77.

Bell, Diane, 1994, 'Representing Aboriginal Women: Who Speaks for Whom?' *in* Mendelsohn, Oliver and Upendra Baxi (eds), *The Rights of Subordinated Peoples*, Delhi: Oxford University Press, pp. 221–50.

Crompton, Rosemary and **Michael Mann,** 1986, *Gender and Stratification*, Cambridge: Polity Press.

Chhachhi, Amrita, 1989, 'The State, Religious Fundamentalism and Women: Trends in South Asia', *Economic and Political Weekly*, Vol. XXIV, No. 11, pp. 567–78.

Choudhury, Prem, 1987, 'Socio-economic Dimensions of Certain Customs and Attitudes: Women of Haryana in the Colonial Period', *Economic and Political Weekly*, Vol. XXII, No. 48, pp. 2060–66.

Connell, R.W., 1994, 'Gender Regimes and the Gender Order', *in The Polity Reader in Gender Studies*, Cambridge: Polity Press, pp. 29–40.

Deva, Indra and **Shrirama,** 1986, *Traditional Values and Institutions in Indian Society*, New Delhi: S. Chand and Co.

Dube, Leela, Eleanor Leacock and **Shirley Ardener** (eds), 1986, *Visibility and Power: Essays on Women in Society and Development*, Delhi: Oxford University Press.

Dube, Leela and **Rajni Palriwala** (eds), 1990, *Structures and Strategies, Women, Work and Family*, New Delhi: Sage Publications.

Forbes, Geraldine H., 1986, 'In Search of the Pure Heathen: Missionary Women in Nineteenth Century in India', *Economic and Political Weekly*, Vol. XXI, No. 17, pp. WS-2–WS-8.

Foucault, Michel, 1980, *Power/Knowledge*, New York: Pantheon.

Ghadially, Rehana (ed.), 1988, *Women in Indian Society*, New Delhi: Sage Publications.

Ghotoskar, Sujata, Rohini Banaji and **Neelam Chaturvedi,** 1983, 'Women, Work, Organisation and Struggle', *Economic and Political Weekly*, Vol. XVIII, No. 10, pp. 334–44.

Gulati, Leela, 1978, 'Profile of a Female Agricultural Labourer', *Economic and Political Weekly*, Vol. XIII, No. 12, pp. A-27–A-35.

Heyzer, Noeleen, 1994, 'Introduction: Market, State and Gender Equity', *in* Heyzer, Noeleen and Gita Sen (eds), *Gender, Economic Growth and Poverty*, New Delhi: Kali for Women, pp. 3–27.

Jain, Devaki, 1990, 'Development Theory and Practice: Insights Emerging from Women's Experience', *Economic and Political Weekly*, Vol. XXV, No. 27, pp. 1454–55.

Jayant, Asha and **Indira Rothermund,** 1989, 'Women, Emancipation and Equality', *Economic and Political Weekly*, Vol. XXIV, No. 30, pp. 1722–23.

Kabeer, Naila, 1995, *Reversed Realities: Gender Hierarchies in Development Thought*, New Delhi: Kali for Women.

Karlekar, Malavika, 1986, 'Kadambini and the *Bhadrolok*: Early Debates over Women's Education in Bengal', *Economic and Political Weekly*, Vol. XXI, No. 17, pp. WS-25–WS-31.

Kazi, Khalid Ahmad and **Rehana Ghadially,** 1979, 'Perception of the Female Role by Indian College Students', *Sociological Bulletin*, Vol. 28, Nos 1–2, pp. 59–70.

Kishwar, Madhu, 1985, 'Gandhi on Women', *Economic and Political Weekly*, Vol. XX, No. 41, pp. 1753–58.

———, 1986, 'Aryasamaj and Women's Education: Kanya Mahavidyalaya Jalandhar', *Economic and Political Weekly*, Vol. XXI, No. 17, pp. WS-9–WS-24.

Kishwar, Madhu and **Ruth Vanita**, 1984, *In Search of Answers: Indian Women's Voices from Manushi*, London: Zed Books.

Kumar, Nita (ed.), 1994, *Women as Subjects: South Asian Histories*, New Delhi: Stree.

Lerner, Gerda, 1986, *The Creation of Patriarchy*, New York: Oxford University Press.

Liddle, Joanna and **Rama Joshi**, 1985, 'Gender and Imperialism in British India', *Economic and Political Weekly*, Vol. XX, No. 43, pp. WS-72–WS-78.

———, 1986, *Daughters of Independence, Gender, Caste and Class in India*, New Delhi: Kali for Women.

Mandelbaum, David G., 1986, 'Sex Roles and Gender Relations in North India', *Economic and Political Weekly*, Vol. XXI, No. 46, pp. 1999–2004.

Mani, Lata, 1986, 'Production of an Official Discourse on Sati in Early Nineteenth Century Bengal', *Economic and Political Weekly*, Vol. XXI, No. 17, pp. WS-32–WS-40.

Mann, Michael, 1986, 'A Crisis in Stratification Theory? Persons, Households/Families, Lineages, Genders, Classes and Nations', *in* Crompton, Rosemary and Michael Mann (eds), *Gender and Stratification*, Cambridge: Polity Press, pp. 40–56.

———, 1994, 'Persons, Households, Families, Lineages, Genders, Classes and Nations', *in* the *Polity Reader in Gender Studies*, pp. 177–94.

Mazumdar, Vina and **Kumud Sharma**, 1990, 'Sexual Division of Labour and the Subordination of Women: A Reappraisal from India', *in* Tinker, Irene (ed.), *Persistent Inequalities, Women and World Development*, New York: Oxford University Press.

Misra, Tilottoma and **Malini Bhattacharya**, 1986, 'Feminism in a Traditional Society?', *Economic and Political Weekly*, Vol. XXI, No. 43, pp. WS-54–WS-58.

Omvedt, Gail, 1995, 'The Awakening of Women's Power: The Rural Women's Movement in India', *in* Savur, Manorama and Indra Munshi (eds), *Contradictions in Indian Society*, Jaipur: Rawat Publications.

Prakash, Padma, 1984, 'People's Science Movement and Women's Struggle', *Economic and Political Weekly*, Vol. XIX, No. 38, p. 1656.

Rajan, Rajeswari Sunder, 1993, *Real and Imagined Women: Gender, Culture and Postcolonialism*, London: Routledge.

Ramu, G.N., 1988, 'Wife's Economic Status and Marital Power: A Case of Single and Dual-earner Couples', *Sociological Bulletin*, Vol. 37, Nos 1 and 2, pp. 49–69.

Saldhanha, Indra Munshi, 1986, 'Tribal Women in the Warli Revolt, 1945–47: Class and Gender in the Left Perspective', *Economic and Political Weekly*, Vol. XXI, No. 17, pp. WS-41–WS-52.

Sangari, Kumkum and **Sudesh Vaid** (eds), 1986, *Recasting Women: Essays in Colonial History*, New Delhi: Kali for Women.

Sangari, Kumkum, 1991, 'Response to Susie Tharu, *Women Writing in India*', *Journal of Arts and Ideas*, 20–21, p. 57, quoted from Rajan, *Real and Imagined Women*.

Saradamoni, X., 1982, 'Women's Status in Changing Agrarian Relations: A Kerala Experience', *Economic and Political Weekly*, Vol. XVII, No. 5, pp. 155–62.

———, 1985, *Women, Work and Society*, Calcutta: Indian Statistical Institute.

Saradamoni, K. and **Joan P. Mencher**, 1982, 'Muddy Feet, Dirty Hands: Rice Production and Female Agricultural Labour', *Economic and Political Weekly*, Vol. XVII, No. 52, pp. A-149–A-167.

Sen, Gita and **Chiranjib Sen**, 1985, 'Women's Domestic Work and Economic Activity', *Economic and Political Weekly*, Vol. XX, No. 17, pp. WS-49–WS-56.

Sen, L. Gina, 1988, 'Class and Gender in Work Time Allocation', *Economic and Political Weekly*, Vol. XXIII, No. 33, pp. 1702–6.

Sethi, Rajmohini, 1976, *Modernisation of Working Women in Developing Societies*, New Delhi: National Publishing House.

Shah, A.M., 1989, 'Parameters of Family Policy in India', *Economic and Political Weekly*, Vol. XXIV, No. 10, pp. 513–16.

Shiva, Vandana, 1988, *Staying Alive: Women, Ecology and Survival in India*, New Delhi: Kali for Women.

Singh, Renuka, 1990, *The Womb of Mind: A Sociological Exploration of the Status-Experience of Women in Delhi*, New Delhi: Vikas Publishing House.

Sircar, Manjusri Chaki, 1984, *Feminism in a Traditional Society: Women of the Manipur Valley*, New Delhi: Vikas Publishing House.

Sood, Rita, 1988, 'Changing Status of Women and Patterns of Adjustment: A Sociological Study in Delhi Metropolis', Ph.D. thesis, Jawaharlal Nehru University, New Delhi.

Stacey, Margaret, 1986, 'Gender and Stratification—One Central Issue or Two?', *in* Crompton, Rosemary and Michael Mann (eds), *Gender and Stratification*, Cambridge: Polity Press.

Standing, Hilary, 1985, 'Women's Employment and the Household: Some Findings from Calcutta', *Economic and Political Weekly*, Vol. XX, No. 17, pp. WS-23–WS-38.

Sundar, Pushpa, 1981, 'Characteristics of Female Employment: Implications of Research and Policy', *Economic and Political Weekly*, Vol. XVI, No. 19, pp. 863–71.

Swaminathan, Padmini, 1987, 'State and Subordination of Women', *Economic and Political Weekly*, Vol. XXIII, No. 44, pp. WS-34–WS-39.

Thorner, Alice and **Jyoti Ranadive**, 1985, 'Household as a First Stage in a Study of Urban Working Class Women', *Economic and Political Weekly*, Vol. XX, No. 17, pp. WS-9–WS-14.

Tinker, Irene (ed.), 1990, *Persistent Inequalities: Women and World Development*, New York: Oxford University Press.

Walby, Sylvia, 1986, 'Gender, Class and Stratification: Towards a New Approach', *in* Crompton, Rosemary and Michael Mann (eds), *Gender and Stratification*, Cambridge: Polity Press.

———, 1994, 'Towards a Theory of Patriarchy', *in The Polity Reader in Gender Studies*, pp. 22–28.

Seven

Social Mobility

Social mobility refers to the change in status of individual(s) or group(s) in relation to a given system of social stratification. This change manifests itself in two forms, either as a threat to the contiguous system and ultimately its displacement by the emergence of a new criterion of status-evaluation (vertical mobility or structural change) or through changes within the parameters of the system (horizontal mobility or positional change). Studies have highlighted positional change in the form of sanskritization and westernization (Marriott 1955; Rowe 1968; Silverberg 1968; Srinivas 1987) emphasizing mobility at the group level while undermining the other levels of social mobility, namely, family and individual (Sharma 1974). The concept of structural change has been emphasized in some recent studies (Bhadra 1989; Breman 1979, 1985; Harriss 1982; Omvedt 1982; Singh 1988). Latent structural changes emanating from cultural processes, and the consequences for further structural changes have remained largely unanalyzed. The cultural and structural approaches have not been adequately interrelated.

Both caste and class affect social mobility at different levels of the social structure (Sharma 1986: 40–76). Apart from these structural determinants, the Indian state has also played a crucial role in social mobility. Caste, class and state besides being the determinants of social mobility have also given cause for social tensions and movements. Besides these institutions, education in particular has contributed to and accelerated the pace of social change and mobility. The contribution of education is borne out by the fact that people from the depressed sections have been in the forefront of the anti-Brahmin and anti-feudal movements.

Approaches to Social Mobility

Broadly speaking, there are three approaches to the study of social mobility, namely, (*a*) the structural–historical, (*b*) the Marxist, and (*c*) the modernization/culturological. A. R. Kamat, Arvind N. Das and Pradhan H. Prasad emphasize on the structural–historical perspective, whereas Bhadra focuses on the relevance of the Marxist approach. Culturological (Indological) approach to social mobility is evident in several studies of the caste system. A. R. Kamat (1980: 1627–30; 1669–75) analyzes the displacement of the old urban-dominated political leadership by a new set of leaders drawn from the advanced rural elements, of which the Marathas (or the Maratha–Kunbis) are the dominant caste-cluster. This social transformation has been possible due to widespread political consciousness and democratization of politics. Besides this, the political leadership hailing from affluent sections in the rural areas has made it *peace* with the Indian big business. Land reforms and massive irrigation schemes have resulted in the embourgeoisiement of the tenants of the pre-independence period. Many of them are rich peasants or kulaks in the post-independence period. Abolition of landlordism has resulted in the exodus of the landed groups (Béteille 1966; Sharma 1974), particularly Brahmins, from rural to urban areas.

Kamat (ibid.: 1673) observes that despite such a structural social change and mobility in the traditional system, various contradictions and conflicts of interests persist. These are: (*a*) regional interests and conflicts between the regions of western Maharashtra, Vidarbha, and Marathwada, and between metropolitan Bombay and the rest of Maharashtra which is overwhelmingly rural; (*b*) between the affluent classes and the indigent sections of society; and (*c*) between the Brahmins and other advanced castes on the one hand and the middle and the lower castes on the other; between the middle caste-cluster of the Maratha–Kunbis and the non-Brahmin non-Maratha middle and lower castes; between the Scheduled Castes and the non-tribal society. The entire gamut of social change and mobility centers around caste, class and state (power). Social change could be gauged in terms of gain and loss by given groups of people, and by the persistence and emergence of tensions, contradictions and conflicts. Arvind Das (1984: 1616–19) describes the Bihar class–caste situation as *class in itself and caste for itself*. *Class for itself* has not emerged. More sharply this class–caste nexus in Bihar is focused by Pradhan H. Prasad (1979: 481–84). The middle castes have registered a stiff opposition to the upper castes and have further legitimized their meteoric rise in the class and power hierarchies leading to rapid decline of the persisting semi-feudalism. Caste-based mobilization by the middle castes in favour of the policy of reservation of jobs rather than diffusing the class contradictions has in fact sharpened and intensified them. Harriss (1982: 9) argues that despite differentiation of the peasantry due to the introduction of the new technology in agriculture in eastern North Arcot district of Tamil Nadu, capitalist transformation has remained at the *intermediate level* because of the blocking of this process by the ideological structures of caste and kinship which reinforce the existing structures of production and the power structure. Gough (1980: 337–64) also encounters a similar role played by caste and kinship and suggests the study of agrarian relations considering their historicity, people and socio-cultural milieu.

The culturological studies and the modernization paradigms are found inadequate to explain the inter-relations between *the mode of production, social classes and the state* (Bhadra 1989: 1–47). The perspective of modernization provides a very limited knowledge of the institutions of caste, joint family and village community. Bhadra (ibid.: 4) discusses,

> the contradictory aspects and effects of the metropolitan capitalist intervention in colonial India by focusing on social change in terms of dependent capitalist development

in colonial India along with three specific dimensions: the capitalist mode of production, the capitalist class structure and the capitalist state.

Obviously Bhadra's analysis incorporates elements of the classical Marxian approach in terms of the base–superstructure–analysis and the Gunder Frank's metropolis satellite hypothesis or the centre–periphery relations in the form of independent capitalism and emergence or creation of dependent capitalism or social formation.

A methodological and ideological bias in the studies of social stratification particularly towards *caste* is hinted at by Uma Chakravarti (1985: 356–60). She observes that study of Buddhist sources would show that instead of the hierarchy comprising the three castes (or Varnas), namely, Brahmins, Kshatriyas and Vaishyas, in the descending order, one might find a different order, namely, Kshatriyas, Brahmins and Gahapatis, and hence power, ritual and economy formed the order from top to bottom. This was perhaps due to social change and mobility emanating from anti-Brahmin movements during the period.

Caste, Class and Social Mobility

There are new castes (Béteille 1969) not really in the hereditary/ascriptive sense of the term caste, but in terms of the emergence of new status groups taking precedence over the traditional upper and middle castes. Social mobility in the caste system has been a historical fact, and every new macro-economic and political development has/had affected the caste system. These changes in the caste system may be seen in the decline of *jajmani* system and emergence of modern occupations (Sharma 1974), and in the form of new dominant groups and families, decline of untouchability and the pollution–purity principle (Kolenda 1986: 106–28). Kolenda (1984: 96–106) while agreeing with the view that there is a change *in* the caste system and not *of* the system, notes upward mobility throughout the history of the caste system. However, downward social mobility (Sharma 1980: 115–34) is largely a recent phenomenon particularly caused by state-sponsored structural changes like the abolition of landlordism, the introduction of the adult franchise and various other legislative measures.

Social mobility within the caste system is dependent upon the manner in which caste is perceived or on functioning of the caste system at a given point of time, in a given context. Dipankar Gupta (1986: 63–78) is of the view that castes are discrete categories, hence do not constitute continuous hierarchies. Mobilizations, movements and social mobility could accrue from both continuous hierarchies based on, for example, income, property, etc., and from discrete categories like caste, nation and language. At an empirical level both caste and class could be present together in mobilizations emanating from discrete categories as well as continuous hierarchies. A. M. Shah and I. P. Desai (1988) uphold the *principle of division* more than the principle of hierarchy. It is the divisions between the groups (castes) and within the castes which have created both horizontal and vertical status–distinctions throughout the history of the caste system.

Caste and class are both rural and urban phenomena, both are hierarchical, and are found interpenetrated into each other (Sharma 1984: 1–28). The very perception of caste has changed over the years since independence. Based on her restudy of a village in west Uttar Pradesh, Pauline Kolenda (1989: 1831–38) characterizes the changes in the caste system by 'micro-ideology and micro-utopia'. However, Franco, Chand and Sarvar (1989: 2601–12) argue that varna–ideology functions merely as a social practice.

Social mobility in the caste system is evident in the ever increasing violations of the traditional criteria of status, namely, hereditary occupations, *jajmani* obligations, observance of certain rituals and in the acceptance of modern secular occupations, education, migration and positions of power in formal political bodies. At times, competition between different castes accentuates into conflicts and violence.

I. P. Desai while commenting upon the report of the Mandal Commission (1978–80) believes that caste cannot be taken as a unit for identifying backwardness (1984: 1106–16). Desai recognizes type of society, role of political power and social mobility movements as significant factors to understand social and educational backwardness, but he does not consider social backwardness as an offshoot of the ascribed status of a community/collectivity. Today, contractual relationship and performance matter a lot in the occupational field. Caste plays a minor role in it. Desai remarks that our minds are possessed by caste. The expressions and articulations of caste have always varied between and within the castes, between different regions and even in the same village. Homo hierarchicus is a myth. Ghanshyam Shah (1985: 132–36) contradicts Desai's argument regarding legitimization of caste by the state and the breakdown of the traditional caste system by the counter-view that caste consciousness in the form of 'we-ness' among the members of castes persists, and the state is not prepared to implement the secular aims incorporated in the Constitution.

Immobility generates contradictions and tensions. These in turn bring about social mobility. The fractions of the depressed castes who are benefited by education and employment demand displacement of the traditional oppressive system and in turn they become a target of the hostility and violence of the entrenched upper castes (Bose 1981: 713–16). Social mobility of the Scheduled Castes in Gujarat was not taken kindly by the upper castes. Bose (ibid.: 713) observes that social mobility can have two consequences on the stability of the structure: (*a*) stabilizing influence on the society and polity; and (*b*) disruptive of social stability. In the first case available opportunity for social mobility is avoided, and in the second case it is monopolized by the upper castes with a view to keep the lower castes at a distance from the positions of prestige and power. I. P. Desai (1981: 819–23) pleads that in today's situation the system of reservation has therefore become a weapon in the hands of the various deprived groups in their struggle against socially entrenched upper caste and class interests. Desai thought of a 'future society without caste' (Baxi 1985: 426–28).

Today social mobility has been possible by way of: (*a*) reservations for the SCs, STs and OBCs, (*b*) competition between these specially advantaged groups, and between them and the upper and the middle castes/classes, and (*c*) seeking new channels of status and power in the changed situation by the traditionally entrenched groups, families and individuals.

Structural variation in economic activity may transform caste consciousness into class consciousness. T. M. Thomas Isaac (1985: PE-5–PE-18) highlights that the coir workers of Alleppey district in Kerala despite the influence of the SNDP Yogam and caste ethnocentrism, decisively reflected class organization replacing the caste organization as the primary claimant of the workers' allegiance (see also Caplan 1980: 213–38; Chandrasekhar 1985; Fernandes 1983). Another way to discard caste as a system of oppressive social stratification was found in religious conversions to Christianity. Underlying all these channels of social mobility have mainly been exploitation, dehumanization and oppressive milieu dominated by the upper and upper middle castes.

Scheduled Castes, Scheduled Tribes and the Other Backward Classes and Social Mobility

The most important testimony of social mobility can be found in the challenge thrown by the SCs, STs and OBCs to the dominance of the upper castes and classes particularly after independence. It is not just a threat, but its actualization is evident in the displacement of the upper strata from their traditional positions of power and dominance and in the transformation of tribal society, emergence of new agrarian stratification, education, migration, employment and new power blocs.

A. R. Kamat (1980: 1279–84) reports that due to education among SCs and STs changes have occurred: (*a*) within the segment of SCs and STs; (*b*) in the wider caste Hindu society; and (*c*) in the interrelations between caste Hindu society and the SC/ST segment. The problem of untouchability and caste discrimination in the case of SCs, and the problem of transition from tribal isolation and backwardness to assimilation into and greater interaction with the rest of the Indian society are discussed by Kamat as definite indicators of social change and mobility. The processes of the demystification of the Brahminic hegemony and egalitarianism have greatly contributed to social mobility among the SCs and STs. New patterns of social stratification due to education and changed agrarian relations have emerged among the STs (Bose 1981: 191–96; Singh 1978: 1221–32; Shah 1986: 149–83).

A comparative study of the Bharuch and Panch Mahal districts in Gujarat (Shah ibid.) reveals that tribal society is neither homogeneous nor egalitarian. People are divided in terms of their own economic interests, mainly *land*. Rich, middle and poor peasants constitute the system of social stratification. Recent developments in the tribal society have eroded traditional institutions. The educated *adivasis* have come closer to the educated *patidars*. However, education and other developments have created new status–distinctions. Land reforms, conversion to Christianity and social movements during the British period considerably altered the hierarchical character of the rural and tribal populace. Constitutional safeguards and the policy of reservation in jobs, education and legislatures, developmental schemes, and check on land-alienation (Sachchidananda 1990: 278–317; Singh: 1982) have brought about structural, cultural and social transformation among the tribes of middle India in the post-independence era.

Social change and mobility among the tribes are a result of their encounters with Christianity and Hinduism in the form of conversion and sanskritization, respectively, and also because of resistance to these socio-cultural forces. Structural change has been caused due to a strong reaction to the interference of the colonial rulers, Hindu zamindars and money-lenders in the past. The nature of encounters has changed today in tribal Bihar. The confrontation is primarily with the north Bihar's middle classes and white-collar populace who are deeply entrenched in the Jharkhand region and who control lucrative jobs and resources, while tribal confrontation with the Punjabi and Marwari traders and industrialists is dormant. Today, tribal discomfort is caused by two other sectors: the tribal elite and the Indian State. Grievances against these two have been articulated in the outbursts of various organizations and groups involved in the Jharkhand movement (see Sengupta 1982; Sharma 1976: 37–43; 1990: 368–81; Weiner 1978: 145–215).

The tribals were forced by the colonial rulers to work as both tenants and labourers. This change led to the process of tribal peasantization in the Thane district (Upadhyaya 1980: A-134–A-146). Singh (1982: 1318–25; 1376–84) reports that 'the major thrust of change has been from tribes into peasants' followed by a rapid growth of urban population and industrialization in tribal areas with a large chunk of immigrants. Alienation of land or displacement due to these economic changes in the tribal areas are reflected in the tribal social stratification. A similar trend of transformation of tribal peasantry to plantation workforce from 1850s to 1947 existed in north-east India (Bhadra and Mondal 1991; Dasgupta 1986: PE-10).

The Scheduled Castes are changing though the process of change is complex, multi-layered and multi-dimensional creating new status distinctions. Initially the lower castes imitated the higher castes in non-economic spheres of social life. Following a considerable degree of socio-political awareness they refused to follow the dictates of their patrons and demanded freedom from the cruel control of the upper caste/class landowners and money-lenders. Anti-upper caste and reform movements by the Scheduled Castes symbolize their aspirations for higher status as well as desire to overthrow the existing system.

Uma Ramaswamy (1984: 1214–17) asks: 'What avenues of mobility are realistically open to the Scheduled Castes?' The policy of protective discrimination has helped some people among the Scheduled Castes, but a large number of them have had to fend for themselves. One of the indicators of social mobility is the changing/unchanging position of the Scheduled Castes over a period of time in agriculture and employment in government departments, public sector undertakings and educational institutions. Data on agriculture and employment from 1961 to 1981 indicates that in agriculture the SCs are stagnating whereas in employment in government and public sector undertakings they have made notable strides. The growth of literacy and the emergence of a small stratum of educated elite (Ramaswamy 1985: 1523–28) is a testimony of social mobility among the Scheduled Castes of Andhra Pradesh.

The Harijan elite have become a distinct entity in relation to the Harijan masses as well as non-Harijan elite in the caste society. Several studies by J. Michael Mahar (1972), Michael Moffat (1979), Sachchidananda (1977), G. Narayan (1978: 1603–8), Nandu Ram (1989) indicate toward limited and uneven impact of the reservation policy. Oliver Mendelsohn's study (1986: 501–9) posits that those who had been better off economically for a generation or two alone could make a dent in politics. The policy of reservation has therefore become an added factor and in fact the sole criterion for their rise in the political arena. However, due to favourable historicity of a select few the reservation policy has helped them alone.

Indian society is characterized by economic inequalities as well as by caste privileges and disabilities. K. C. Alexander (1989: 363–64) writes: 'An essential feature of the caste hierarchy is the social separation among castes, which divides economically homogeneous classes, particularly the lower classes, along caste lines.' Caste being the primary basis of identity, it remains a major source of mobilization. Upper-caste agricultural labourers often look at the Scheduled Castes with humiliating expressions. The SC labourers observe caste hierarchy among their sub-castes. Atrocities against Harijans are also an offshoot of such a divide among the Scheduled Castes. The Jats and Yadavas in Uttar Pradesh adopted an exclusively aggressive posture against the Dalits (Hasan 1989: 133–203) when the oppressed Harijan castes showed their reluctance to work as agricultural workers on their farms. Caste-based mobilization (Alexander 1989: 370–79) was the only answer to the Brahminical order in Kerala and Tamil Nadu. Several unions of agricultural labourers with pre-eminence of the labourers hailing from the Scheduled Castes were formed in these two southern states.

An approving statement of the reservation policy by G. Ram Reddy (1989: 298–302) lists compensation for the past inequalities, participation in the politico-administrative system and government employment as the net benefits for the SCs. In Andhra Pradesh in 1981, 14.5 per cent of jobs went to the SCs, 2 per cent to the STs and 28.6 per cent to the backward castes. Today the new elite consist of the SC, ST and the backward caste segments along with the upper caste/class elite in an absolutely visible form. The present situation is characterized by James Manor (1989: 356–59) as 'divisions in dominance'. Thus power is a relative phenomenon and not an absolute entity.

Ghanshyam Shah (1990: 59–114) reports that about 11 per cent of the total class III jobs are held by the SCs in Gujarat. There are more than 40,000 clerks and typists in Gujarat from among the SCs and STs. For the increasing unemployed among the educated upper and middle castes men and women, the reservation policy for the SCs and STs is being blamed particularly since the beginnings of eighties. The anti-reservation agitation of 1985 in Gujarat took a toll of more than 200 lives. Caste-based organizations have also flourished due to the conflicts between the upper/middle castes and the lower castes.

The beneficiaries of development are mainly the upper stratum of the OBCs. The rich and the middle peasants have been on the rise simply because they have access to modern benefits accruing to the countryside (Blair 1980: 64–74; Prasad 1980: 215–19). It may be inferred that in the first two decades after independence the major beneficiary groups consolidated their economic gains, and from the late sixties began their effective entry into electoral politics. They took nearly a decade to put it to the wider political forces that they could not be ignored or sidelined because numerically they were a formidable segment and economically they stood on a sound footing. Since the late 1970s the OBCs have become a political force which no political party could afford to undermine and hence had to make adjustments of a varying nature with the leadership of the OBCs.

In the context of change in the agrarian stratification, K. L. Sharma (1983: 1796) posits three questions: (*a*) whether the abolition of landlordism has resulted in the transfer of landholdings from one group to another?, (*b*), whether technological devices in agriculture, in particular, have helped in further consolidating the traditional inequalities or have reduced them?, and (*c*) whether political power has shifted from one group of people to another irrespective of the change in the pattern of land-ownership?

A redistribution of land and power has not taken place, but considerable change has occurred in the traditional arrangements of society. Thus sharecroppers and agricultural labourers of yesteryears have become after independence high, middle and low peasants without correspondingly sanskritizing their cultural modes of living as a pre-requisite to this basic economic transformation. However, economic change and consolidation of its gains have significant socio-cultural consequences affecting life-styles, cultural patterns, education, etc. In-migration, out-migration and income from any other source including employment in the Middle East (Gulati 1983: 2217–26) would affect family including marital status, dowry, family networks, living standards, etc.

The emergence of agrarian classes like rich, middle and poor peasants and agricultural labourers from the traditional rural class structure comprising zamindars, *jagirdars*, *ryots* and *tenants* is a significant development after independence (Bose 1984; Xaxa 1980). The change in agrarian relations has altered the nature of caste relations and family ties as the middle castes (consisting of *ryots* and major tenantry) now comprise the upper echleons of the agrarian hierarchy sidetracking the ex-landlords and other previously privileged groups.

Carol Upadhya (1988: 1376–82; 1433–42) analyzes the manner in which a new class of businessmen has arisen from the class of capitalist farmers in coastal Andhra Pradesh. The main factors for the rise of this new class are: (*a*) the development of a productive and commercialized agrarian economy, (*b*) the emergence of a rich peasant class, (*c*) the integration of town and countryside, (*d*) education among the rural elite, (*e*) the politicization of caste identity, and more recently, (*f*) the green revolution and (*g*) land reforms. The capitalist farmers have sought to invest in more profitable enterprises in urban areas. In this way, the rural capitalist class and elite have transformed themselves into urban entrepreneurs. New patterns of rural–urban connections, flow of resources from rural to urban and occupational mobility are some of the obvious social consequences of such an economic diversification. The capitalist farmers-turned-businessmen belong to several castes, for whom agriculture and not trade was traditional occupation. They belong to the class of the landed cultivators. Class rather than caste was the basis of social mobility implying change from agriculture to entrepreneurship and the form of migration from rural to urban area. The emergence of the new business class is not only because of the economic forces, but social, political and cultural processes, particularly the social and political history of the region and of the dominant land-owning castes (Omvedt 1981: A-140–A-159) have also played an important role.

The backward castes are traditionally divided into (*a*) the agricultural castes, and (*b*) the service (functionary) and artisan castes. The agricultural or peasant castes have fought for land reforms and technological advances like the green revolution, and the benefits derived have resulted in their upward social mobility in the economic field in the first instance, and in the political sphere later on. The functionary and artisan castes have not only been deprived of the economic benefits, they also lost their traditional callings in this process of change, and political patronage in the form of reservation of jobs has also eluded them because the upper castes have obstructed the filtering of benefits.

In a recent study (Singh 1988) the elite approach has been preferred than the class approach to the study of rural society in eastern Uttar Pradesh. Singh poses three questions: (*a*) What was/is the nature of social hierarchy in the north Indian countryside? (*b*) In what ways does social hierarchy overlap with the hierarchies of land and power? (*c*) What is the normative basis of the agrarian social structure? The emerging elites, partly displacing the established elites, are the new entrants and they are the beneficiaries of certain social, political and agrarian reforms. The electoral process, open competition and achievement–ideal are the main bases of the positions which they hold under the new dispensation. They are not necessarily from the upper castes, aristocratic and priestly families.

Jan Breman (1985: 191–259) lists factors which stimulate mobility and also those which retard it thereby resulting into immobility. Out-migration is taken as the main yardstick of social mobility. The popular view regarding social mobility is that rural migration occurs because of urbanization and this results in socio-economic development, and finally rural development takes place. Aspirations for social climbing are the basis of such a premise but Breman does not subscribe to this hypothesis. The villagers are driven, not by a higher level of aspiration than their non-migrating fellow villagers, but by economic necessity. However, it is a fact that people have constant desire for higher status and prestige particularly by distancing from manual work (Navlakha 1989: 78; Singh 1985). Inter-generational differences in occupations indicate such a pattern of social mobility.

Education and Social Mobility

Though education cannot be the sole criterion of social change and mobility, in certain situations it can contribute to the social awakening among people (may be a small section) who may be 'harbingers of social change' (Kamat 1982: 1327–44). Education creates a divide between the educated and the uneducated or semi-literate people. This divide makes a society *unequal*. The educated become a class by itself as they have an access to white-collar jobs and channels of upward social mobility. Educated middle class consists of upper and middle caste clusters in the form of managers, teachers, doctors, engineers, clerks, administrators, etc. André Béteille refers to such status groups as new castes.

Krishna Kumar (1985: 1280–84) rightly poses the question about the role of education: reproduction or change? Because education reproduces elites by circumventing the opportunities to education and subsequently to the positions of high status and power. Early selection for a coveted school education itself determines all other opportunities in life. The rural middle castes which have gained access to political and economic dominance are in a position to take advantage of education for further upward social mobility (Desai 1984; Sivakumar 1982). These middle castes comprise the upper stratum of the backward castes, and have even become volatile in their demand for reservation of jobs (Béteille 1981).

Education is faced with the dilemma of equity vs elitism, and it produces both for different sections of society at different points of time in their life-histories. Participation of different sections of people in education is also unequal, and this inequality is reflected at different levels, in types of schools and colleges and in the streams of education (Jayaram 1987; Singh 1983). Jayaram believes that *formal* equity is fallacious in conception as well as unjust in reality. Nirmal Singh (1983) in his study of seven colleges in Kanpur finds a siege of public education by private control. Despite this the SCs in particular have shown upward social mobility (Chitnis 1981: 12–72) through the policy of protective discrimination in the field of education.

Social Movements and Social Mobility

Social movements are specific goal-oriented plans of fast actions with involvement of a specific section(s) of society. When the people are oppressed, suppressed and exploited, they organize themselves by launching protest movements. Likewise, people organize reform movements to discard their dysfunctional and obsolete activities, to adopt or imitate the life-styles and cultural ethos which would accord them higher status in the society. Based on the *socio-economic characteristics* and the *issues* involved, Ghanshyam Shah classifies social movements (1990: 27–28) into eight categories comprising the peasants, tribals, Dalits, backward castes, women, students, middle classes and industrial working class clearly indicating the efforts by each of these groups, through their respective movements, to improve their position in the wider society.

Several studies of peasant movements indicate that peasants are not docile and caste and religion do not necessarily blur their identity as peasants and their militancy to fight their oppressors. Consciousness among the peasants has been the basis of their success in several struggles (Desai 1981: 1986). But the peasant movements like Bharatiya Kisan Union (BKU) and Shetkari Sanghathan, and the movements involving women, students, industrial workers and middle classes have articulated the demand of these sections of society. They do not suffer the agony arising out of the structurally determined forces like colonialism, feudalism, caste and religion as inflicted upon the SCs, STs, OBCs. Movements related to these sections do not insist upon contingent demands because their problems have persisted over a long time.

The tribals in India have derived the advantages of the secular sources of status like education, white-collar jobs, land reforms and adult franchise. But the process of sanskritization which started in the colonial period still persists in various forms (Singh 1985: 282–83). The movements for political autonomy, agrarian and forest-based movements and cultural movements based on script and language (ibid.: 268–88; 1982) have immensely contributed to social change and mobility among the tribes of the middle India. The question of aspiration for higher status is not so important for the tribals as it is the restoration of what was the good in their life which they have lost due to onslaught of colonialism and other external influences. To compensate for the loss and to keep up pace with the changing tide, tribals are now having movements for structural as well as cultural transformation of their society and culture.

In general the magnitude of culturological transformation has dwindled among the peasants. A large number of studies of peasant movements stress upon the mobilization of peasantry based on caste, class, affiliation with political parties, organizational support (Alexander 1981; Desai 1986; Dhanagare 1983; Gupta 1988: 2688–96; Pathy 1984; Ram 1986; Rao 1979; Sen 1982; Sharma 1986; Surana 1983). There are also protest and reform movements against the state and its policies (Rao 1979; Shah 1977) having bearing upon mobilization around caste, class and some other allied bases.

State and Social Mobility

The State in India has effected major changes in the social formation of society through its policy of protective discrimination, land reforms, adult franchise, panchayat raj, and planning and development. Since the entrenched sections of society have adversely been affected by some of these structural developments, tensions between the upper and the lower castes, landlords and tenants, rich and poor, possessed and deprived, powerful and weak have emerged leading to resistance, reconciliation and rearrangements. A sort of a struggle has been going on during the past few decades since independence between the traditionally entrenched groups and families, and the newly upwardly mobile sections from among the middle and the lower castes and tribal groups.

Land reforms, abolition of feudalism and green revolution have created social tensions and have also brought about social mobility (see Barik 1988; Breman 1985; Lal 1982; Rosin 1987; R. A. P. Singh 1985; Singh 1986). As mentioned earlier the abolition of feudalism proletarianized and even pauperized some sections of the previously landed families and enriched some who had been deprived of status and power. Such a structural mobility has weakened the traditional arrangements like the *jajmani* system and inter-caste relations. The upwardly mobile groups and families soon started claiming their share in education, white-collar jobs and political power at different levels. Elections held in 1994 for six state assemblies reinforce the demand of the erstwhile weaker sections for status and power. The middle and lower castes have by way of their mobilization come to the centre-stage in the states of Bihar, Uttar Pradesh and Karnataka.

It is evident that the state-sponsored programmes have made caste weak. It is also quite obvious that class has lost its haziness. To promote further its interests a class leans heavily on caste for mobilization, and as such caste has become weak and strong both simultaneously due to implementation of some of the provisions provided in the Indian Constitution. Thus it shows both the tendencies in the context of electoral politics, migration and education. A new form of casteism (Breman 1985: 361–401) has also emerged due to such a process of change.

Political power creates its own legitimacy, and the latter is derived from different class reference groups and different balance of class forces by power-seekers (Petras 1989: 1955–58). Power revolves around class interests and control over the state. A class-view of Indian society refers to two ruling classes: (*a*) having base in agriculture, and (*b*) with base in large industry (Rudra 1989: 142–50; Bardhan 1984). Rudra observes that the *intelligentsia* has become a member of the ruling coalition by co-option rather than through any struggle for power like the agrarian and industrial classes. The intelligentsia is a product of social mobility in their respective castes and families over a period of few generations. According to Rudra, all the white-collar workers in the organized section, all office workers in administrative services, all teachers, doctors and nurses, lawyers and judges, engineers and architects, writers, journalists, artists and other skilled workers, and professionals, politicians, trade union leaders, etc., constitute the intelligentsia.

There is no uniform pattern of social mobility in terms of caste, class and power. A study of *panchayat* leaders in a West Bengal district (Lieten 1988: 2069–73) indicates that a new type of leadership has come to dominate at the lower levels in the system of political devolution. Poor peasants and agricultural labourers (also the SCs and STs) have come to the forefront of local politics. But another study of the *Zila Parishad* presidents in Karnataka suggests that the caste composition of the local government leadership does not seem to have significantly changed (Ray and Kumpatha 1987: 1825–30). The Lingayats and the Vokkaligas, the two dominant land-owning castes, dominate the rural political scene even now as they did in the past.

A third pattern emerges from Rajendra Singh's study of the Basti district in Uttar Pradesh. Ownership of *land* and support of *people* (numerical strength of caste[s]) together have made it smooth for the middle peasant-castes to reach the corridors of power. Since the upper castes have lost control over land and were never numerically preponderant, they could not continue with their traditional supremacy in the changed circumstances in the post-independence era. These traditionally dominant castes/classes have become jealous of the new entrants from the traditionally low castes (Shah 1987: AN-155–AN-172). In Gujarat anti-reservation agitations have gained ground in the past because of the displacement of the upper/middle caste/class people from the positions of power. The inability to cope with the forces of social change and mobility in today's context has forced the upper castes to withdraw from contests for positions of power and authority.

Thus, the State in India has brought about economic and political changes having consequences for social mobility eliminating some old persisting tensions and creating some new ones. Undifferentiated mechanisms of transformation to wipe out uneven structures of inequality have produced differential consequences, hence new and differential forms of inequality have emerged. Today, there are definite indications of a change in the traditional arrangements and of the emergence of a new system of social stratification.

References

Alexander, K.C., 1981, *Peasant Organisations in South India*, New Delhi: Indian Social Institute.

———, 1989, 'Caste Mobilization and Class Consciousness: The Emergence of Agrarian Movements in Kerala and Tamil Nadu', *in* Frankel, F.R. and M. S. A. Rao (eds), *Dominance and State Power in Modern India: Decline of a Social Order, Vol. I*, Delhi: Oxford University Press, pp. 362–414.

Bardhan, Pranab, 1984, *Land, Labour and Rural Poverty: Essays in Development Economics*, New York: Columbia University Press.

Barik, Bishnu C., 1988, *Class Formation and Peasantry*, Jaipur: Rawat Publications.

Baxi, Upendra, 1985, 'Caste, class and reservation', *Economic and Political Weekly*, Vol. XX, No. 10, pp. 426–28.

Béteille, André, 1966, *Caste, Class and Power*, Bombay: Oxford University Press.

——— (ed.), 1969, *Social Inequality*, Penguin Books.

———, 1981, *The Backward Classes and the New Social Order*, Bombay: Oxford University Press.

Bhadra, Bipul Kumar, 1989, *The Mode of Production, Social Classes and the State*, Jaipur: Rawat Publications.

Bhadra, R.K. and **S. R. Mondal** (eds), 1991, *Stratification, Hierarchy and Ethnicity in North-East India*, Delhi: Daya Publishing House.

Blair, Harry W., 1980, 'Rising Kulaks and Backward Classes in Bihar: Social Change in the Late 1970s', *Economic and Political Weekly*, Vol. XV, No. 2, pp. 64–74.

Bose, P.K., 1981, 'Stratification among tribals in Gujarat', *Economic and Political Weekly*, Vol. XVI, No. 6, pp. 191–96.

———, 1984, 'Peasant production and capitalist enterprise', *Economic and Political Weekly*, Vol. XIX, No. 40, pp. 1742–44.

Breman, Jan, 1979, *Patronage and Exploitation: Changing Agrarian Relations in South Gujarat*, New Delhi: Manohar Publications.

———, 1985, *Of Peasants, Migrants and Paupers: Rural Labour Circulation and Capitalist Production in West India*, Delhi: Oxford University Press.

Caplan, Lionel, 1980, 'Caste and Castelessness among the South Indian Christians', *Contributions to Indian Sociology* (NS), Vol. 14, No. 2, pp. 213–38.

Chakravarti, Uma, 1985, 'Towards a historical sociology of stratification in ancient India: Evidence from Buddhist sources', *Economic and Political Weekly*, Vol. XX, No. 9, pp. 355–60.

Chandrashekhar, S., 1985, *Dimensions of Socio-Political Change in Mysore, 1918–1940*, New Delhi: Ashish Publishing House.

Chitnis, S., 1981, *A Long Way to Go...*, New Delhi: Allied Publishers.

Das, Arvind N., 1984, 'Class in Itself, Caste for Itself: Social Articulation in Bihar', *Economic and Political Weekly*, Vol. XIX, No. 37, pp. 1616–19.

Dasgupta, Ranjit, 1986, 'From peasants and tribesmen to plantation workers', *Economic and Political Weekly*, Vol. XXI, No. 4.

Desai, A.R., 1981, 'Relevance of the Marxist approach to the study of Indian society', *Sociological Bulletin*, Vol. 30, No. 1, pp. 1–20.

Desai, A.R., 1984, 'G. S. Ghurye', *Economic and Political Weekly*, Vol. XIX, No. 1, pp.

————— (ed.), 1986, *Violation of Democratic Rights in India, Vol. I*, Bombay: Popular Prakashan.

Desai, I.P., 1981, 'Anti-reservation Agitation and Structure of Gujarat Society', *Economic and Political Weekly*, Vol. XVI, No. 18, pp. 819–23.

—————, 1984, 'Western Educated Elites and Social Change in India', *Economic and Political Weekly*, Vol. XIX, No. 15, pp. 1106–16.

Dhanagare, D.N., 1983, *Peasant Movement in India 1920–1950*, Delhi: Oxford University Press.

Fernandes, Walter, 1983, *Caste and Conversion Movements in India: Religion and Human Rights*, New Delhi: Indian Social Institute.

Franco, F., Sherry Chand and **V. Sarvar**, 1989, 'Ideology as Social Practice: The Functioning of Varna', *Economic and Political Weekly*, Vol. XXIV, No. 47, pp. 2601–12.

Gough, E. Kathleen, 1980, 'Modes of production in southern India', *Economic and Political Weekly* (AN), Vol. XV, Nos. 5, 6 & 7, pp. 227–64.

Gulati, Leela, 1983, 'Male Migration to Middle East and the Impact on the Family: Some Evidence from Kerala', *Economic and Political Weekly*, Vol. XVIII, Nos. 52 and 53, pp. 2217–26.

Gupta, Dipankar, 1986, 'Continuous Hierarchies and Discrete Castes: Social Mobilization among Peasants', *in* Sharma, K.L. (ed.), *Social Stratification in India*, Delhi: Manohar Publications, pp. 63–78.

—————, 1988, 'Country-Town Nexus and Agrarian Mobilisation: Bharatiya Kisan Union as an Instance', *Economic and Political Weekly*, Vol. XXIII, No. 51, pp. 2688–96.

Harriss, John, 1982, *Capitalism and Peasant Farming: Agrarian Structure and Ideology in Northern Tamil Nadu*, Delhi: Oxford University Press.

Hasan, Zoya, 1989, 'Power and Mobilization: Patterns of Resilience and Change in Uttar Pradesh Politics', *in* Frankel, F.R. and M. S. A. Rao (eds), *Dominance and State Power in Modern India: Decline of a Social Order, Vol. I*, Delhi: Oxford University Press, pp. 133–203.

Isaac, T.M. Thomas, 1985, 'From Caste Consciousness to Class Consciousness: Alleppey Coir Workers during Inter-war Period', *Economic and Political Weekly*, Vol. XX, No. 4, pp. PE-5–PE-18.

Jayaram, N., 1987, *Higher Education and Status Retention*, New Delhi: Mittal Publications.

Kamat, A.R., 1980, 'Politico-economic development in Maharashtra: A review of the post-independence period', *Economic and Political Weekly*, Vol. XV, No. 39, pp. 1627–30, and No. 40, pp. 1669–75.

—————, 1982, 'Education and Social Change: A Conceptual Framework', *Economic and Political Weekly*, Vol. XVII, No. 31, pp. 1327–44.

Kolenda, P., 1984, *Caste in Contemporary India: Beyond Organic Solidarity*, Jaipur: Rawat Publications.

—————, 1986, 'Caste in India since independence', *in* Basu, Dilip K. and Richard Sisson (eds), *Social and Economic Development in India, A Reassessment*, New Delhi. Sage Publications, pp. 106–28.

Kolenda, P., 1989, 'Micro-ideology and Micro-utopia in Khalapur: Changes in the discourse on caste over thirty years', *Economic and Political Weekly*, Vol. XXIV, No. 32, pp. 1831–38.

Kumar, Krishna, 1985, 'Reproduction or change: Education and elite in India', *Economic and Political Weekly*, Vol. XX, No. 30, pp. 1280–84.

Lal, S.K. (ed.), 1982, *Sociological Perspectives of Land Reforms*, New Delhi: Agricole Pub. Academy.

Lieten, G.K., 1988, 'Panchayat leaders in a West Bengal district', *Economic and Political Weekly*, Vol. XXIII, No. 40, pp. 2069–73.

Mahar, J.M., 1972, *The Untouchables in Contemporary India*, Tuscon: University of Arizona Press.

Manor, James, 1989, 'Karnataka: Caste, class, dominance and politics in a cohesive society', *in* Frankel, F.R. and M. S. A. Rao (eds), *Dominance and State Power in Modern India: Decline of a Social Order*, Vol. I, Delhi: Oxford University Press, pp. 322–61.

Marriott, M. (ed.), 1955, *Village India: Studies in the Little Community*, Chicago: Chicago University Press.

Mendelsohn, Oliver, 1986, 'A Harijan elite? The lives of some untouchable politicians', *Economic and Political Weekly*, Vol. XXI, No. 12, pp. 501–9.

Moffatt, Michael, 1979, *An Untouchable Community in South India: Structure and Consensus*, Princeton: Princeton University Press.

Narayan, G., 1978, 'Social background of Scheduled Caste Lok Sabha members, 1962–71', *Economic and Political Weekly*, Vol. XIII, No. 14, pp. 1603–8.

Navlakha, Suren, 1989, *Elite and Social Change: A Study of Elite Formation in India*, New Delhi: Sage Publications.

Omvedt, Gail, 1981, 'Capitalist agriculture and rural classes in India', *Economic and Political Weekly*, Vol. XVI, No. 51, pp. A-140–A-159.

—— (ed.), 1982, *Land, Caste and Politics in India*, Delhi: Authors Guild Publications.

Pathy, Jaganath, 1984, *Tribal Peasantry: Dynamics of Development*, New Delhi: Inter-India Publications.

Petras, James, 1989, 'Class politics, state power and legitimacy', *Economic and Political Weekly*, Vol. XXIV, No. 34, pp. 1955–58.

Prasad, Pradhan H., 1979, 'Caste and Class in Bihar', *Economic and Political Weekly* (AN), Vol. XIV, Nos. 7 & 8, pp. 481–84.

——, 1980, 'Rising middle peasantry in north India', *Economic and Political Weekly*, Vol. XV, No. 4, pp. 215–19.

Ram, Nandu, 1989, *Mobile Scheduled Castes: Rise of a Middle Class*, Delhi: Hindustan Publishing Corporation.

Ram, Pema, 1986, *Agrarian Movement in Rajasthan*, Jaipur: Panchsheel Prakashan.

Ramaswamy, Uma, 1984, 'Preference and Progress: The Scheduled Castes', *Economic and Political Weekly*, Vol. XIX, No. 30, pp. 1214–17.

Rao, M.S.A., 1979, 'Sociology in the 1980s', *Economic and Political Weekly*, Vol. XIV, No. 44, pp. 1810–15.

——, 1985, 'Education and Inequality', *Economic and Political Weekly*, Vol. XX, No. 36, pp. 1523–28.

Ray, Amal and **Jayalakshmi Kumpatla**, 1979, *Social Movement and Social Transformation*, Delhi: Macmillan Co.

Ray, Amal and **Jayalakshmi Kumpatla**, 1987, 'Zila Parishad Presidents in Karnataka', *Economic and Political Weekly*, Vol. XXII, Nos. 42 & 43, pp. 1825–30.

Reddy, G. Ram, 1989, 'The Politics of Accommodation: Caste, Class and Dominance in Andhra Pradesh', *in* Frankel, F.R. and M. S. A. Rao (eds), *Dominance and State Power in Modern India: Decline of a Social Order, Vol. I*, Delhi: Oxford University Press, pp. 265–321.

Rosin, R. Thomas, 1987, *Land Reform and Agrarian Change*, Jaipur: Rawat Publications.

Rowe, William L., 1968, 'The New Chauhans: A Caste Mobility Movement in North India', *in* Silberberg, James (ed.), *Social Mobility in the Caste System in India*, The Hague: Mouton, pp. 66–77.

Rudra, A., 1989, 'Emergence of the Intelligentsia as a Ruling Class in India', *Economic and Political Weekly*, Vol. XXIV, No. 3, pp. 142–50.

Sachchidanand, 1977, *The Harijan Elite*, Faridabad: Thomson Press.

———, 1990, 'Patterns of Politico-economic Change among Tribals in Middle India', *in* Frankel, F.R. and M. S. A. Rao (eds), *Dominance and State Power in Modern India, Vol. II*, Delhi: Oxford University Press, pp. 278–315.

Sen, Sunil (ed.), 1982, *Peasant Movements in India*, New Delhi: K. P. Bagchi and Company.

Sengupta, Nirmal (ed.), 1982, *Fourth World Dynamics: Jharkhand*, Delhi: Delhi Authors Guild.

Shah, A.M. and **I. P. Desai** (eds), 1988, *Division and Hierarchy: An Overview of Caste in Gujarat*, Delhi: Hindustan Publishing Corporation.

Shah, Ghanshyam, 1977, *Protest Movements in Two Indian States*, New Delhi: Ajanta Publications.

———, 1985, 'Caste, Class and Reservation', *Economic and Political Weekly*, Vol. XX, No. 3, pp. 132–36.

———, 1986, 'Stratification among the Scheduled Tribes in the Bharuch and Panch Mahals districts of Gujarat', *in* Malik, S.C. (ed.), *Determinants of Social Status in India*, Delhi: Motilal Banarsidas.

———, 1987, 'Middle Class Politics: Case of Anti-reservation Agitation in Gujarat', *Economic and Political Weekly*, Vol. XXII, Nos. 19, 20 & 21 (AN), pp. 155–72.

———, 1990, 'Caste Sentiments, Class Formation and Dominance in Gujarat', *in* Frankel, F.R. and M. S. A. Rao (eds), *Dominance and State Power in Modern India: Decline of a Social Order, Vol. II*, Delhi: Oxford University Press, pp. 59–114.

———, 1990, *Social Movements in India—A Review of the Literature*, New Delhi: Sage Publications.

Sharma, K.L., 1974, *The Changing Rural Stratification System*, New Delhi: Orient Longman.

———, 1976, 'Jharkhand Movement in Bihar', *Economic and Political Weekly*, Vol. XI, No. 1, pp. 37–43.

———, 1980, *Essays on Social Stratification*, Jaipur: Rawat Publications, pp. 115–34.

———, 1983, 'Agrarian Stratification: Old Issues, New Explanations and New Issues, Old Explanations', *Economic and Political Weekly*, Vol. XVIII, Nos. 42, 43, pp. 1796–1802; pp. 1851–55.

Sharma, K.L., 1984, *Sociology of Law and Legal Profession*, Jaipur, Rawat Publications.

———, 1986, *Caste, Class and Social Movements*, Jaipur: Rawat Publications, pp. 40–76.

———, 1990, 'Jharkhand Movement: The Questions of Identity and Sub-nationality', *Social Action*, pp. 368–81.

Silverberg, James (ed.), 1968, *Social Mobility in the Caste System in India*, The Hague: Mouton.

Singh, Charan, 1986, *Land Reforms in U.P. and the Kulaks*, New Delhi: Vikas Publishing House.

Singh, Gurchain, 1985, *The New Middle Class in India*, Jaipur: Rawat Publications.

Singh, K.S., 1978, 'Colonial Transformation of Tribal Society in Middle India', *Economic and Political Weekly*, Vol. XIII, No. 30, pp. 1221–32.

———, 1982, 'Transformation of Tribal Society: Integration v/s Assimilation', *Economic and Political Weekly*, Vol. XVII, Nos 33, 34, pp. 1318–25; 1376–84.

———, 1985, *Tribal Society in India: An Anthropo-Historical Perspective*, Delhi: Manohar Publications.

Singh, Nirmal, 1983, *Education under Siege*, New Delhi: Concept Publishing Company.

Singh, Rajendra, 1988, *Land, Power and People: Rural Elite in Transition, 1801–1970*, New Delhi: Sage Publications.

Singh, R.A.P., 1985, *Kin, Clan and Land Reforms*, Jaipur: Rawat Publications.

———, 1987, *Sociology of Rural Development in India*, Delhi: Discovery Publishing House.

Sivakumar, C., 1982, *Education, Social Inequality and Social Change in Karnataka*, New Delhi: Hindustan Publishing Corporation.

Srinivas, M.N., 1987, *The Dominant Caste and Other Essays*, Delhi: Oxford University Press.

Surana, Pushpendra, 1983, *Social Movements and Social Structure*, New Delhi: Manohar Publications.

Upadhyaya, Ashok K., 1980, 'Peasantisation of Adivasis in Thane District', *Economic and Political Weekly*, Vol. XV, No. 51, pp. A-134–A-146.

Upadhya, Carol Boyack, 1988, 'The Farmer-capitalists of Coastal Andhra Pradesh', *Economic and Political Weekly*, Vol. XXIII, Nos. 27, 28, pp. 1376–82; 1433–42.

Weiner, Myron, 1978, *Sons of the Soil: Migration and Ethnic Conflict in India*, Princeton: Princeton University Press.

Xaxa, Virginius, 1980, 'Evolution of Agrarian Structure and Class Relations in Jalpaiguri District, West Bengal', *Sociological Bulletin*, Vol. XXIV, No. 1.

Eight

New Dimensions in the Studies of Caste, Class, Ethnicity and Power

The Main Issues

Caste has been analyzed as an all-inclusive system of social ranking. It has also been understood as a basis of the division of labour and the allocation of positions of power. This uniqueness is exemplified by cultural exclusiveness and particularism of the caste system. A host of scholars and writers (Dumont 1970; Furnival 1939; Ghurye 1950; Hocart 1950; Hutton 1946; Ketkar 1979; Risley 1969; Senart 1930; Sherring 1974; Srinivas 1952, 1955) have dealt with the following aspects of the caste system:

1. Theories of origin of the caste system;
2. Exclusiveness and inclusiveness of the system; and
3. Functionality of the caste system.

Caste was thought of as an example of a non-contractual status–society. Stability even under resistance to change was considered as a desirable value emanating from the caste system. The questions which need to be debated are:

1. Was caste synonymous to the system of social stratification in India?
2. What has been the nature of social stratification in India?
3. What changes have occurred in the structure and process of social stratification in contemporary India?
4. What have been the factors of change and social mobility in the system of social stratification?

Caste and class have been perceived as polar opposites and antithetical constructs and practices (Bottomore 1964: 118; D'Souza 1968: 192–211; Dumont 1970; Ghurye 1950: 18; Leach 1960: 1–10; Srinivas 1952, 1966; Weber 1948: 396–415). Caste and class have also been characterized as rural and urban phenomena, respectively (Rosen 1966). Another view is that caste is an explosive class (Desai 1948). Caste stratification is also equated with the stratification based on race (Berreman 1960: 120–27; 1967: 45–73). Flexibility or elaboration of the caste system (Marriott 1965) is used as a scale for analyzing caste in different parts of India.

The reality of Indian society as seen by some social and economic historians (Desai 1948, 1975; Habib 1974: 264–316; Mencher 1974; Pannikar 1955; Stein 1968: 78–94; Thapar 1974: 95–123) is somewhat contrary to the above characterizations. Social mobility and structural changes have occurred in the stratification system. Migration and mobility were caused by several factors including conflicting claims and feuds regarding land, property and resources. The various accounts of caste system and social mobility suggest that both structural and positional changes and upward and downward social mobility have taken place at different levels such as group, family, and individual in historical time (Sharma 1980: 27–50; 1986: 16–39). The nexus between caste and class and its continuity and change could explain the structural and processual aspects of social stratification in Indian society. Unfortunately these remain understudied as stratificational phenomena.

More than anything else historicity of the nexus between caste and class (power implied in both) needs to be studied seriously and carefully. Though members of a caste compete with each other yet they exhibit mutual co-operation and harmony. Class-like distinctions within a given caste are found to be quite prominent in some cases; the conspicuous display of class distinction is considered to be an anti-caste activity, but at the same time an indicator of high social status. Such class distinctions are reflected in matrimonial alliances though these do not violate the caste-based rules of marriage. Caste continues to function as an imagined status group and as a referent for evoking collective mobilizations and actions on certain occasions. It operates as a device of social arrangement of people in the local context. At the macro-level caste is used as a means of identity, not necessarily paving way for commonalities and intimate interpersonal relations. Caste functions at times both formally and informally as an interest group. It becomes a resource, and a means of establishing as well as expanding social networks. From the viewpoint of the functions it used to perform earlier, it could be said that caste is dying out as an institution (Sharma 1986: 16–39). Caste–class–power nexus and levels of social mobility need to be studied in terms of both space (context) and time (historicity).

Today the dominant castes are not necessarily the twice-born castes. The dominant caste could well signify a section of a particular caste group, not necessarily the entire caste-group. The caste system is not uniformly rigid/flexible, hence different patterns of social mobility exist in the caste system. In a given context, caste might work as a cultural phenomenon or it may denote structural features resembling with the systems of social stratification in a global context. In a situation caste may exhibit structural and cultural features in varying proportions. Thus the crucial questions are:

1. What is India's social formation today?
2. Whether—even heuristically—caste, class, ethnicity, and power can be defined independent of each other?
3. What are main factors and forces which have brought about changes in India's social formation?
4. What has been the nature of historicity of the nexus between caste, class, ethnicity, and power?

There have been some studies on the dimensional nature of social stratification covering caste, class and power (Aggarwal 1971; Béteille 1966; Bhatt 1975), but the theoretical and methodological issues concerning social stratification as an integral part of India's social formation still remain unresolved (Sharma 1980: 1–27; 1986: 16–39; 1986: 29–62). The questions of theory, ideology and method for understanding the structure and process of social stratification have attracted the attention of a number of scholars during the past three decades (Sharma 1985: 82–114). In a comprehensive review of the studies on social stratification from the perspective of sociology of knowledge Sharma outlines the main questions and theoretical constructs. Yogendra Singh provides systematic two reviews (1974; 1985) of the main points relating to caste, class, ethnicity, power, and social mobility.

Caste

Unlike Henry Maine (1970), Dumont (1970) does not consider caste as 'the most dangerous and blighting of all human institutions'. But like Bougle (1958; 1971) and Hutton (1946: 111–32), Dumont does not defend caste. However, Dumont's treatment of caste amounts to its defence and perpetuation (Madan 1971: 1807). A discussion on hierarchy, change, ideology of caste, pure and impure, division of labour, and egalitarian society is presented by Dumont in a highly scholastic manner. The first question here is: How does Dumont define caste? For Dumont, the inequality of the caste system is a special type of inequality. It is determined by the ideas and values which people express related to interrelations among them. These ideas and values regarding inequality are found both in theory and practice because they are practised and legitimized in real life by the people themselves.

The notion of the fundamental opposition between the pure and the impure, as in the case of Bougle, is the hallmark of Dumont's analysis of the caste system. Both Bougle and Dumont define caste system in terms of hierarchically arranged hereditary groups, segregation and interdependence. These are mutually entailed principles, and are based on the fundamental principle of the opposition between the pure and the impure—a single true principle. This opposition underlines hierarchy in terms of the superiority of the pure over the impure. The hierarchy of the pure and the impure also implies their separation, thus the categorization of occupations and activities as pure and impure. Hierarchy is the relationship between 'that which encompasses and that which is encompassed', and whole system comprises the hierarchical existence of the two opposites—the pure and the impure.

Granting primacy to 'values and ideas' as the essence of hierarchy, Dumont focuses on the differentiation between status and power and the subordination of the *king* (rulership) to the *priest* in Hindu society. Hierarchy involves gradation, but it is different from both power and authority. It is an all-embracing, comprehensive concept. However, the connection between hierarchy and power remains problematic. Hierarchy cannot give a place to power without contradicting its own principle.

Singh (1985: 37–79) discusses four main points rather appreciatively in Dumont's structuralism. These are: (*a*) ideology, (*b*) dialectics (binary opposition), (*c*) transformational relationship, and (*d*) comparison. T. N. Madan (1971: 1807) has all the praise for Dumont's *Homo Hierarchicus* stamping it as an unusual work in its conception, design and execution. To an extent Dumont's view on the caste system reaffirms the caste model of Indian society. Dumont has invited a great deal of criticism from the Marxist scholars as well as from those who are engaged in a critical rethinking of the concepts and approaches to the study of caste, class, ethnicity, and power (Sharma 1985: 48–51, 82–114).

Caste and Class

A significant and quantifiable departure on the study of caste and class as found in the Annual Number of *Economic and Political Weekly* (Vol. XIV, Nos 7 and 8, 1979) is on 'Class and Caste in India' consisting of twenty-three articles under seven heads, namely, rationalizing inequalities, dialectical relationships, 'the more things change...', peninsular movements, protection by discrimination, on the periphery of Hinduism, and emerging alliances. M. N. Srinivas (1979: 237–42) recognizes competition, though reluctantly, between various urban castes for access to power and resources, and argues that even today agricultural production requires the co-operation of several castes. The use of the caste idiom is widespread despite rejection of the idea of hierarchy by the lower castes. Caste fuzziness permeates the entire system. In no way class and power are recognized by Srinivas as independent phenomena because caste encompasses the two as an overriding principle and practice of social relations in the Indian society. For Srinivas caste is a compelling facticity.

A look at other essays included in the above Annual Number of the *EPW* is unavoidable. Satish Saberwal (1979: 243–54) highlights the sociologist's lack of sensitivity to the magnitudes of poverty and inequality in India. Cultures of deprivation rather than caste and/or class as frames of reference for describing the lower strata would include explanation of both social and economic elements. Caste as a frame of analysis (Juergensmeyer 1979: 255–62) implies a cultural continuity between the lower and the higher strata of society; but it obfuscates the radical differences which have emerged between the two, and even these differences may exist due to the labouring class character of the lower caste community. To accept class as a frame of reference amounts to neglect of cultural solidarity (Sivakumar and Sivakumar 1979: 263–86).

Sivakumar and Sivakumar note that caste cannot be confined to a superstructural role, and at the same time caste bears economic significance to a great extent. Caste and class together define the structure of interests. Cognitive world is not characterized by class consciousness alone. Consciousness is a highly complex phenomenon. It emanates from distribution of income and *jati* hierarchy and from the intermixture of the two. The world of politics enters into economic and social realms through patron–client relationship. Caste and class nexus is understood by Sharad Patil (1979: 287–96) in terms of relations of various castes to land, expropriation of its surplus, and military and bureaucratic sharing of wealth and power. The colonial society was basically representative of mercantile economy.

A similar analysis of the interlinking of caste and class (Roy 1979: 297–312) stresses on the substitution of the concept of class by the concept of caste/varna which is basically a form of class differentiation, hence a structural phenomenon, and not unique to Indian society. The ongoing caste tensions in India are in essence class conflicts. Georges Kristoffel Lieten (1979: 313–28) finds Indian society constituted of multiple opposites like Hindu/Muslim, Hindi/non-Hindi, Sunni/Shia, tribal/non-tribal, caste/Harijan, male/female, urban/rural, agricultural/industrial, employed/unemployed, worker/capitalist, landless labourer/rich peasant, sharecropper/landlord. The role played by caste associations and the programmes of the left political parties throw some light on how caste and class are related to each other in practice. A similar view is expressed by E. M. S. Namboodiripad (1979: 403–8) and B. T. Ranadive (1979: 337–48). Saraswati Menon in her study of the kisan movement in Thanjavur district in Tamil Nadu finds that peasantry faced a historically developed landlord class, which belonged to a caste that had adopted itself to the class structure, and also retained its own dimensions of oppression.

Thus besides class–caste nexus, caste has remained as an institution independent of class. Articles, such as *Caste and Class in Maharashtra* (Pandit 1979: 425–36), *Tribal Identity and Class Differentiations* (Shah 1979: 459–69), *Class and Caste in a Tribal Movement* (Kulkarni 1979: 465–68), *Caste, Class and Economic Opportunity in Kerala* (Sivanandan 1979: 475–80) and *Caste and Class in Bihar* (Prasad 1979: 481–84) highlight the nexus between caste and class. These studies also underline the fact that despite the nexus, caste has its own character independent of class in domains such as religion, politics, economic formation, migration, mobility, change and conflicts.

Conceptualizing the Caste–Class Nexus

Dipankar Gupta (1981: 2093–2104) places the caste and class debate in the framework of culturological and Marxist approaches. According to the culturological approach caste is a primordial reality of Indian society, and the Marxist approach questions the theoretical and historical assumptions underlying the culturological approach. Dumont as the chief architect of the culturological approach considers caste as a system of ideas and values overriding all the aspects of society. Maurice Godelier (1978) argues that caste is part of the infrastructure of the society. However, according to Gupta, both Dumont and Godelier tend to argue on the pre-eminence of caste as a determining factor of social reality in India. Even Godelier takes a middle position between those who argue that caste is part of the sub-structure and those who argue that it is part of the superstructure.

There is no uniform pattern of the nexus between caste and class. Castes occupying leading positions in the competitive economy of Punjab are also leading castes in two religions of the state, namely,

the Sikhs and the Hindus (D'Souza 1982: 1783–93). These dominant castes/communities are in a position to mobilize their respective fellowmen to defend their economic and political interests.
However, the situation is somewhat different in Bihar where caste
is used openly and unhesitatingly in most virulent form to divide
the society in real life situations. Besides mobilization and solidarity/
loyalty at one's own caste level, there are confederational expressions and activities. Entire state is divided into the forwards, backwards, Harijans, *adivasis* and Muslims (Das 1984: 1616–19; 1983).

A. N. Das addresses to such a situation in Bihar as class in itself,
caste for itself (1984: 1616–19). Caste has become a means of close
and constant encounters, and such a situation has made it (caste)
both a familiar factor of social existence in Bihar and a convenient
concept for social reporting and analysis. 'On the other side, there
is much less obvious evidence of social being articulating itself in
terms of class.' Now the questions are: What sort of ideology does
caste represent? Does caste incorporate economic and political
relations within and between castes or not? Is the non-class behaviour not really rooted into class relations and conflicts? Das blames
social scientists for not providing conceptual clarity regarding the
concept of class and its relevance for studying the Bihar situation.
Following E. P. Thompson (1968), Das (ibid.: 1616) writes: 'Class,
therefore, is a political process, not a cataloging category.' Class
is both a concept and a process. To use class merely as a concept
makes it abstract, inappropriate and confusing, hence its use as a
political process may help critical examination of the well-tried
caste concepts.

Class is not a mere category; in everyday life it is a relationship,
not a thing. Class, as history has borne out, is a historical phenomenon; a social and cultural formation (ibid.: 1617). In Bihar
everyday something or other happens in the name of caste war,
caste atrocities, caste mobilization, etc., but it is in fact a class war
(Sinha 1982). Changes in the caste stratification have occurred
from *tribe to caste to class* (ibid.: 1982). The idiom of expression
of interests may be caste, tribe or religion; the issues are economic
and political. The emergent formations, organizations, *senas* and
sabhas are all obviously class organizations (Das 1984: 1619).
A number of scholars (Dirks 1989: 59–77; Driver 1982: 225–53;
Raheja 1989: 79–101; Shah 1982: 1–33; Srinivas 1984: 151–67;
Veer 1985: 303–21) hardly touch upon the opposites such as caste

and class and their underlying background assumptions. In the context of elections caste-based mobilization is more of a resource for achieving political power than economic gains. However, political power may latently lead to economic power as well of those who occupy political offices.

A Note on the Notion of Hierarchy

A conceptual formulation on castes which Dipankar Gupta (1984: 1955–58; 2003–5; 2049–53) names as continuous hierarchies and discrete castes is an alternative to the traditional ideological–cum–sociological view and to the empirical view of the caste system. Empirical studies of the caste system contradict many of the premises of the traditional indological view, yet, the latter persists without reformulation (Gould 1988: 143–85). Gupta grants his concurrence to the criticisms of Dumont's view as the ideal representation by Veena Das (1982) and the indological-cum-sociological view of the caste system by Morton Klass (1980). Das is concerned with a close scrutiny of Brahminical *Puranas*. Klass's chief objective is to understand the origin of the caste system and its residual essence. Gupta bases his analysis on the study of myths and traditions of the subaltern castes. Gupta critically examines Dumont's view on caste as a hierarchical system; he also provides facts which contradict Dumont's view of caste as an encompassing ideological system. The criticisms are offered in the form of discrete ideologies, discrete castes and muddled hierarchies, multiple binding and hyper-symbolism and the Brahmin as a fiction. Two conclusions drawn by Gupta (ibid.: 2049) are as follows:

1. Any notion of hierarchy is arbitrary and is valid from the perspective of certain individual castes. To state that the pure hierarchy is one that is universally believed in, or one which legitimizes the position of those who participate in the caste system is misleading.
2. The separation between castes is not only on matters which connote the opposition between purity and pollution. Distinctions and diacritical notches which are not even remotely suggestive of purity and pollution are observed strictly. Obversely, distinctions related to purity and pollution do not systematically affect caste status.

Further Gupta defines caste (ibid.: 2051) as follows:

> We would define the caste system as a form of differen-
> tiation wherein the constituent units of the system justify
> endogamy on the basis of putative biological differences
> which are semaphored by the ritualisation of multiple
> social practices. The above definition according to us gives
> the essence of the caste system.

There is no uniform rule for all the *jatis* in the observance of
rituals. No doubt different *jatis* enjoyed a certain amount of autonomy with the protection provided by their respective *caste councils*;
however, they were not beyond the umbrella of the system itself
which demanded from each *jati* performance of certain functions
and duties which were supposedly assigned to them under the
customary law of the land. Violation of this rule was taken as an
offence against the system, hence *jajmani* system functioned and
persisted as an integral part of the caste system. Gupta has undermined this systematic aspect of the caste system perhaps *consciously* to highlight the discrete nature of *jatis*. No caste could
ever perceive itself in the rank-order without perceiving other
castes in the same social arrangement. This is true in today's
changed context as well. Even if a caste functions as an interest
group or a faction in a given situation, it does so in relation to
other caste(s) which are themselves behaving as interest groups
and factions. Today castes also perceive themselves in terms of
their numerical strength in one context, and education, economic
resources, etc. in other context, and ritual hierarchy in a third
context.

Kolenda (1984) examines caste almost in its totality taking into
consideration its formation, origins, local groupings, ideological
basis, social and cultural mobility, anti-caste movements, caste and
politics, untouchability and the role of the state, decline of the
jajmani system and the nature of caste in India's urban centres.
Several structural factors (Kolenda 1986: 110–11) have contributed
to the change in the caste system resulting into decline of the
jajmani system and the emergence of new dominant castes, inter-
caste marriages, modern occupations, caste blocks, renewed violence against untouchables and reaction against such atrocities, etc.
Emergence of *Caste Senas* in Bihar indicates at the transformation

of caste into warring groups for political power and supremacy. However, such a situation has not been witnessed in other parts of the country.

A. M. Shah and I. P. Desai (1988) make yet another important contribution on the study of caste. Shah has used excellently ethnography of Gujarat upholding the indological and ethnographic tradition of Ghurye, Dumont, Peacock, Karve, etc. However, Desai has a marked preference for the analysis of economic and political factors in the study of caste system. A. M. Shah discusses (1982; 1988) the internal structure of the castes such as Brahmins, Vanias, Rajputs, Patidars and Kolis. He argues that along with *hierarchy, division* is the basis of competition within the caste system. All the castes have several sub-castes mainly based on *endogamy*, but there is hardly any organized hierarchy within a given caste. In fact, Shah finds hierarchy, hypergamy and endogamy with much less pollution–purity principle in practice. There are also sub-castes of the same order within the castes of Brahmins and Vanias without having a sense of higher or lower to one another. Shah seems to emphasize the principle of *division* more than hierarchy because it has remained underplayed, and also it can be accepted as a competing principle within and between different castes. For this reason, Shah stresses on the need for the study of caste in urban areas. However, Shah certainly underplays Dumont's notion of hierarchy. Whether the division of labour itself could be the basis of hierarchy is not explicit in Shah's analysis of the caste system.

I. P. Desai's critique of A. M. Shah's view pleads for an empirical view of the caste system. Desai states that caste is disintegrating, getting secularized, and it has become a new system of social stratification. Caste elites have emerged in modern era to exploit members of their own castes. Due to various processes of structural transformation caste is changing fast into a new economic and political force. But for Shah caste continues still as a social institution adapting itself to the new forces of social change.

Pauline Kolenda (1989: 1833–38) analyzes changes in the discourse on caste over the past thirty years based on her study of a village in western Uttar Pradesh. Thirty years ago people used to debate on the issues related to educational and occupational access for the lower castes and untouchables and on other practices concerning untouchability. Today, they discuss about the ideas related to equal etiquette and equal rights, inter-caste marriage, utility of the caste system itself and social change. However, subjectively experienced views on caste by a cross-section of the village people in no way are congruent with the indological-cum-sociological view of the caste system.

F. Franco and Sarvar V. Sherry Chand (1989: 2601–12) observe that varna ideology is found as a social practice. The notion of varna is subjectively formed among all Hindus/Indians as it is not a localized phenomenon like a *jati* in the form of an endogamous group found operating in a given territory. The presence of varna is denied, but it subsists within the power matrix of affirmation of sanction. It is seen through expressions and activities involving the forwards, the backwards, the Harijans and so on. It is pervasive as a social practice at all levels of social life. It is constantly reproduced by the cognitive and *nomic* structure constantly shaping the consciousness of all members of society (ibid.: 2610). Thus, caste could be seen from several viewpoints as it refers to a variety of aspects of social life in many different ways. This complex and absorbing and adaptive nature of the caste system has allowed debate and discourse of a wide ranging magnitude.

Class

Class and power are the economic and political dimensions of social stratification, respectively. Several scholars and ideologues have studied caste and power from a class perspective, thereby applying a wide range of Marxian concepts and paradigms. The limitations of the Marxian approach to the study of class and class-conflict in Indian society are evident when V. M. Dandekar (1978: 102–24) and K. L. Sharma (1994; 1995) discern the four classes in India, not just the bourgeoisie and the proletariat. The classes are as follows:

1. Agrarian classes,
2. Industrial classes,
3. Professional classes, and
4. The business and mercantile classes.

Dandekar questions the Marxist approach on several counts including the absence of the fully developed monopoly of capitalism and emergence of trade unions and their power of collective bargaining, class harmony, middle class, intra-class differentiation, welfare policies of the state, and an overlap between caste, class and occupation and mixed classes. Even for the realization of economic or class interests, the use of caste idiom is found to be a convenient means of articulation. The following patterns of social mobility (Sharma 1986: 50) have both caste and class in the background:

1. Downward mobility and proletarianization,
2. Upward mobility and embourgeoisiement,
3. Urban migration and income for the rural people and social mobility in the village, and
4. Rural non-agricultural income and intra-village social mobility.

Both the reality and perception of class have changed over the years. Class is no more understood simply as a grouping of people having common economic and occupational interests. It is not merely an attributional phenomenon understood in terms of income, occupation, education, etc. Competition alone cannot be the sole criterion of the emergence of class in a caste-society. A couple of studies (Jha 1987) in particular analyze the prevalence of private landholding, interaction between socio-economic classes, trade and society, and agrarian growth and social conflicts in ancient and medieval Indian society. Sabyasachi Bhattacharya and Romila Thapar (1986) bring out relationship between class and the colonial state in India. It is evident from various accounts that class has/had always been embedded in caste and wider social formation throughout Indian history.

The Indian Capitalist Class and Political Power

The economic development of the Indian capitalist class in the colonial period was quite noticeable and substantial. The Indian capitalist class grew from about the mid-nineteenth century with largely an independent capital base, not as junior partners of foreign capital or as compradors. The capitalist class on the whole was not tied up in a subservient position with pro-imperialist feudal interests either economically or politically (Chandra et al.: 1988: 375–85).

Bipan Chandra also observes that the capitalist class grew rapidly in the period between 1914 and 1947 particularly by waging a constant struggle against colonialism and colonial interest. The Indian capitalists did this to make space for themselves, and in the long-run within India's political economy, they perceived a state which would eventually not include the colonialists. However, the Indian capitalist class did their best to accord supremacy to their own class interests over and above the national interests. Their relationship with the Indian National Congress (INC) was guided by this motive force. Bipan Chandra (ibid.: 385) writes: 'Clearly the Indian capitalist class was anti-socialist and bourgeois but it was not pro-imperialist ' This view is also reaffirmed by Aditya Mukherjee (1978: 1516–28; 1986: 239–87). The Indian capitalist class constituted itself as a class with an independent class base and with an organization on an all-India basis. Mukherjee (1986: 239) writes: 'It became constituted politically as "a class for itself" and developed a hegemonic ideology vis-à-vis other classes and the nation'. The capitalist class was ahead of any other class in India, and influenced the state and society by way of contributing to the establishment of an independent bourgeois order. But the capitalist interests remained wedded to nationalism, and projected its own interests as that of the Indian nation.

Sabyasachi Bhattacharya (1986: 171–93) discusses the relationship between the colonial state, capital and labour. Interest representation from these structures and their relationship emerged in such a way that it divided the Indian society in various layers at different levels. It created new forms of socio-economic and political inequality. The capitalist class is identified by Bhattacharya within the parameters of this complex nexus of the trinity, namely, state, capital and labour. In the thirties the colonial government identified the following classes:

1. Political classes,
2. Commercial classes,
3. Landholders and agricultural classes, and
4. Industrial labour.

Charles Betteleheim (1968: 54–83; 84–105), R. K. Hazari (1966) and Pavlov (1964) have also emphasized the emergence of the capitalist class during the post-independence period. Some steps were initiated on the basis of studies on the increasing control/ influence of the capitalist class (big business) in decision making. However, the big business may not always occupy a superordinate position.

Lloyd and Susanne Rudolph (1987) also argue that both organized workers and private financial and industrial capital are politically marginal because the two are constrained by their specific interests. The state is more influenced by small-scale, self-employed 'bullock capitalists'. The bullock capitalists oppose both industrial capital and urban capital workers. The Congress party has played centrist politics. No doubt class politics and inequality, poverty and injustice exist in Indian society, but class politics 'is not likely to become the principal medium for representing India's weaker sections, wage workers, and capitalists or for expressing conflicts among them' (ibid.: 20). However, the Rudolphs may not be quite right in their observation because caste, untouchability, joint family and other institutions have become quite weak since independence. Stanley A. Kochanek (1974) too believe that big business never succeeded in blocking or even modifying a major distributive policy in India. It could not stop or mould the nationalization of banks and other institutions in 1969.

M. S. A. Rao (1989: 21–45) spells out three approaches to the study of caste, class, ethnicity and dominance. These are: (*a*) the class-approach; (*b*) the caste approach; and (*c*) the subaltern approach. Conceptual issues in the study of caste, class, ethnicity and dominance are discussed by Rao within the larger framework of these approaches under the headings—caste; caste and sect; economic and political dimensions of caste; caste and power; class, ethnicity, and political power; and dominance and authority. Contributors to the first volume edited by Frankel and Rao (1989) are mainly concerned with the breakdown or decline of the Brahmanical social order in Bihar and with patterns of resilience in Uttar Pradesh, non-Brahminism, Dravidianism and Tamil nationalism in Tamil Nadu, accommodation and resilience in Andhra Pradesh, cohesion in Karnataka, the emergence of caste mobilization and class consciousness as reflected through agrarian movements in Kerala and Tamil Nadu. The essays in the second volume (1990) analyze political backwardness in Rajasthan, caste–class amalgamation and upper caste revitalization in Gujarat, emergence of anti-Brahminism in the form of Dalit consciousness and mobilization in Maharashtra, the slow pace of social change among 'tribes' of middle India, the continuity of backwardness in Orissa, the state of reform communism in West Bengal and ethnicization of politics in Punjab.

A few tentative conclusions may be drawn from the narrative–descriptive-cum-analytical essays published in the two volumes. In most of the essays the emphasis is on the caste approach. There are hardly any subaltern descriptions in the contributions. The class approach, though figuring in some of the essays, finds a second or third place in the analytical scheme of most of the articles. Both class and dominance are viewed from the caste approach. The need for a shift from the caste approach to the class approach is clearly undermined as the contributors reset and reverse the trend of analysis in the study of social stratification.

A synthesis of òrthodox Hinduism, Vaishnav sectarianism and tribalism (Bhadra: 1979; 1995: 256–78) has moulded the stratification system in Assam in a unique form, thereby displaying simultaneously rigidity, flexibility, mobility and egalitarianism. The forces of modernization have further liberalized the traditional system. The congruence that exists between caste, class and power elsewhere in India is not found in Assam. Instead of group (caste), family and individual are the units of status-determination because social status is determined by economic standing, and positions of power and authority are enjoyed by a given individual family.

Family as the basis of social status is discussed by Sophie Baker (1990) in her biographical accounts of a princely family of Rajputs, a Marwari family, a weaver's family, a Brahmin family, a Harijan family and a middle-class family in a Rajasthan village, in Bombay, Andhra Pradesh, Tamil Nadu, Bihar and Delhi respectively.

The second inference is about the nature of dominant causality. No single factor is a determining force. No factor is independent of or insulated from the macro-structural changes in the Indian society. Class and dominance are seen from the caste perspective, but the caste perspective itself has changed rapidly, and caste is also seen from the perspectives of class and dominance.

Lastly, no uniform paradigm can be proposed for the study of social stratification. The emergence of middle castes as dominant castes/classes in Bihar and eastern Uttar Pradesh provides a new model compared to the situation in western Uttar Pradesh and Haryana partly because of the historical reasons and partly due to new processes of social change since independence. Tamil Nadu and Maharashtra have a long history of anti-Brahminism. Gujarat represents an ethos and culture of entrepreneurship, trade and commerce, and hence the polity is not beyond the grip of these forces. Rajasthan continues to remain, to some extent, under the influence of the feudal bourgeoisie and the new class of dominants belonging to upper and upper middle castes. Kerala and Bengal have been different at least politically from other states.

Ethnicity

Can ethnicity be treated as a significant dimension of social stratification just like caste, class and power? A satisfactory answer to this question depends upon the understanding of the word ethnicity. An ethnic group may be considered as a *stratum* in a given system of social stratification. It is possible because ethnicity is accompanied with class and power. Ethnicity is also considered as an extension of kinship sentiments, and hence the synthesis of the primordial and the instrumentalist views on ethnicity (Van der Berghe 1981). M. S. A. Rao (1989: 38–41) opines that ethnicity may have a structural basis in several primordial ties like caste, kinship, religion, sect, language, tribe and race, and as a social formation it is not immutable. Rao argues that ethnic ties can be changed or acquired by discarding/having sectarian and even linguistic affiliations by acquiring new caste identities based on new symbolic legitimations, spatial mobility, etc. Situational factors may also change ethnic status and power. In actual life ethnicity as a functioning phenomenon can be seen in terms of a collectivity of people sharing common values and norms in relation to the wider society.

S. K. Acharya while discussing the ethnic processes in northeastern India (1988: 1068–77) dwells upon the concept of *ethnicity* at length. Since the word *ethnos* means *people*, it could mean the English, Japanese, Eskimos, Assamese, Gonds, Oriyas, etc. Thus communities both small and large, and archaic and modern alike may be called *ethnos*. The term ethnos may be used in a broad as well as in a narrow sense. An *ethnicos* refers to an *ethnos* in a restricted sense, for example, in the context of a specific community such as Manipuris, Bodos and Santhals. Besides some common attributes which an ethnicos possesses, ethnic consciousness is an indispensable feature. Self-identification is realized by the ethnic consciousness, and it is termed as *ethnonym* or *endoethnonym*, and when it is done by others it is known as *exoethnonym*.

Today, a plethora of literature is available on ethnicity and its entrenchment into various aspects of social, political and economic life of the people. Caste associations participate in political arena as distinct ethnic entities. Caste clusters like AJGAR (Ahirs, Jats, Gujars and Rajputs), forwards, backwards, Dalits, minorities, etc., have emerged as bigger ethnic blocs in today's politics. Hindu–Muslim relations, native people–outsiders, cultural identities like the Sikhs, Jains, Buddhists, Gorkhas and Bodos, have also been articulated in ethnic terms. Even regional identities like Oriya, Tamil, Telugu, Assamia, Marathi and Gujarati, are expressed in the ethnic idiom. There are studies like politics of ethnic and communal identities (Puri 1990: 703–5), ethnic politics in municipal corporation (Kamalakar 1988: 945–46), capitalist development and ethnic tension (Engineer 1988: 409–12), ethnic dimension of subcontinental Muslims (Puri 1987: 126–28), and class base of the Swaminarayan sect (Hardiman 1988: 1907–12).

Shahida Lateef (1980: 2086–87) uses the words communalism and ethnicity interchangeably in the Indian context. Religion, language or caste may form a sufficient but not necessary reason for ethnic grouping. The contingent economic, political or even cultural interests may be necessary factors along with the primordial ties as a sufficient base for ethnicization of social relations. 'Ethnicity denotes strife between groups as does communalism' (ibid.: 2086). Ethnicization has necessarily been accentuated by wide ranging economic, social and political changes in Indian society.

The depressed groups and communities find ethnic solidarity and mobilization as a convenient means of their quest for equality and share in resources of the society. George Mathew (1982: 1027–34; 1068–72) argues that conversion to Islam in Tamil Nadu in 1981 by the Harijans of Meenakshipuram village was caused by the persistent discrimination and inequality they had been suffering for a long time. It was a reaction to the socio-economic situation that existed in the village. Thus conversions became a threat to status quo. Conversion by the lower castes certainly implies a threat to the upper castes' hegemonic control of the society's resources. Mathew observes that 'conversion in India is a structural question', because 'economic issues and status questions are not divorced from each other for the lower class'.

Conversions to Christianity by the tribal people in Bihar and some other parts of India have created two social categories: (*a*) the converts, and (*b*) the non-converts. The *adivasis* who converted to Christianity became a superior class in terms of access to better education, employment, health facility, etc. Those who did not opt for conversion have lagged behind because they did not have access to some of these amenities that could change their *status* in society (Sharma 1986: 9–34).

Migration is the main basis of ethnic diversity as well as endo-ethnonym and exoethnonym (Weiner 1978). The subjective expression and articulation by the people themselves and the analysis of ethnicity by outsiders substantiate correlation between migration and ethnic diversity. The problem in Assam arose because of Bengali migrants; the encounters in Bihar's Chhota Nagpur surfaced due to north Bihar's Hindu migrants and Christians; and in Andhra Pradesh there were problems between the *mulkis* (natives) and the migrants. The questions of employment, resource distribution, right of access to local infrastructural assets and above all the question of *status* and *legitimacy* have arisen in all the three states of Assam, Bihar and Andhra Pradesh which have been discussed in detail by Myron Weiner.

Myron Weiner (ibid.: 4) finds three concepts quite useful in the study of ethnic demography: (*a*) territorial ethnicity, (*b*) dual labour market, and (*c*) ethnic division of labour. A dual labour market is generally accompanied by an ethnic division of labour. The dual labour market may be *ethnically stratified*, that is, each person in a given occupation may be recruited from a specific ethnic group. Ethnic division of labour implies that some people work in the subordinate or peripheral sectors or positions whereas members of some other ethnic groups control access to the core sectors of economy. Migration is thus *ethnically selective* (ibid.: 4–5). The Marwaris and the Punjabis in Bihar have practically monopolized the core sector of industry, trade and commerce at the exclusion of the north Biharis and the tribals and other locals. The north Biharis have taken over the core sector of government services excluding the tribals and others. Such a situation besides generating 'ethnic conflict' also produces an ethnically stratified society commensurate with class stratification.

The migrants in Bihar, Assam and some other states of India are generally entrepreneurs, shopkeepers, traders and independent professionals. If the migrants work as unskilled labourers, there may be less ethnic strife and antipathy against the outsiders, as against a situation in which the outsiders have practically taken over the core areas of economic activities. Questions of exploitation, cultural differences and domination of the locals by the aliens arise once there is an awareness about the significance of the control of resources by the migrants.

In a situation where the migrants occupy top positions in the occupational and income hierarchy ethnic distinctiveness is emphasized by the natives reflecting their class relationships with the migrants. Ethnic/class conflict outfaces, and efforts are made by the natives to displace the migrant economic dominants by political means such as elections, legislations and movements. Ethnic infrastructures like restaurants, religious institutions, newspapers, neighbourhood associations, schools, and a lot of other ameliorative institutional and organizational structures are created and used by the conflicting migrants and the locals (ibid.: 10–11).

Jaganath Pathy (1984) pleads for the development of the tribes of India because they constitute ethnic minorities like any other religious and linguistic minorities. S. L. Doshi (1990: 227–38) believes that ethnicity imparts continuity and identity to the tribal people. 'Ethnicity runs like a cord at different levels of development and social formation' (ibid.: 230). There is always an interplay between ethnicity and class, and also there are multiple identities of the same ethnic group (Badgaiyan 1986: 293–308). A given ethnic group may have many class identities, and within the group class-based antagonisms may be expressed frequently.

Dominance and Power

The questions of caste, class and ethnicity have remained vitally alive to the Indian political scene since independence, but their forms and formats have changed from variants of the functionalist stance to Marxist formulations to ethno-social and pragmatic concerns. Caste and politics remain closely interlinked despite the weakening of the caste system in the context of ritual practices and the emergence of a new language of politics from time to time.

Three types of political mobilization characterize the relationship between caste and politics (Rudolph and Rudolph 1987: 24–29). These are: vertical, horizontal, and differential. For the Rudolphs horizontal mobilization geared by caste associations is the most effective means in power–politics. However, Kothari strongly refutes the dichotomous view regarding caste and politics as unrealistic and mechanical (1970: 224–44). Caste is something like interest-gratifying means in politics. Kothari no longer holds this view (1986: 210–16).

M. N. Srinivas's concept of dominant caste (1955; 1959; 1987) could be used for analyzing the rural power structure. However, its many limitations make it unsuitable for the study of the rural social stratification and power (Dube 1968: 58–71; Dumont 1970; Gardner 1968: 82–97; Oommen 1970: 73–83; Sharma 1980: 135–54, 1986). A complex set of criteria of dominance and power at different levels and layers is suggested in several critiques of Srinivas's concept of the dominant caste. Caste and power, and not power and caste, and class and power or power and class, are significantly inter-related, and this hypothesis itself is a serious limitation of the concept of dominant caste. K. N. Sharma's concepts of resource networks and resource groups (1963: 47–52) for explaining social mobility and access to positions of power and dominance are quite useful as they refer to the traditional as well as the new bases of networks.

John MacDougall's poser 'Dominant Castes or Rich Peasants?' (1979: 625–34) may be taken as a direct critique of Srinivas's concept of dominant caste. After marshalling a lot of facts regarding dominance of castes/peasants and after a careful comparison of the two theories rather hypotheses, MacDougall prefers the rich peasants theory. 'The rich-peasant theory allows for a variation in the form and presence of change, and can explain the apparently slow but irreversible pace of change in many of India's villages' (ibid.: 633). It explains better the class element in rural conflicts which at times are passed as caste conflicts. The dominant-peasant theory can explain not only what the concept of dominant caste does, but also the processes of legitimizing rural power structures and the nature of supra-village processes (ibid.: 633). Even in an apparent situation of caste tensions and violence *class* is the main factor in the background (Bose 1981: 713–16). Those sections of the Scheduled Castes who were relatively better educated, more mobile and had some access to modern jobs were most seriously affected by the caste riots of 1981 in Gujarat. The *class element* is existent even among the Scheduled Caste members of Parliament as most of them belong to the second generation of the educated beneficiaries having a fairly high degree of political awakening (Mendelsohn 1986: 501–9).

Rajni Kothari (1986: 210–16) hypothesizes about the increasing encounters between the masses and the classes in which the state remains a mute spectator. The classes cherish status quo, and the masses are restless for bringing about change and transformation. Kothari unlike his earlier analysis of Indian politics and the role of caste (1970) lays emphasis on the multiple dimensions of domination, exploitation and marginalization by the monolithic elite and the role of state in tackling these basic problems (Kothari 1988: 2223–27). Power revolves around class interests and control over the state, hence legitimacy is of different class reference groups and of different balance of class forces (Petras 1989: 1955–58). Thus a critique of the concept of dominant caste is undoubtedly rooted into class as the basis of power. But then the question is: What is class? Is it not entrenched into caste? Can caste be just a system of stratification based on ritual distance among the people? The paradigm of caste as it was used in the fifties and sixties has lost much of its significance. Change in the nature of issues, development strategies, styles of politics and mass mobilizations and the decline of the traditional literate castes and communities and the emergence of the middle castes and middle classes peasantry have changed the nature of relationship between caste, class and politics of power.

In a scathing attack on the democratic–pluralistic theory of the state Moin Shakir (1986: 1–30) pleads for the application of the materialist theory as propounded by Karl Marx to understand the entrenchment of the propertied classes in Indian society. It is the state which protects the interests of the classes and not the masses, and the classes both rural and urban (bourgeoisie) exercise control on the State. Shakir (ibid.: 31–62) discusses the class character of the Indian state covering the entire array of rural and urban propertied classes and the petty bourgeois classes.

Class politics is marginal at the national level (Rudolphs 1987: 1–15; 19–59) despite much inequality, poverty and injustice. It is not a principal medium for representing India's class structure and class conflicts. Cultural and caste groups play a decisive role in India's power politics. Demand groups such as minorities, bullock capitalists and backward classes, Scheduled Castes, Scheduled Tribes, farmers, agricultural labourers, entrepreneurs, students and women, are involved consciously or unconsciously in the game of extrication of maximum benefits from the State. The very nature of the Indian State allows the articulation of the *art of interests*. These groups are engaged in economic pursuits clearly visualizing the possibility of claiming a share as their due in the state's resource structure.

Caste, Class and Dominance

Caste, land and politics are found closely interlinked throughout India (Omvedt 1982) because they have a common ingredient, namely, economic power. A caste is a class and yet it remains a caste; land is related closely to caste hierarchy and power; and those who have the support of caste (in the sense of both caste and class) and have control over economic resources such as land, have entry to the game of power politics in rural India. Thus, both caste and class are resources for gaining access to political power. Once political power is gained, it proves to be a further resource for the consolidation and improvement of status and class positions. This is how the relationship between land, caste and politics is found in Indian villages today.

Rajendra Singh (1988) distinguishes between the 'established elites' and the 'emerging elites'. The former are drawn from the upper castes, aristocratic families and priestly classes, and the latter are a product of the electoral process, open competition, achievement–ideal and political awakening. The agrarian power structure determines to a large extent the nature and composition of the new elite. The two exist side by side and they also interact, intermingle providing a way for a sort of circulation of elites and social mobility.

The situation in other states of India is not the same as it is in eastern Uttar Pradesh. 'Just below the surface of caste conflict, the outline of a new class polarization became perceptible' is stated about Bihar by Frankel (1989: 124). Zoya Hasan (1989: 133–203) while discussing the 'patterns of resilience and change in Uttar

Pradesh' finds commonality of economic interests of the rich and the middle peasants. The middle peasants in particular lured the marginal farmers and agricultural labourers on their side preventing them to act on class lines by arousing caste loyalty as most of them belonged to the castes of the middle peasants.

The south Indian and Maharashtrian political drama is somewhat different from the one we have reported about Bihar and Uttar Pradesh. The politics and contradictions of the regional forces have resulted into conflicts within the power structures in Tamil Nadu (Washbrook 1989: 204–64). *Accommodation* in politics in Andhra Pradesh (Reddy 1989: 265–321), cohesive divisions based on caste, factionalism and ideology in Karnataka (Manor 1989: 322–61), and class consciousness based on caste mobilization in Kerala (Alexander 1989: 362–413) amply demonstrate the distinctiveness of the operational mechanisms of power-politics in terms of caste and class. Despite a lack of uniformity in the pattern of caste, class and dominance in the south Indian states, it is different from the north Indian socio-political system obviously due to historical and structural reasons.

Rajputs in an alliance with wealthy Vaishyas and Jains relegating the Brahmins in the background occupied the apex of the social ladder in Rajasthan (Narain and Mathur 1990: 1–58). A more or less similar situation existed in Gujarat (Ghanshyam Shah 1990: 59–114). In Rajasthan, conflicts between the traditional rivals like Jats and Rajputs surfaced initially, but cooled down slowly in course of time. Indifference and a sort of lack of trust still continue among these groups at various socio-political levels. 'Ambivalence of status' is one of the consequences preventing their integration in the same political fora. Orissa is another backward state like Rajasthan where despite several socio-political movements the dominance of the Brahmin-Karan middle classes continues because of the persistence of pro-capitalist agriculture and economic backwardness (Mohanty 1990: 321–66). Consolidation of conservative economic forces in Bengal (Kohli 1990: 367–415), ethnicization of politics in Punjab (Wallace 1990: 416–81), and entrenchment of the neo-rich in the state's politics in Maharashtra (Lele 1990: 115–211) are some of the other patterns which can be noted on India's political horizon in the context of social formation of the caste-class nexus.

Lastly, the State in India—*colonial* as well as the post-1947—has interfered with lives of people in varying degrees depending upon their caste, religion, economic status and educational attainments. State's policies by creating new cleavages in the established social order have generated negative reactions and protests particularly from those who have had been affected adversely. A large number of peasant movements (Desai 1979; 1987; Dhanagare 1983; Jeffery 1978: 131–48; MacDougall 1985; Miller 1978: 105–30) have explained mobilization by the peasantry and political groups and parties mainly as a reaction against the state's policies and the entrenched sections of society who benefited from these legal enactments. The capitalist mode of production in agriculture has not only polarized the rural class structure further in terms of the *rich* and the *poor*, the *dominant* and the *weak*, the *upper* and the *lower* segments of society, their relationship with the state is being redefined in favour of the beneficiaries of the state's policies and programmes (Berreman 1979; Bhadra 1989; Harris 1982; Robb 1986; Rudolph and Rudolph 1984: 281–344; Singh 1990).

The following conclusions may be arrived at from the above discussion:

1. Caste, class and dominance are not monolithic structures of social, economic and power relations.
2. There is no exclusivity of these phenomena as one cannot be comprehended in actual social life without the other(s).
3. The state has been a crucial factor in shaping and reshaping the social, economic and political arrangements.
4. Efforts in the form of social movements supporting/opposing the state's policies and programmes have crystallized the structural contradictions and paved the way for social transformation.

Concluding Remarks

Social stratification is a multi-faceted and multi-causal phenomenon. It requires a multidisciplinary analysis and understanding. A critical examination of the theoretical and methodological issues may hint at the shifts in the study of social stratification. The caste model used to study social stratification has ensured the application of class and power approaches mainly due to its own contradictions and decreased relevance as a frame of reference. Instead of *caste and class*, the phrase *class and caste* has been in vogue to signify class as the dominant dimension of social stratification while relegating caste to a secondary position. This shift may be understood as a critique and negation of caste as an all-encompassing ideational system. Today, the emphasis has shifted considerably from the cultural to the structural criteria of social stratification. The revival of interest in the cultural perspective in the study of social stratification is taking a different form and substance.

Caste has not remained confined to ritual ranking and rules of marriage; it has shown flexibility in these spheres and has acquired new grounds for its survival and interpenetration into other domains like religion, economy and politics. A couple of studies on the caste system have signalled that caste was never a static system, and it was also not confined to ritual and religious functions alone. Status–mobility was reflected in migration, competition for power, gap between the ideal and the actual status, and the emergence of the new and mixed castes. Thus, social stratification was not uniformly structured as it had diverse forms and expressions in different structural and historical contexts. A mix of interactional and attributional criteria of social ranking has persisted from ancient period till today. This processual nature of social stratification can be characterized by the dynamics of differentiation, evaluation, ranking and reward patterns.

Shifts in the studies of social stratification were noticed earlier through the application of structural–functional, structuralist and Marxist approaches. Today, not only is the dimensional analysis of social stratification under serious scrutiny, the very concepts of caste, class, and power are being reformulated to make them relevant for analyzing historically specific Indian situations. Emphasis is laid on the study of dialectics, history, culture, and structure of Indian social formation with a view to minimize the paradigmatic inadequacies and empirical gaps in the studies of social stratification. Caste was used to study class relations and power structure. Now through class and power approaches, caste is being studied and not really as a cultural phenomenon, but as a concomitant inseparable structural entity.

In the present analysis of social stratification in the contexts of rural–agrarian and urban–industrial settings, the studies undertaken by historians, economists, political scientists and anthropologists besides the sociological studies and analyses have provided substantial empirical inputs. It is evident that both macro- and micro-structural forces and processes of social change have weakened the traditional summation of statuses paving a way for the emergence of a new system of social stratification with political power and better off economic standing as the dominant causality in status–determination. Such a pattern of status–relationships is also witnessed in the analysis of the weaker sections and women. An image of a desirable society devoid of rigid inequalities based on caste, religion, gender, etc., has not only become an integral feature of people's consciousness, but its realization is underway particularly since independence. Despite persisting inequalities and emerging new hierarchies, the constitutional provisions, legal enactments and social movements in particular have reduced social inequalities as reflected in the structural transformation and normative reorientation during the past few decades.

There is enough evidence available to prove that caste was never a monolithic, closed, organic, ritualistic and unidimensional hierarchical system. We now know that caste embedded class and power, and the latter even dominated over the caste. Historicity of the nexus between caste, class and power in varied forms and contexts has become the focal point in recent studies of social stratification. Conceptualizing caste–class–power nexus, rather than analyzing caste, class and power as three orders or dimensions of social stratifications has become a necessity as borne out by the studies of social mobility and change in the system of social stratification (Sharma 1996: 130–46). Obverse structural processes of social change and mobility have occurred simultaneously implying the emergence of a new social formation in the context of social stratification.

Social stratification deals with social differences and distances among the people. These may be both overtly visible and invisible. It is not just differences that form the basis of stratification; hierarchization of differences also creates social inequality. People have a tendency to hierarchize their relations, and seek expression and articulation of the same in actual life with due legitimacy. This is how a particular system of social stratification emerges. Thus, social stratification incorporates a semblance of both differences, i.e., division of labour and hierarchy. These two are found in one form or other in different combinations in all human societies.

References

Acharya, S.K., 1988, 'Ethnic Processes in North-Eastern India', *Economic and Political Weekly*, Vol. XXIII, No. 21, pp. 1068–77.

Aggarwal, P.C., 1971, *Caste, Religion and Power*, New Delhi: Shriram Centre for Industrial Relations.

Alexander, K.C., 1989, 'Caste Mobilization and Class Consciousness: The Emergence of Agrarian Movements in Kerala and Tamil Nadu', *in* Frankel, F.R. and M. S. A. Rao (eds), *Dominance and State Power in Modern India: Decline of a Social Order, Vol. I*, Delhi: Oxford University Press.

Badgaiyan, S.D., 1986, 'Class and Ethnicity: Chota Nagpur in the 19th Century', *in* Sharma, K.L. (ed.), *Social Stratification in India*, Delhi: Manohar Publications.

Baker, Sophie, 1990, *Caste: At Home in Hindu India*, London: Jonathan Cape.

Berghe, Van der, 1981, *The Ethnic Phenomenon*, New York: Elsevier.

Berreman, G.D., 1960, 'Caste in India and the United States', *American Journal of Sociology*, Vol. 66, pp. 120–27. Also reproduced *in* Heller, Celia S. (ed.), 1969, *Structured Social Inequality*, New York: The Macmillan Co., pp. 74–81.

———, 1967, 'Stratification, pluralism and interaction: A comparative analysis of caste', *in* de Reuck, Anthony and Julie Knight (eds), *Caste and Race: Comparative Approaches*, London: Churchill.

———, 1979, *Caste and Other Inequalities*, Meerut: Folklore Institute.

Béteille, André, 1966, *Caste, Class and Power*, Bombay: Oxford University Press.

Bettelheim, Charles, 1968, *India Independent*, London: MacGibbon and Kee.

Bhadra, Bipul Kumar, 1989, *The Mode of Production, Social Classes and the State*, Jaipur: Rawat Publications.

Bhadra, R.K., 1979, 'Rural class structure in post-independent Assam', *Economic and Political Weekly*, Vol. XIV, No. 4, pp. 165–67.

———, 1995, 'Caste and Class in Assam', *in* Sharma, K.L. (ed.), *Social Inequality in India*, Jaipur: Rawat Publications, pp. 256–78.

Bhatt, Anil, 1975, *Caste, Class and Politics*, Delhi: Manohar Publications.

Bhattacharya, Sabyasachi, 1986, 'The Colonial State, Capital and Labour', *in* Bhattacharya, S. and Romila Thapar (eds), *Situating Indian History*, Delhi: Oxford University Press, pp. 171–93.

Bose, Pradip Kumar, 1981, 'Social Mobility and Caste: Study of Gujarat Riots', *Economic and Political Weekly*, Vol. XII, No. 16, pp. 713–16.

Bottomore, T.B., 1964, *Sociology*, London: ELBS and Allen and Unwin.

Bougle, C., 1958, 'The essence of reality of caste system', *Contributions to Indian Sociology* (Old Series), No. 2.

———, 1971, *Essays on the Caste System*, Cambridge: Cambridge University Press.

Chandra, Bipan, Aditya Mukherjee, Midula Mukherjee and **Sucheta Mahajan**, 1988, *India's Struggle for Independence, 1857–1947*, New Delhi: Viking, Penguin Books India Ltd.

Dandekar, V.M., 1978, 'Nature of class conflict in the Indian society', *Artha Vijnana*, Vol. 20, No. 2, pp. 102–24. Reprinted in Sharma, K.L. (ed.), 1995, *Social Inequality in India*, New Delhi: Rawat Publications.

Das, Arvind N., 1983, *Agrarian Unrest and Socio-Economic Change in Bihar, 1900–1980*, New Delhi: Manohar Publications.

———, 1984, 'Class in Itself, Caste for Itself: Social Articulation in Bihar', *Economic and Political Weekly*, Vol. XIX, No. 37, pp. 1616–19.

Das, Veena, 1982, *Structure and Cognition: Aspects of Hindu Caste and Ritual*, Bombay: Oxford University Press.

Desai, A.R., 1948, *Social Background of Indian Nationalism*, Bombay: Popular Book Depot.

———, 1975, *State and Society in India*, Bombay: Popular Prakashan.

——— (ed.), 1979, *Peasant Struggles in India*, Bombay: Oxford University Press.

———, 1987, 'Rural Development and Human Rights in Independent India', *Economic and Political Weekly*, Vol. XXII, No. 31, pp. 1291–96.

Dhanagare, D.N., 1983, *Peasant Movement in India 1920–1950*, Delhi: Oxford University Press.

Dirks, Nicholas B., 1989, 'The Original Caste: Power, History and Hierarchy in South India', *Contributions to Indian Sociology*, Vol. 23, No. 1, pp. 59–77.

Doshi, S.L., 1990, *Tribal Ethnicity, Class and Integration*, Jaipur: Rawat Publications.

Driver, Edwin D., 1982, 'Class, Caste and Status Summation in Urban South India', *Contributions to Indian Sociology*, Vol. 16, No. 2, pp. 225–53.

D'Souza, V.S., 1968, *Social Structure of a Planned City—Chandigarh*, New Delhi: Orient Longman.

———, 1982, 'Economy, Caste, Religion and Population Distribution: An Analysis of Communal Tensions in Punjab', *Economic and Political Weekly*, Vol. XVII, No. 19, pp. 783–92.

Dube, S.C., 1968, 'Caste Dominance and Factionalism', *Contributions to Indian Sociology*, New Series, No. 2.

Dumont, Louis, 1970, *Homo Hierarchicus*, London: Paladin, Granda Pub. Ltd.

Engineer, Asghar Ali, 1988, 'Capitalist Development and Ethnic Tension', *Economic and Political Weekly*, Vol. XXIII, No. 9, pp. 409–12.

Franco, F. and **Sherry Chand, V. Sarvar**, 1989, 'Ideology as Social Practice: The Functioning of Varna', *Economic and Political Weekly*, Vol. XXIV, No. 47, pp. 2601–12.

Frankel, Francine R. and **M. S. A. Rao**, 1989/1990, *Dominance and State Power in Modern India: Decline of a Social Order, Vol. I*, and *Vol. II*, Delhi: Oxford University Press.

Furnivall, J.S., 1939, *Netherlands–India: A Study in Plural Economy*, Cambridge: Cambridge University Press.

Gardner, Peter M., 1968, 'Dominance in India: A Reappraisal', *Contributions to Indian Sociology* (NS), No. 2.

Ghurye, G.S., 1950, *Caste and Class in India*, Bombay: Popular Book Depot.

Godelier, Maurice, 1978, *Perspectives in Marxist Anthropology*, Cambridge: Cambridge University Press.

Gould, Harold A., 1988, *Caste Adaptation in Modernizing Indian Society*, Delhi: Chanakya Publications.

Gupta, Dipankar, 1981, 'Caste Infrastructure and Super-structure: A Critique', *Economic and Political Weekly*, Vol. XVI, No. 51, pp. 2093–2104.

Gupta, Dipankar, 1984, 'Continuous Hierarchies and Discrete Castes', *Economic and Political Weekly*, Vol. XIX, Nos. 46, 47 and 48, pp. 1955–58; 2003–5; 2049–53.

Habib, Irfan, 1974, 'The Social Distribution of Landed Property in Pre-British India', *in* Sharma, R.S. (ed.), *Indian Society: Historical Probings*, New Delhi: Peoples Publishing House, pp. 264–316.

Hardiman, David, 1988, 'Class Base of Swaminarayan Sect', *Economic and Political Weekly*, Vol. XXIII, No. 37, pp. 1907–12.

Harriss, John, 1982, *Rural Development: Theories of Peasant Economy and Agrarian Change*, London: Hutchinson University Library.

Hasan, Zoya, 1989, 'Power and Mobilization: Patterns of Resilience and Change in Uttar Pradesh Politics', *in* Frankel, F.R. and M. S. A. Rao (eds), *Dominance and State Power in Modern India: Decline of a Social Order, Vol. I*, Delhi: Oxford University Press, pp. 133–203.

Hazari, R.K., 1966, *The Structure of the Corporate Private Sector: A Study of Concentration, Ownership and Control*, London: Asia Publishing House.

Hocart, A.M., 1950, *Caste: A Comparative Study*, London: Metheun and Co

Hutton, J.H., 1946, *The Caste in India*, Oxford: Oxford University Press.

Jeffery, Robin (ed.), 1978, *People, Princes and Paramount Power: Society and Politics in the Indian Princely States*, Delhi: Oxford University Press.

Jha, D.N. (ed.), 1987, *Feudal Social Formation in Early India*, Delhi: Chanakya Publications.

Juergensmeyer, Mark, 1979, 'Culture of Deprivation: Three Case Studies in Punjab', *Economic and Political Weekly* (AN), Vol. XIV, Nos. 7 and 8.

Kamalakar, Jaya, 1988, 'Ethnic Politics in Municipal Corporations', *Economic and Political Weekly*, Vol. XXIII, No. 19, pp. 945–46.

Ketkar, S.V., 1909, *History of Caste in India* (reprinted 1979), Jaipur: Rawat Publications.

Klass, Morton, 1980, *Caste: The Emergence of the System in South Asia*, Philadelphia: Institute for the Study of Human Issues.

Kochanek, Stanley A., 1974, *Business and Politics in India*, Berkeley and Los Angeles: University of California Press.

Kohli, Atul, 1990, 'From Elite Activism to Democratic Consolidation: The Rise of Reform Communism in West Bengal', *in* Frankel, F.R. and M. S. A. Rao (eds), *Dominance and State Power in Modern India: Decline of a Social Order, Vol. II*, Delhi: Oxford University Press.

Kolenda, P., 1984, *Caste in Contemporary India: Beyond Organic Solidarity*, Jaipur: Rawat Publications.

———, 1986, 'Caste in India since Independence', *in* Basu, Dilip K. and Richard Sisson (eds), *Social and Economic Development in India, A Reassessment*, New Delhi: Sage Publications.

———, 1989, 'Micro-ideology and Micro-utopia in Khalapur: Changes in the Discourse on Caste over Thirty Years', *Economic and Political Weekly*, Vol. XXIV, No. 32, pp. 1833–38.

Kothari, Rajni, 1970, *Politics in India*, Delhi: Orient Longman. See also Kothari, Rajni (ed.), 1970, *Caste in Indian Politics*, Delhi: Orient Longman.

———, 1986, 'Masses, Classes and the State', *Economic and Political Weekly*, Vol. XXI, No. 5, pp. 210–16.

Kothari, Rajni, 1988, 'Integration and Exclusion in Indian Politics', *Economic and Political Weekly*, Vol. XXIII, No. 43, pp. 2223–27.

Kulkarni, S.D., 1979, 'Class and Caste in Tribal Movement', *Economic and Political Weekly*, Vol. XIV, Nos. 7 and 8, pp. 465–68.

Lateef, Shahida, 1980, 'Ethnicity and Social Change', *Economic and Political Weekly*, Vol. XV, No. 50, pp. 2086–87.

Leach, Edmund R., 1960, 'What Should We Mean by Caste?', *in* Leach, E.R. (ed.), *Aspects of Caste in South India, Ceylon and North-West Pakistan*, London: Cambridge University Press, pp. 1–10.

Lele, Jayant, 1990, 'Caste, Class and Dominance: Political Mobilization in Maharashtra', *in* Frankel, F.R. and M. S. A. Rao (eds), *Dominance and State Power in Modern India, Decline of a Social Order, Vol. II*, Delhi: Oxford University Press.

MacDougall and **John Douglas**, 1979, 'Dominant castes or rich peasants', *Economic and Political Weekly*, Vol. XIV, Nos. 12 and 13, pp. 625–34.

Madan, T.N., 1971, 'On Understanding Caste' (Review article on L. Dumont's *Homo Hierarchicus*), *Economic and Political Weekly*, Vol. 6, No. 34.

Maine, H.J.S., 1890, *Village Communities in the East and West*, London: J. Murray.

Manor, James, 1989, 'Karnataka: Caste, Class, Dominance and Politics in a Cohesive Society', *in* Frankel, F.R. and M. S. A. Rao (eds), op. cit., pp. 322–61.

Marriott, M., 1965, *Caste Ranking and Community Structure in Five Regions of India and Pakistan*, Poona: Deccan College.

Mathew, George, 1982, 'Politicisation of Religion: Conversions to Islam in Tamil Nadu', *Economic and Political Weekly*, Vol. XVII, No. 25, pp. 1027–34 and No. 26, pp. 1068–72.

Mencher, Joan P., 1974, 'The caste system upside down, or the not-so-mysterious east', *Current Anthropology*, Vol. 15, No. 4.

Mendelsohn, Oliver, 1986, 'A Harijan elite? The lives of some untouchable politicians', *Economic and Political Weekly*, Vol. XXI, No. 12, pp. 501–9.

Miller, D.B. (ed.), 1978, *Peasants and Politics: Grassroots Reaction to Change in Asia*, New York: St. Martins Press.

Mohanty, Manoranjan, 1990, 'Class, caste and dominance in a backward state Orissa', *in* Frankel, F.R. and M. S. A. Rao (eds), *Dominance and State Power in Modern India: Decline of a Social Order*, Delhi: Oxford University Press.

Mukherjee, Aditya, 1978, 'Indian Capitalist Class and Congress on National Planning and Public Sector 1930–47', *Economic and Political Weekly*, Vol. XIII, No. 35, pp. 1516–28.

————, 1986, 'The Indian Capitalist Class: Aspects of its Economic, Political and Ideological Development in the Colonial Period, 1927–47', *in* Bhattacharya, S. and Romila Thapar (eds), *Situating Indian History*, Delhi: Oxford University Press.

Namboodiripad, E.M.S., 1979, 'Caste conflicts v/s growing unity of popular democratic forces', *Economic and Political Weekly*, Vol. XIV, Nos. 7 and 8, pp. 403–8.

Narain, Iqbal and **P. C. Mathur**, 1990, 'The Thousand Year Raj: Regional Isolation and Rajput Hinduism in Rajasthan Before and After 1947', *in* Frankel, F.R. and M. S. A. Rao (eds), *Dominance and State Power in Modern India: Decline of a Social Order, Vol. II*, Delhi: Oxford University Press, pp. 1–58.

Omvedt, Gail (ed.), 1982, *Land, Caste and Politics in India*, Delhi: Authors Guild Publications.

Oommen, T.K., 1970, 'Rural Community Power Structure in India', *Social Forces*, Vol. 49, No. 2, pp. 73–83.

Pandit, Nalini, 1979, 'Caste and Class in Maharashtra', *Economic and Political Weekly*, Vol. XIV, Nos. 7 and 8, pp. 425–36.

Panikkar, K.M., 1955, *Hindu Society at the Cross Roads*, Bombay: Asia Publishing House.

Pathy, Jaganath, 1984, *Tribal Peasantry: Dynamics of Development*, New Delhi: Inter-India Publications.

Pavlov, V.I., 1964, *The Indian Capitalist Class*, Bombay: People's Publishing House.

Petras, James, 1989, 'Class Politics, State Power and Legitimacy', *Economic and Political Weekly*, Vol. XXIV, No. 34, pp. 1955–58.

Prasad, Pradhan H., 1979, 'Caste and Class in Bihar', *Economic and Political Weekly*, Vol. XIV, Nos. 7 and 8, pp. 481–84.

Puri, Balraj, 1987, 'Ethnic dimension of sub-continental Muslims', *Economic and Political Weekly*, Vol. XXII, No. 4, pp. 126–28.

———, 1990, 'Politics of ethnic and communal identities', *Economic and Political Weekly*, Vol. XXV, No. 14, pp. 703–5.

Raheja, Goloria Goodwin, 1989, 'Centrality, Mutuality and Hierarchy: Shifting Aspects of Intercaste Relationships in North India', *Contributions to Indian Sociology* (NS), Vol. 23, No. 1, pp. 79–101.

Rao, M.S.A., 1989, 'Some conceptual issues in the study of caste, class, ethnicity, and dominance', *in* Frankel, F.R. and M. S. A. Rao (eds), *Dominance and State Power in Modern India: Decline of a Social Order, Vol. I*, Delhi: Oxford University Press.

Reddy, G. Ram, 1989, 'The Politics of Accommodation: Caste, Class and Dominance in Andhra Pradesh', *in* Frankel, F.R. and M. S. A. Rao (eds), op. cit., pp. 265–321.

Risley, H.H., 1969, *The People of India* (2nd Edition), Delhi: Orient Books.

Robb, Peter (ed.), 1986, *Rural India*, New Delhi, Segment Book Distributors.

Rosen, George, 1966, *Democracy and Economic Change in India*, Berkeley: University of California Press.

Roy, Ajit, 1979, 'Caste and Class: An Interlinked View', *Economic and Political Weekly*, Vol. XII, Nos. 7 and 8, pp. 297–312.

Rudolph, S.H. and **L. I. Rudolph**, 1984, *Essays on Rajputana: Reflections on History, Culture and Administration*, New Delhi: Concept Pub. Company.

———, 1987, *In Pursuit of Lakshmi: The Political Economy of the Indian State*, New Delhi: Orient Longman.

Saberwal, Satish, 1979, 'Inequality in Colonial India', *Contributions to Indian Sociology (NS)*, Vol. 13, pp. 241–64.

———, 1979, 'Sociologists and Inequality in India: The Historical Context', *Economic and Political Weekly*, Vol. XIV, Nos. 7 and 8, pp. 234–54.

Senart, E., 1930, *Caste in India: The Facts and the System*, London, Metheun and Co.

Shah, A.M., 1982, 'Division and Hierarchy: An Overview of Caste in Gujarat', *Contributions to Indian Sociology*, Vol. 16, No. 1, pp. 1–33.

Shah, A.M. and **I. P. Desai** (eds), 1988, *Division and Hierarchy: An Overview of Caste in Gujarat*, Delhi: Hindustan Pub. Corp.

Shah, Ghanshayam, 1979, 'Tribal Identity of Class Differentations: A Case Study of the Chauduri Tribe', *Economic and Political Weekly* (AN), Vol. XIV, Nos. 7 and 8, pp. 459–69.

——, 1990, 'Caste Sentiments, Class Formation and Dominance in Gujarat', *in* Frankel, F.R. and M. S. A. Rao (eds), op. cit., pp. 59–114.

——, 1990, *Social Movements in India—A Review of the Literature*, Delhi: Sage Publications.

Shakir, Moin, 1986, *State and Politics in Contemporary India*, New Delhi: Ajanta Publications.

Sharma, K.L., 1980, *Essays on Social Stratification*, Jaipur: Rawat Publications.

——, 1986, *Caste, Class and Social Movements*, Jaipur: Rawat Publications, pp. 16–39.

—— (ed.), 1986, *Social Stratification in India*, Delhi: Manohar Publications, pp. 29–62. See also Sharma, K.L, 1994, *Social Stratification and Mobility*, Jaipur: Rawat Publications; *Caste and Class in India* (ed.), 1994, Jaipur: Rawat Publications and *Social Inequality in India: Profiles of Caste, Class, Power and Social Mobility* (ed.), 1995, Jaipur: Rawat Publications.

——, 1996, 'Conceptualisation of Caste-Class Nexus as an Alternative to Caste-Class Dichotomy', *in* Momin, A.R. (ed.), *The Legacy of G. S. Ghurye, A Centennial Festschrift*, Bombay: Popular Prakashan.

Sharma, K.N., 1963, 'Panchayat Leaders and Resource Groups', *Sociological Bulletin*, Vol. XII, No. 1, pp. 47–52.

Sharma, Surendra, 1985, *Sociology in India*, Jaipur: Rawat Publications, pp. 82–114.

Sherring, M.N., 1974, *Hindu Castes and Tribes* (Reprint), New Delhi: Cosmos Publications.

Sinha, Arun, 1982, Class War, Not Atrocities Against Harijans', *Journal of Peasant Studies*, Vol. 9, No. 3.

Singh, P.C., 1992, *Mode of Production in Indian Agriculture*, Jaipur: Rawat Publications.

Singh, Rajendra, 1988, *Land, Power and People: Rural Elite in Transition, 1801–1970*, New Delhi: Sage Publications.

Singh, Yogendra, 1974, 'Sociology of Social Stratification: A Trend Report', *in A Survey of Research in Sociology and Social Anthropology*, ICSSR, Vol. I, Bombay: Popular Prakashan.

——, 1985, 'Sociology of Social Stratification', *in A Survey of Research in Sociology and Social Anthropology*, Vol. II, New Delhi: Satvahan Publications.

Sivakumar, S.S. and **Chitra Sivakumar,** 1979, 'Class and Jati at Asthapuram and Kanthapuram: Some Comments Towards a Structure of Interests', *Economic and Political Weekly* (AN), Vol. XIV, Nos. 7 and 8, pp. 263–86.

Sivanandan, P., 1979, 'Caste, Class and Economic Opportunity in Kerala: An Empirical Analysis, *Economic and Political Weekly*, Vol. XIV, Nos 7 and 8, pp. 475–80.

Srinivas, M.N., 1952, *Religion and Society among the Coorgs of South India*, Bombay: Oxford University Press.

—— (ed.), 1955, *India's Villages*, Calcutta: Govt. of West Bengal.

Srinivas, M.N., 1959, 'The Dominant Caste in Rampura', *American Anthropologist*, Vol. 61, No. 1, pp. 1–16.

————, 1966, *Social Change in Modern India*, Berkeley and Los Angeles: University of California Press.

————, 1979, 'Future of Indian Caste', *Economic and Political Weekly* (AN), Vol. XIV, Nos 7 and 8, pp. 237–42.

————, 1984, 'Some Reflections on the Nature of Caste Hierarchy', *Contributions to Indian Sociology*, Vol. 18, No. 2, pp. 151–67.

————, 1987, *The Dominant Caste and Other Essays*, Delhi: Oxford University Press.

Stein, Burton, 1968, 'Social Mobility and Medieval South Indian Sects', *in* Silverberg, James (ed.), *Social Mobility in the Caste System in India*, The Hague: Mouton Publishers, pp. 78–94.

Thapar, Romila, 1974, 'Social Mobility in Ancient Indian Society', *in* Sharma, R.S. (ed.), *Indian Society: Historical Probings*, New Delhi: Peoples Publishing House, pp. 95–123.

Veer, Peter Van der, 1985, 'Brahmans: Their Purity and their Poverty in the Changing Values of Brahman Priests in Ayodhya', *Contributions to Indian Sociology*, Vol. XIX, No. 2, pp. 303–21.

Wallace, Paul, 1990, 'Religious and Ethnic Politics: Political Mobilization in Punjab', *in* Frankel, F.R. and M. S. A. Rao (eds), *Dominance and State Power in Modern India: Decline of a Social Order, Vol. II*, Delhi: Oxford University Press.

Weber, Max, 1948, *From Max Weber: Essays in Sociology*, London: Routledge and Kegan Paul.

Weiner, Myron, 1978, *Sons of the Soil: Migration and Ethnic Conflict in India*, Princeton: Princeton University Press.

Washbrook, D.A., 1989, 'Caste, Class and Dominance in Modern Tamil Nadu: Non-Brahminism, Dravidianism and Tamil Nationalism', *in* Frankel, F.R. and M. S. A. Rao (eds), op. cit., pp. 204–64.

Index